MARGINALITY

MARGINALITY
The Key to Multicultural Theology

JUNG YOUNG LEE

Fortress Press   Minneapolis

To Sue and Jonathan

The author gratefully acknowledges the following publishers of poems quoted in this work: Washington Square Press, a division of Pocket Books, Simon & Schuster, for Diana Chang's poem "Saying Yes" in *Asian-American Heritage: An Anthology of Prose and Poetry* (1974), edited by David Hsin-Fu Wand; City Lights Books for Francis Naohiko Oka, *Poems* (1970); Calyx Books for Genny Lim, "Children Are Color-Blind," in *The Forbidden Stitch: An Asian American Women's Anthology* (1989), edited by Lim, Tsutakawa, and Donnelly; UCLA Asian American Studies Center for Joanne Miyamoto's poem "What Are You?" from *Roots: An Asian American Reader* (1971).

Cover graphic: Garden II, oil on linen by Dan Mason
Cover design: Evans McCormick Creative

Library of Congress Cataloging-in-Publication data

Lee, Jung Young.
    Marginality : the key to multicultural theology / Jung Young Lee
      p. cm.
    Includes bibliographical references.
    ISBN 0-8006-2810-1 :
      1. Christianity and culture. 2. Marginality, Social—Religious aspects—
Christianity. 3. Multiculturalism—Religious aspects—Christianity.
    4. Lee, Jung Young. I. Title.
    BR115.C8L44 1995
    230'.046—dc20   94-31475
                                             CIP

Manufactured in the U.S.A.   AF 1-2810

99   98   97   96   95   1   2   3   4   5   6   7   8   9   10

CONTENTS

ACKNOWLEDGMENTS

I am grateful to many people who have helped me in preparing this book and understanding marginality. Most of all, I am thankful to the prominent sociologists who have attempted the difficult task of defining the concept of marginality, particularly Robert E. Park and Everett Stonequist for their pioneering study of ethnicity and marginality in America. However, because their views reflect the perspective of the dominant groups, their work can only be complemented by the perspective on marginality that I offer in this book.

I am greatly indebted to many Asian-American scholars and friends. I cannot mention everyone, but I should not fail to name the following persons: Won Moo Hurh, Jung-ha Kim, Kwang Chung Kim, Sang Hyun Lee, Warren Lee, Paul Nagano, David Ng, Roy Sano, Ben Silva-netto, Ronald Takaki, and Wesley Woo. I am grateful to the Pacific Asian Center for Theology and Strategies for providing me with many valuable materials during my stay on the campus of the Pacific School of Religion. I am especially thankful to Julia Estrella, who, during my stay at Berkeley, assisted me immensely with resources. I am grateful for the services provided me by the Pacific School of Religion, Graduate Theological Union, and the University of California at Berkeley.

I express my special thanks to Robert Bellah of the University of California at Berkeley and Eleanor Scott Meyers of the Pacific School of Religion. They read parts of my manuscript with "sociological" eyes and gave me helpful suggestions for improvement. I am also grateful for encouragement and support given by Thomas Ogletree of Yale Divinity School, Robin Lovin of Perkins School of Theology, and Janet Fishburn of Drew University. I am grateful to the Association of Theological

vii

Schools for the grant that allowed me to continue my research in California during my sabbatical year.

The germinal idea for this book came from a matriculation address I gave to the incoming students at Drew University Theological School in the fall of 1990. I would like to thank my colleagues at Drew University for their support. Their discussion of my paper at the fall retreat encouraged me to undertake this project. I am grateful to students who were in my "Marginality" class. Their perspectives were quite helpful in reassessing my concept of marginality.

My special gratitude goes to Judith Kurth, Nancy Schluter, and Ann Shaw, who have provided me with an indispensable service of preparing the manuscript for publication. Their eagerness to assist me facilitated my work. I am also grateful to So-Young Park and Jae-Shik Shin, who compiled the index. Most of all, I am deeply indebted to J. Michael West, Senior Editor of Fortress Press. He was not only enthusiastically supportive of my project but also truly empathetic with my concerns. Without his assistance the publication of this book would not have been possible. I am most grateful to my wife, Gy, who provided me with relevant materials and essential summaries of what she read on Asian-American work while I was in California. Without her cooperation I could not have completed this project. Perhaps my greatest teachers for the living wisdom of marginality have been my two children, Sue and Jonathan, who have taught me more than all of the books and articles on marginality. I dedicate this book to my children as living exemplars of new marginality.

INTRODUCTION

We live in a pluralistic society where different cultural and ethnic groups must coexist. In North America the demographic picture of ethnic minorities has changed drastically in recent years.[1] The minority population in North America is growing at a faster rate than the population as a whole. Ethnic minorities will occupy one-third of the total American population by the year 2000, and "by the end of the next century there will be a new majority population in America—a majority of minorities."[2] Marvin Cetron, a futurist and author of *American Renaissance: Our Life at the Turn of the Twenty-First Century*, predicts an increasingly multicultural society, in which minorities will make up the majority by the year 2030.[3] This new mosaic society, with its cultural and racial pluralism, demands a radically new approach to doing theology. Concentrating on liberation from economic and political injustice alone, for example, is not a sufficient theological task. The roots of oppression are not only in class and gender struggle but in racial and cultural misunderstanding in a pluralistic society. I propose in this book a new theology based on marginality, which serves not only as a hermeneutical paradigm but as a key to the substance of the Christian faith.[4]

A theology of marginality is an alternative to a centralist approach to theology. A marginal approach is an inevitable outcome of the marginal context, while a centralist approach is based on the context of centrality. The latter does not replace the former. They are not competitive, because their approaches are different. Theological critiques and arguments presented analytically are inappropriate, because a theology of marginality is not based on the norm of centralist theology. Since a theology of marginality has its norm to validate itself, I refrain from citing

1

the work of centralist theologies which have dominated the theological world. This is necessary to make a theology of marginality truly creative in its own right. Moreover, I am not interested in critical exegesis, for my primary emphasis is on a creative reflection of Christian symbols emerging from marginality.

Although this book is addressed to all marginal people in our society, it is not written on their behalf, for no one can write theology for someone else. While I am a Korean-American, I cannot write theology for all Korean-Americans, because I do not represent every one of them. In the same context, I cannot write theology for all Asian-Americans, even though I am an Asian-American. For me, being Asian-American means being one of many Asian-Americans. Thus, this book is written from my perspective, an Asian-American perspective, which means one of many Asian-American perspectives. A theology of marginality is, then, one of many ways a marginalized person could understand theology.

No theology is free of personal bias. Our sociological, psychological, political, economic, ethnic or cultural backgrounds determine our personal theological orientations. Theology, like all other disciplines, including the so-called "exact sciences," cannot dismiss the personal factor.[5] No pure rational and logical abstraction of objective truth is possible. Reality must be related to our life situations. Any theology that is not in touch with our life experience cannot be a living theology. Just as theory and praxis are inseparable, so theology is inseparable from life, as it is a faith reflection on life.

The theology that I have attempted to construct in this book is my faith reflection on my life experience. As Paul Knitter said, "All theology is, we are told, rooted in biography."[6] My theology is rooted in living as an Asian in North America, and is best characterized by marginality. I am a marginal person. As that, I write theology that is marginal and autobiographical. I write this book to articulate my faith from the perspective of a marginalized existence. While I write this to assist my understanding of marginality and to help determine a way to cope with my marginal status in North America, I hope this work may become a catalyst for others to reflect on their experience. Since marginality is a relative and dynamic term, it is not confined to the experience of ethnic minorities. Marginality is experienced by white Americans who have been marginalized by gender, class, economy, or religion. My study may appeal to all marginalized people. Although I cannot speak for all of them, I believe that marginality is a common ground that unites us, regardless of class, gender, cultural, or ethnic differences in the United States.

My life experience, which becomes the primary source of my theological work, also includes my way of thinking. Rooted in a Northeast Asian culture and trained in theology in North America, I think differently from white Americans. When I submitted the first draft of my doctoral dissertation, my advisor called me and said: "I have a copy of your dissertation with me. I am now reading it a third time to make sure that I understand it correctly. Your style of writing is quite different from ours [western style]. You have a tendency to repeat, but you repeat in such a way that your repetitions are not repetitious."[7] Reading a different style of writing is in itself a learning experience of another culture.

Although theology is personal, it is more than private property because it is derived from common experiences which connect us with one another. Because of this inter-relatedness, I am not isolated from others. I am a part of others, just as they are a part of me. I share the experience of others, just as others share my experience. I have been nurtured and shaped by a group of people. I am like a part of the ripple that expands over the water. My experience of marginality is defined clearly when I see myself in this group. Seeing myself from within the total picture of Asian-Americans, I may recognize a pattern in Asian-American experience. So in the first chapter I introduce the history of Asian-American experience after first introducing my own experience in the United States. By Asian-Americans, I mean Northeast Asian-Americans, mainly Chinese-Americans, Korean-Americans, and Japanese-Americans with whom I closely identify. I introduce the parable of "Dandelion" to tell my own story. This chapter serves as the *context* for understanding my theology of marginality.

Marginality is not only the context of marginal theology but also the *method* of marginal theology. To provide the method of marginal theology, I first define the meaning of marginality through the use of cultural and racial determinants. To move toward a comprehensive approach to marginality, in chapter 2 I consider negative and positive aspects of the definition. In defining the negative aspect of marginality I evaluate in the work of Robert E. Park and Everett Stonequist, who were responsible for its classical definition.[8] I evaluate their definition from a marginal perspective. Since their idea does not have universal implication[9] and to complement the classical self-negating definition of marginality, I propose the contemporary self-affirming definition of marginality.

Negative and positive aspects of marginality are joined in chapter 3 to define a new marginality—a new marginal person who is *in-beyond* two or more worlds. Based on this comprehensive definition of marginality, I have attempted to discover a certain pattern of thinking which can serve as a hermeneutical paradigm for doing theology in the genuinely pluralistic society emerging in North America. In this book the theological paradigm shifts from centrality to marginality: marginality becomes the norm of theological interpretation.

Marginality is not only the hermeneutical principle but also the *content* of the Christian faith. Here, the method and content of theology are inseparably united. The reinterpretation of theological themes, therefore, is none other than the rediscovery of marginality intrinsic to the Christian faith. One of the most important theological themes in Christianity is christology. In chapter 4, I discuss Jesus-Christ, who is the margin of marginality. I avoid the technical term *Christology,* because the study of Jesus-Christ is also "Jesusology." I intentionally hyphenate the words *Jesus-Christ,* because he is always Jesus *and* Christ. It is also fitting to use a hyphen because he is a new marginal person *par excellence.*[10]

If God was in Jesus-Christ, the people of God must also be marginal people. I therefore discuss in chapter 5 the marginal people of God. We are called to be the marginal people because marginality is an intrinsic part of creation, which continues because of marginality. The history of Israelites and Christians needs to be reinterpreted from the perspective of marginality.

The fellowship of God's marginal people is known as the church, or the body of Christ. In chapter 6 from a marginal perspective I attempt to rediscover the concept of the church as the community of marginality. One fundamental problem that the church faces today is its tendency to seek a central place in our society. The church becomes authentic when it is situated at the margins of the world.

The way to overcome marginality is through the creative transformation of marginal and dominant people into a new marginality. In chapter 7 I discuss the creative power of marginality for overcoming itself. Change and transformation take place at the margins because creativity flourishes there. Finally, in the concluding chapter, I state the challenges of this theology for a pluralistic society.

I attempt to provide a new perspective on the Christian faith and a way of making marginality creative in our Christian life. Marginality touches a wide dimension of human life, particularly in our pluralistic society. It deals with social, economic, and political issues as well as racial, cultural, and psychological issues. I hope this book will help Christians find meaning and vitality in the pluralistic world.

1. I Am

The Autobiographical Context of Theology

> By faith Abraham obeyed when he was called to set out
> for a place that he was to receive as an inheritance; and
> he set out, not knowing where he was going. By faith he
> stayed for a time in the land he had been promised, as in
> a foreign land . . . For he looked forward to the city that
> has foundations, whose architect and builder is God.
>
> *(Heb 11:8-10)*

Theology is Autobiographical

Theology is autobiographical, but it is not an autobiography. My theology is not just a story of my life. It is the story of my faith journey in the world. It is my story of how God formed me, nurtures me, guides me, loves me, allows me to age, and will end my life. It is my story of seeking who I am in relation to the community, the natural environment, time and history, and the ultimate reality of my existence which I accept by faith. It is my story of seeking to understand how God acts in my life and in the lives of those who are part of my life. It is a faith-reflection on my life, whether it is told in poetry, in parable, or in narrative. Theology is certainly autobiographical, because I alone can tell my faith story. However, it is not an autobiography. Telling my story is not itself theology but a basis for theology, indeed the primary context for doing my theology. This is why one cannot do theology for another. If theology is contextual, it must certainly be at root autobiographical.

I am Becomes *We Are*

Theology begins with my life, but my life is related to the lives of others. Thus, "I am" is always also "we are." In Asia, and particularly in Korea, "I" and "we" or *Oori* are synonymous. For example, my parents are our parents, my home is our home, my dog is our dog, and my children are our children.[1] I am is "pluralistic," even though it is not the combination of I with others. It is pluralistic because it is relational. The story of my life is the story of many lives. In Asia we-are takes precedence over I-am, because the latter is always relative to the former. In other words, I-am is defined in terms of we-are, because we-are is considered to be more fundamental than I-am. However, living in the United States, I have learned to think of the importance of I-am. I-am is more important than we-are. As an Asian-American, I value them equally. I-am is possible because we-are, just as we-are is inseparably related to I-am. It is not possible for me to put one before the other. To be a marginal person is to be a both/and person, one who is an Asian and an American. That is, my story is not complete without our story. I know who I am only in the context of who we are. Knowing one Asian in America well is not possible without knowing other Asians in America. Thus, in the history of Asian-American experience, I find my story of life in America.

History of Asian-American Experience

First of all, it is important to understand that Asians are not one ethnic group. They are many different ethnic groups who originated on the same continent. Placing all Asians into a single ethnic category is misleading. Chinese, Japanese, Koreans, Vietnamese, Hmongs, Malaysians, Pakistanis, Hindus, and others, are different ethnic groups in Asia. They speak Chinese, Japanese, Korean, Vietnamese, Bahasa Malaysia, Hindi, and others. They have dissimilar cultural, religious, and racial origins. They have some common sense, however, of being Asian. Connectedness among them exists because of their common continental tie or because they are called Asians regardless of differences. Among the ethnic groups of Asia, the Chinese, Japanese, and Koreans seem to share more common cultural and religious heritages, and it is with these that I most closely identify. They are representative of Asian people, so I introduce the American experience largely from the Chinese, Japanese, and Korean perspective. However, be cognizant that the American experiences of Asians are not all the same nor is the first generation's exactly that of the second or the third generation's life situation. Geographic location of each group also affects its American experience. With an autobiographical approach, I am the primary source of my understanding of the marginal experience, yet my experience is supported and reflected in the Asian marginal experience especially of Chinese-Americans, Japanese-Americans, and Korean-Americans. As I study the history of Asian-American experience, I see my own history; all of us are marginal people. Marginal status in America necessarily includes suffering, rejection, discrimination, and oppression. My Asian-American predecessors are my teachers, pioneers, and the roots of my Asian-American identity. The more I study their history, the more deeply I have been drawn into it. In fact, I feel that I am an extension of the lives of early Asians in this country. Their stories tell me something that I did not know about myself. Their history seems to repeat in my history in a different way. In their story I see myself, as my life reflects on their past lives. As I study more of their lives, I understand more of my own predicament as an Asian in the United States. If my life is the context for my theology, it is vital to introduce the history of Asian-Americans.

Although the history of Asian immigration is complex, I hope to highlight some patterns of Asian-American experience which help me understand my life better. I can delineate this if I understand that a dominant group often stereotypes characteristics of a minority group. The reverse is also true. When I came to teach in the University of North Dakota, I realized I was defined no differently from Korean wives of American servicemen, the Asian imagemakers in that area. Wherever I went, people treated me as they treated these Korean wives. For North Dakotans, I was not a professor, I was simply an Asian. So my Asian predecessors became the Asian imagemakers in this country. Consciously or unconsciously, non-Asian Americans project onto me their stereotypical image of Asians, regardless of who I am, merely because I am an Asian in this country.

Asians originally came to this country as sojourners rather than as immigrants. This is perhaps why people ask me, "When are you going back to your country?" There does not seem to be another explanation for this question, since they know that I have a job in this country. They never ask this question of a Caucasian European who comes to work here. Before I studied the history of Asian immigration, I did not know why people expected me to return to Asia. However, it is now quite clear that the expectation arises not only from the Caucasian bias toward Asian people, but also comes from the image that the early Asians created. As we will notice later, among other images of Asians, this stereotype is a permanent scar that still hurts Asians in America.

I would like to think of myself as one of those who came here to share the American dream of equality and justice for all people. My life experience in this country is like a small drop of water in the stormy ocean of Asian experiences in America. Let me share this small drop of experience in the parable of a dandelion.[2] The story of marginal people is a parable of a dandelion in a broad, beautiful lawn. This story is a parable because it does not belong to the dominant group, and it is absurd. The parable is the primary context for my theological perspective.

The Dandelion

"It is already spring," I said, while opening the front door. I almost felt the spring. The cold winter was gone, and cosmic resurrection was already taking place outside. Through the storm door I watched events outside. Things were starting to live again. The front lawn was turning green. "What a beautiful lawn we have!" I thought to myself.

Suddenly, I discovered a yellow flower at the far corner of the front lawn. Unconsciously, I kicked the storm door. I opened it vigorously and dashed out into the yard with bare feet and picked the dandelion. I tried to pull it out completely, but some of its roots refused to loosen. I gazed at the dandelion in my hand. It was golden yellow, like the rising sun. "Why don't I like you?" I questioned myself. In its smile was the cynical message: "You hate me because I represent you." I felt sad and lost the courage to question any more. I sat on the lawn and looked mindlessly at the lonely dandelion. Gradually I returned to my early childhood in Korea.

I lived in a small farming village about fifty miles north of Pyongyang, the capital of North Korea. When spring came, the first things I saw were the dandelions blooming all over the countryside. I liked the bright yellow flowers, and picked them one by one to make a bouquet, then brought them home and placed them in a water-filled cup. The yellow flowers helped to brighten our dark rooms.

In the early summer, when all other plants were beginning to produce their green leaves, the dandelion was already producing its seeds. The golden flowers changed to white like cotton in the midst of a green field. On my way home from school, I would sometimes pick one and put it close to my mouth and blow on it as hard as I could. Then I would see the white seeds fly up in the air and come down like parachutes. Most of the seeds came down nearby, but a few, driven by the wind, rose high into the sky.

Among them was one brave seed that went farther away than the others. Summoning the courage to go as far as it could, it had faith that it could find a better place to live. Soaring skyward, it floated like a cloud and flew over the mountains, crossed the rivers and ocean, and finally arrived on the great continent of North America.

It was certainly a strange place for the dandelion seed when it landed in the beautiful front lawn of a house. The dandelion seed was afraid to land there, but it had no choice. The wind had calmed down, and the seed could stay in the air no longer. The dandelion seed noticed that the green grasses were curious about its coming; they were somewhat excited at seeing something new. The dandelion seed was delighted with its reception.

However, when the seed started to settle by covering itself with rich soil, the grasses said: "You had better not settle here. As you know, this is only for us." The seed thought they were joking. "You are not serious, are you?" it said. The dandelion thought that, since they had welcomed its coming, they would welcome its settling down. The grass said: "We'll tell you the truth. You belong at the roadside, where many wild plants grow."

"But every dandelion has the right to live wherever it chooses. I don't understand." A final warning came from the grass: "When spring comes, you will know what we mean." Regardless of what the grass said, the seed settled in the yard and covered itself, preparing for the cold winter in a strange land.

The cold winter did not last too long. Soon the warmer sunlight began to melt down the dusty snow, and spring approached in the yard where the dandelion had settled down. While the grasses and trees in the yard were still sleeping, the dandelion was working to root itself deeply into the soil, while sending its sprouts up faster than any other plants. The dandelion worked harder and longer than any others, because it had to prove itself in the new place. By the time the other plants and grasses had started to come up from the ground, the dandelion already stood above the others. When they sprouted leaves, the dandelion had already produced a bright, golden, round flower, resembling the rising sun. The dandelion was so proud of its flower, the only flower in the whole yard. The dandelion did it to brighten up the yard and please its owner.

When the owner came out into the yard and saw the dandelion flower, he did not appreciate it. Rather, he hated it. He said to himself, "I thought I weeded out all the dandelions last year, but there comes a new one up again." He then came all the way over to the corner and pulled the dandelion up. He wanted to pull out its root, but the plant was embedded so deeply that it broke instead; only half of its root came out. The man was frustrated, but decided to give up. Rather than dig further, he threw away the dandelion along the roadside. The grass, seeing what had happened to the dandelion, said: "We told you so last fall. You do not belong here. Go away!" But the dandelion said nothing. Half of its root was already taken away. It could not go anywhere.

In spite of what had happened to the dandelion, it did not lose faith in God, who it believed called it to settle in this land. "I must work harder than ever before," the dandelion said to itself. It worked and worked to grow its root back to full size and then to come up from the ground. Again, the dandelion did its best to produce a beautiful flower. This time it produced a better flower, thinking that the owner was not pleased with the first one. The dandelion had confidence that this time the owner would be pleased with its flower, which was huge and bright. Nevertheless, the man was angrier than before. "I hate to see that dandelion again," he said to himself. He pulled it out, but again failed to remove it completely; the root was broken again. The dandelion was greatly hurt but did not lose faith. It rooted itself deeper and deeper. The more it suffered, the more its root penetrated into the ground. Its faith was expressed in its root. The dandelion's faith became stronger and stronger as it faced the hardship of its existence. The faith that God had called it to dwell in this land gave it an indomitable courage to pursue its goal. Nothing could thwart its purpose.

In due course another springtime came to the place where the dandelion dwelt. During the wintertime the dandelion had done its best to strengthen its root. It came out really strong this time and did its best to produce the most splendid flower in the yard. The dandelion thought that the owner of the house would be pleased with its flower. But again, the owner came out and pulled it out. This time he said, "I hate to see this yellow color in my green yard." When the dandelion heard that, it finally realized that the reason the owner hated it was because of its yellow color. The dandelion therefore decided not to display its yellowness. "I will have to conform to the color that the lawn has," the dandelion said to itself. To save itself and to please the owner, the dandelion no longer produced its flower. It stayed green, like the rest of the plants in the yard. In this way it was able to survive another year without being picked by the owner.

The dandelion survived, but it was not happy at all; it had lost the meaning of its existence. The dandelion tried to change its appearance to be like the grass, but it was not possible. However much it wanted to become like the grass in the yard, it could not do so. The dandelion knew that it was different from the others, and it could not disguise its nature. "I fool myself in trying to become like the grass. The grass is not going to accept me as one of them," the dandelion thought.

During the long winter the dandelion thought and thought, and finally decided to allow its nature, which was yellowness, to blossom. "Without a flower my life is not worth living," the dandelion thought. So as soon as the spring came again, the dandelion flourished, stretching its long and handsome stem to the sky and producing its yellow and golden flower. "If I can live a few weeks, I can produce hundreds of white seeds and send them off from here," the dandelion dreamed. But its dream ended with a dream. In the dream the man came out and took the flower in his hand. He was an Asian-American, a yellow man, who also was dreaming. In his dream he became the dandelion.

Suddenly, I heard a familiar voice, "Daddy, Daddy." It was my child's voice. I was brought back to the present, then saw the yellow flower in my hand. I looked at it anew. It was no longer ugly. "How beautiful!" I exclaimed to myself. Instead of throwing it away, I brought it into my house and put it in a plastic cup filled with fresh water. I placed it on the dining table to brighten up the room. Like the golden sun, the flower shined on in my house for a long time. Several days later its head turned white. I took it outside, and blew on it as hard as I could. The white seeds sailed high and began to fall like parachutes all over the rich green yards. "Let them live; let them live anywhere they want. It is God's world, and they are God's creatures," I said as I watched them.

Chinese-American Experience

The earliest group of Asians who came to this country were Chinese.
They were recruited by white Americans, who needed the labor force
to build railroads, to work in factories and mills, to reclaim swampland,
and to serve as domestic servants. The Chinese people also needed
work. China in the mid-nineteenth century was in turmoil and people
suffered widely from starvation. This was a time when the ruling Man-
chus had fallen into the hands of corrupt officials who were demand-
ing higher taxes from the peasants. Through the opium war of 1839–
42, the British demanded that China open itself to the West. Americans
used this opportunity to bring the cheap Chinese laborers to their
country. Attractive advertisements recruited the Chinese people. An
American clergyman who was in China came across this advertisement:

> Americans are very rich people. They want the Chinaman to come and
> will make him very welcome. There you will have great pay, large
> houses, and food and clothing of the finest description. You can write
> to your friends and send them money at any time, and we will be re-
> sponsible for the safe delivery. . . . There are a great many Chinamen
> there now, and it will not be a strange country. China god is there, and
> the agents of this house. Never fear and you will be lucky. Come to
> Hong Kong, or to the sign of this house in Canton, and we will instruct
> you. Money is in great plenty and to spare in America.[3]

Many Chinese responded to this advertisement because they needed
work.

American-Asian history began in 1848 when eager young Chinese responded to the demand for labor in California's gold mines, in Oregon
and other western locations. The 1868 Burlingame Treaty was signed
by the U.S. and China to formally recruit labor; the treaty remained in
effect only as long as the U.S. needed Chinese laborers.[4] Within a few
years, thousands of Chinese had arrived in California, and by 1860
more than 34,000 Chinese were living on the West Coast. Twenty years
later, more than 120,000 Chinese had come to America. The first wave
of Chinese "sojourners" in California dreamed that in the *Gun-san*, the
Mountain of Gold, they would acquire quick fortunes and return to
their families in China. Gunther Barth characterized the Chinese as essentially "sojourners" who eventually became immigrants.[5]

Why did the sojourners become immigrants? First of all, their dreams were seldom realized. Few quick fortunes were to be made. Second, they hadn't realized the high expense of living in the United States. Many couldn't save enough money to buy a return ticket of forty dollars. They became indebted to get the ticket money, and remained to pay their debt. Many dishonest employers took advantage of the Chinese inability to read a contract. Those who received the ticket money through agents in Hong Kong or San Francisco had to pay more than $100 for high interest rates.[6] They therefore had no choice but to remain in the United States. Thus, sojourners became immigrants. Stanford Lyman agrees with Gunther Barth's conclusion that the Chinese in America prior to the Second World War were regarded as sojourners.[7]

This reminds me of my life. I came as a sojourner, to study, but became an immigrant. I had no intention of remaining here. However, things did not turn out as I expected. After finishing my education, I found a job and finally settled here.

As sojourners and laborers, most Chinese men came alone, despite that most of them were married.[8] In 1890, only 3,868 Chinese women were reported in this country, while there were 102,620 Chinese men working here.[9] The ratio of Chinese was 100 males to one female in 1890. The low percentage of Chinese women in America had disastrous effects on the social structure of the Chinese community in which marriage and family life is central. The extreme imbalance in the gender ratio among Chinese in America's Chinatowns created problems with regard to prostitution and concubinage, and gambling and opium sales were often conducted by secret societies. Between 1882 and 1943, the Chinese were unable to bring their families to America, and were prohibited from visiting their families in China. This low ratio of Chinese women to Chinese men deliberately controlled the Chinese population. "In 1890, forty years after the Chinese had begun to migrate to the United States, the American-born Chinese consisted of only 2.7 percent of the Chinese population in America."[10] This unfortunate event in Chinese emigration history became a primary cause for the dehumanization, violence, and stereotypical image of Asian people in America.

Such stereotyping influences the Chinese-American historical perspective. Our children do not read textbooks that describe early Chinese immigrants' contributions in building America. Historically, Chinese laundries and restaurants come to mind when we think of Chinese people. But interestingly, these occupations became "Chinese"

by chance. The California gold-seekers were men; men needed someone to do their washing, cooking, and cleaning. Some Chinese were
ready to do this work, while other Chinese labored in mines and mills.
They set up laundries and opened restaurants for other prospectors
and laborers. By 1920, more than half of all employed Chinese worked
in laundries or restaurants. Laundries outnumbered restaurants, because they required little capital for start-up and lesser use of English to
do business.[11] The Chinese filled a service demand few white Americans were willing to provide.

The Chinese also labored to build the railroads. In 1865, Central Pacific Railroad started hiring Chinese. More than 12,000 Chinese, who
made up 90 percent of the working force, constructed the transconti-
nental railroad, which connected the Union Pacific and Central Pacific
railroads. Many Chinese lost their lives doing this work. "One newspaper claimed 20,000 pounds of bones were collected from shallow
graves lining the railroad tracks where Chinese workers had fallen. The
bones were sent home to China for burial."[12] They sacrificed their lives
in the building of America, but they were hardly recognized by American society or American history.

Despite their hard and honest labor, the Chinese often were recipients of harsh and violent treatment because of their cultural differences. The Chinese cooked differently, dressed differently, ate
differently, and acted differently. An American reporter described the
scene as a ship arrived in San Francisco:

> Her main deck is packed with Chinamen—every floor of space being
> occupied by them. . . . A living stream of the blue-coated men from
> Asia, bearing long bamboo poles across their shoulders, from which
> depend packages of bedding, matting, clothing, and things of which
> we know neither the names nor the uses, pours down the plank the
> moment the word is given. All ready.[13]

They became objects of harassment and assault. White workers often
called the Chinese "nagurs," and one magazine cartoon depicted the
Chinese as "a bloodsucking vampire with slanted eyes, a pigtail, dark
skin, and thick lips."[14] Their long pigtail or queue was cut off. Mobs of
white Americans sporadically burned and sacked Chinatowns, killing
inhabitants. In Los Angeles in 1871, a mob of whites beat, hanged, and
killed about twenty Chinese in one night.[15] The Chinese were considered inferior, and culturally and biologically incapable of assimilation.

Feared as competitors, they worked harder and longer than white laborers for low pay, which subsequently lowered the living standard of American labor. Labor unions criticized them. A popular song, "Twelve Hundred More," published in 1877 conveys the mood of that era and explains emotions of white laborers:

Oh, damn this long-tailed race! . . .
Twelve hundred honest laboring men
Thrown out of work today.
By the landing of these Chinamen
In San Francisco Bay . . .
'Drive out the Chinamen!'[16]

Dennis Kearney, an immigrant from Ireland and founder of the Workingmen's Party, developed a series of resolutions condemning the importation of coolies. He threatened, in the name of America, to "drive every greasy-faced coolie from the land. We must take this insidious monster by the throat," he shouted, "and throttle it until its heart ceases to beat, and then hurl it into the sea!"[17] In 1882, under pressure from powerful labor unions, the Chinese Exclusion Act was passed to curtail Chinese immigration and naturalization. Six years later, the Scott Act was passed to prohibit Chinese workers from returning after a visit to China unless they had relatives in the United States or owned land worth $1,000. A second Exclusion Act was passed in 1892 and the third in 1902, which was to be in force indefinitely. In 1920 the Chinese population stood at 86,000, 40,000 fewer than its 1890 population. The exclusion acts and inhuman treatment of the Chinese were psychologically harmful to their personality. As a group, they became shy and withdrawn, and retreated into their Chinatowns.

A new generation of Chinese-Americans came into its own with the Second World War. When Japan bombed Pearl Harbor in 1941, the relationship between Chinese-Americans and other Americans changed. These Asians suddenly became allies against Japan. In 1943 the Chinese Exclusion Act was repealed, an annual quota of 105 Chinese immigrants was established, and they were allowed to become naturalized. By 1945, the War Brides Act brought Chinese women into the United States as wives of U.S. military men, followed by the Supreme Court's 1947 overruling of the state alien land laws. In 1952, immigrants of any nationality could become citizens. By 1970, the gender ratio of Chinese reached equilibrium, and they began to

establish a normal family life. Education became of paramount importance and was a means of advancement for their children, and toward
assimilation and ethnic pride. With it Chinese-Americans became solid
members of the middle class, seeking and attaining positions in the
fields of engineering, teaching, medicine, law, and other white-collar
professions. Today more Chinese-Americans hold Ph.D. degrees from
prestigious institutions than do whites per capita, and many success
stories exist among this population. Yet they are still recipients of discrimination from other American ethnic groups. They work harder and
longer to overcome the stereotyped image created by a century of misunderstanding and bias. Overcoming discrimination is the task of all
Asian-Americans and white Americans.

Japanese-American Experience

The history of the Japanese in America followed a similar path as the
Chinese, yet the Japanese suffered less in the beginning of their migration but were humiliated more near its end. Japanese migration began
in national crisis. The isolationist perspective of Shogun Tokugawa
began to erode with the arrival of U.S. Naval Commodore Perry in
Tokyo Bay on July 8, 1833.[18] About thirty years later, the restoration of
the Meiji era marked the beginning of trade with the West, which
brought 148 Japanese contract laborers to Hawaii's sugarcane fields in
1868. Following the 1882 Chinese Exclusion Act, America needed
other laborers to replace the Chinese on its Hawaiian and Californian
plantations. The initial laborers came from Japan's cities, and were not
used to working in the field. When employers in Hawaii complained
about them, the Japanese government immediately intervened and re-
patriated some workers. In 1886 Japanese migration heightened because of worsening conditions in Japan's economy. Most Japanese who
came were young males who wanted to make good money and return
to Japan. Fewer than 200 Japanese lived in the United States during the
1870s, 2,000 moved to the U.S. mainland during the 1880s, and this
figure tripled during the 1890s. The year 1910 saw more than 100,000
Japanese in America.[19] In contrast to the Chinese, Japanese workers
were skilled in agriculture, and about 40 percent worked as farm laborers on the mainland while the rest were employed on railroads, and in
mines, lumber mills, and canneries. Their determination to succeed is
well-illustrated in Noriko Oma's remark:

The first immigrants who came to this country came for economic gain. They came with that dream and worked very hard for success. Because this is the Japanese culture, you must go out and either you are going to die, or come back with success. You don't come back as a failure. When you go to war, you either come back dead, or in victory.[20]

They proved industrious, honest, and reliable workers. Many Japanese were ambitious to become farmers. They reclaimed areas of swampland disregarded by white farmers, thus acquiring more farmlands. Their success on the land created widespread fear among white farmers, and like the Chinese, Japanese in California became a target for hostility. In 1900, white American racism demanded an extension of the Chinese Exclusion Act to include the Japanese as well. Their attack on the Japanese, as on the Chinese, was based on racism. Like the Chinese, the Japanese were regarded as culturally and biologically incapable of assimilation. The 1913 Alien Land Law forbade alien ownership of California land, and Japanese were ineligible for citizenship.[21] To protect their holdings, Japanese immigrants transferred ownership to their children—native-born citizens. By 1930, about half of all Japanese-Americans were nisei, second-generation. Another decade saw one-third of all Californian commercial crops being produced by the Japanese. The Alien Land Law became a symbolic act of an anti-Japanese American movement on the West Coast.

Anti-Japanese sentiment seeped into education. In 1906, the San Francisco School Board decided that Chinese, Japanese, and Korean students must attend the Oriental school on Chinatown's Clay Street. The School Board claimed that local laws supported segregation. When the Japanese government heard this, it waged an official protest in Washington, D.C.; the result was the famous "Gentlemen's Agreement" with Japan. To save face on both sides, California was forced to back down on the segregation issue while Japan agreed to limit emigration to those with American relatives. After this agreement, only women, largely "picture brides," came. Still, white Americans harassed the Japanese for their picture brides, because they feared Japanese population increase. Since the Japanese people were thought to be culturally and racially inassimilable in the melting pot idea of America, the increase of their population was seen as a threat to America. American xenophobia was expressed concerning picture brides:

The intent on the part of the Japanese that is quite evident now is to secure upon this continent a foothold for their race, not as individual units to be absorbed and assimilated in the great American melting pot, but as a compact body of loyal subjects of the Mikado [the ancient title of the Japanese emperor], to serve his interest in every possible way.[22]

Picture brides helped redress the Japanese male/female imbalance.[23] However, the Gentlemen's Agreement was broken in 1924, when the Asian Exclusion Act included the Japanese, and Asian immigration was completely cut off for some time.

The most tragic experience of the Japanese in America began with the Japanese bombing of Hawaii's Pearl Harbor on December 7, 1941. Within days, the FBI rounded up 2,000 nisei leaders and ransacked their homes; Japanese were dismissed from jobs, and professional licenses were revoked. The Japanese became pariahs. Grocers would not sell them food; banks declined to honor their checks; gas stations refused them gas; and hospitals failed to admit Japanese-Americans. Despite General DeWitt's public declaration that "a Jap's a Jap, and it makes no difference whether he is a citizen or not,"[24] and rigorous FBI searches, no Japanese-American was ever convicted of an act of sabotage during the Second World War.

On February 19, 1942, President Franklin Delano Roosevelt signed Executive Order 9006 authorizing the establishment of military defense zones to exclude persons considered a threat to the U.S. military effort. The language excluded Italian-Americans and German-Americans. It authorized curfews, the use of federal troops, and special housing for evacuees. Some 117,000 Japanese-Americans were removed from their homes and interned; of these 70,000 were nisei— American citizens. The government refused these citizens information, often gave them fewer than forty-eight-hours notice to leave their communities, ordered them to report to any of fifteen specified locations for removal to evacuation camps, and allowed them to bring only what they could carry. Consequently, they received little for what they sold, and California farmers—strong supporters of internment—quickly purchased vast acreage of rich, Japanese-owned land.

Once they arrived at the centers, actually prison camps, their prospects were equally grim. Barracks became their residences and were partitioned into six rooms; one room for each family, furnished with a stove, a light, and straw-mattressed beds. All families in a barracks shared a bathroom and showers, while there were common laundries and dining rooms in each camp. The roads were unpaved. All the camps were surrounded with barbed-wire fences and equipped with searchlights and armed sentries.

During this period, family life among evacuees disintegrated. One of the second generation described the disintegration as follows:

> My own family, after three years of mass hall living, collapsed as an integrated unit. Whatever dignity or feeling of filial strength we may have known before December 1941, was lost. . . . Not only did we stop eating at home, there was no longer a home to eat in. The cubicles we had were too small for anything you might call "living." Mama couldn't cook meals there. It was impossible to find any privacy there. We slept there and spent most of our waking hours elsewhere.[25]

During the detainment, many nisei volunteered for the U.S. Army to convince the American public they were loyal Americans willing to fight for the United States, and in 1943 a special regiment was formed for the Japanese-Americans. Some 26,000 nisei joined the Army, many of them in the nisei 442nd Regiment, which demonstrated heroism and became one of the most decorated units in America's military history. Clearly they proved that non-whites were equally valuable citizens.

On December 17, 1944, the relocation camps were closed, and Japanese-Americans were allowed to travel nationwide. Why didn't Japanese-Americans resist internment? Why did they go so quietly and obediently to fill buses and trains to an unknown destiny? Could it have been because they saw themselves as marginal people? Did white racism and xenophobia diminish their confidence? If so, racism created an unfortunate legacy for America and instilled Asian mistrust in American government.

Internment caused psychological trauma that would be neither compensated nor healed. One nisei, almost thirty years after returning to the Manzanar relocation center, said:

> I had nearly outgrown the shame and the guilt and the sense of unworthiness. This visit, this pilgrimage, made comprehensible, finally, the traces that remained and would always remain, like a needle. That hollow ache I had carried during the early months of internment had shrunk over the years to a tiny sliver of suspicion about the very person

I was. It had grown so small I'd forgotten it was there. Months might pass before something would remind me. When I first read, in the summer of 1972, about the pressure Japan's economy was putting on American business, and how a union in New York City had printed up posters of an American flag with MADE IN JAPAN written across it, then that needle began to jab. Mama's soft weary voice from 1945 said, "it's all starting over." . . . Manzanar would always live in my nervous system, a needle with Mama's voice.[26]

The memory of that internment still arouses shame and anger, but its memory is important. We must not allow the same atrocity to be repeated. After the war, in 1948, President Harry Truman signed the Evacuation Claims Act to compensate for the material loss Japanese-Americans endured because of relocation. Japanese-Americans asked for $132 million and the government paid $38 million (about 10 cents for every dollar they lost). Finally, the 1952 MaCarran-Walter Act updated the U.S. immigration and naturalization law and abolished racial qualification for citizenship. This was important for first generation, issei, and other Asian immigrants, who had been ineligible for citizenship because of their racial origin.

After the Second World War, a new generation of Japanese in America emerged. The center and authority of its communities shifted from the issei to the second generation, nisei, the third generation, sansei. The emergence of the sansei provides new hope for Japanese-Americans. They, unlike the nisei, are interested in rediscovering their ethnic heritage with pride and have attained extremely high educational and professional levels. Today the average Japanese-American has a better education and higher income than the national average, while criminal activity and juvenile delinquency rates remain low. They have even turned their farmland losses during the internment around. Today 99 percent of all celery crops and 95 percent of all strawberry crops produced in Los Angeles County are grown by the Japanese.[27] They have also succeeded in engineering, business, social services, law, and medicine, as well as many other occupations, and have made outstanding contributions to America's development. Nevertheless, to most Americans, Japanese-American citizens, like other Asians, are still "foreigners." We do not know how long it will take for them to be accepted as Americans. Until non-Asian Americans get to know Asian-Americans, they will remain marginal people.

Korean-American Experience

The history of Korean-Americans is similar to the other two stories. They share a similar pattern of suffering, rejection, and humiliation. However, Koreans distinguish themselves from other Asians with their strong political interests and their religious affiliation with Protestant denominations.

The first Koreans in America were students and political refugees. They arrived in 1883, a year after the signing of the Shufeldt Treaty, which opened Korea to the West. By 1887 sixty-four Koreans had arrived, most of whom had been encouraged by Christian missionaries in Korea to come to study. This group included many great leaders who fought for Korean independence from Japanese occupation.[28]

Large-scale Korean migration to America and its territories began in 1903. It was initiated by American sugar planters in Hawaii and Horace D. Allen, an American missionary to Korea. Allen met with the Hawaii Sugar Planters' Association and became interested in bringing Korean laborers to Hawaii. Korea was in the throes of severe drought, floods, locust plagues, and Japanese occupation. Through Allen's initiation, most who came to Hawaii were Christians. The first ship left Inchon Harbor on December 22, 1902. Fifteen additional ships arrived in 1903; another thirty-three came in 1904. By 1905, more than 7,000 Korean immigrants had come to Hawaii.[29] Since that year Japan decided that further Korean immigration to America threatened its newly established political control over Korea, and halted it. The 1907 Gentlemen's Agreement[30] with Japan included Korea, a Japanese protectorate, yet the agreement did not include students. Small groups of Korean scholars were able to escape Japanese political control.

Like other Asians in America, most Koreans in Hawaii were males, previously from port cities, and Christian. They came to Hawaii's cane fields from diverse occupational backgrounds: domestic, service, mining, and police work.[31] More than half remained in Hawaii, while a thousand returned to Korea, and two thousand moved to the West Coast. Nearly half of the first 101 immigrants on the first shipload were the original members of Reverend Jones' Yongdong Church in Inchon.

Korean laborers worked sixty-hour weeks for sixty-nine cents in daily wages on the plantations. They repaid their passage loans, saved what they could, and often left Hawaii for the mainland to work on the railroads and farms, and in fisheries and mines. Because Koreans in America were a relatively small group in comparison to the Chinese or

Japanese, they were not given any special place in the American labor forces. They were often humiliated, harassed, shamed, and hurt, as were other Asians in America. However, they also had an advantage; Koreans as a small ethnic group retained their sense of community and mutual support through patriotic societies and religious organizations. An example of their intense nationalist feelings was demonstrated in 1908. In San Francisco a protest was organized against Durham White Stevens, a pro-Japanese American working in the Korean diplomatic service. Stevens was sent to America to explain Japan's policy on Korea, and he made a speech later published in the *San Francisco Chronicle*. Korean nationalists demanded that his statement on Korean policy be retracted. Stevens refused. He was assassinated shortly after, while accompanying the Japanese Consul in the city. The assassin made the following remarks:

> I was born on March 30, 1875, in Pyeng Yang, Korea, and became a baptized Christian in my early days. When I saw my country fall into the hands of Japanese aggressors, I was filled with sorrow, but unable to do much to help. I applied for the status of an immigrant and came to Hawaii hoping to learn something in order to help my country. As a traitor to Korea, Stevens should die for his betrayal, since, through his deception, he made the Japanese occupation of Korea possible. I wish that I could have killed the traitor for my people. What is life? It is not enough to die, but one ought to know how to die. To die for having shot a traitor is glory, because I did it for my people.[32]

The Stevens case was the first demonstration of Korean nationalism in America; the incident had a profound impact on that community. Political activities accelerated, and the immigrants won considerable national support for Korean independence from Japan. Meanwhile, Japan tightened Korean student visa requirements.[33] The immigrants kept the issue alive until Korea gained its independence from Japan at the end of the Second World War.

Besides political involvement, Korean immigrants built community through religious affiliation. The first Korean church service was held at Mokolia plantation in Hawaii on July 4, 1903, barely six months after their arrival. Soon Korean immigrants established Methodist, Presbyterian, Episcopal, and other Christian churches in Hawaii, San Francisco, and Los Angeles.[34] After a decade, they had established more than thirty-one churches and church schools in Hawaii with 2,800 members. Nearly every Christian mission in Hawaii provided a Sunday school and Korean language classes for children. In the 1920s Korean churches were established in Chicago, New York City, and other major cities; the churches became the foci of community life for Koreans in America. Today more than 2,000 Korean churches exist nationwide. This means one Korean church for every 350 Koreans. A popular saying among Korean-American churchgoers is: "When two Japanese meet, they set up a business firm; when two Chinese meet, they open up a Chinese restaurant; and when two Koreans meet, they establish a church."[35] Korean churches grow faster than any other churches in America. According to a study on Asian-Americans in the Chicago area, about 32 percent of Chinese-Americans and 28 percent of Japanese-Americans participate in the life of the church, whereas 71 percent of Korean-Americans are affiliated with churches.[36] To meet the need of the growing churches, an increasing number of Korean students are entering theological seminaries.[37] The Korean church may continue to grow and affect the lives of other congregations.

After the Second World War, the demography of Koreans in America changed drastically. Korea became an independent nation, although divided between North and South. Twenty-eight thousand Korean women came to this country with American soldiers from 1947 to 1975, an increasing number of students came to study, and war orphans were placed for adoption. Changes in immigration laws in 1965 resulted in the elimination of rigid quotas and broadened immigration opportunities for professionals and students. The majority of the latecomers were between the ages of twenty and forty-five, and came with more education than other immigrant ethnic minorities. Moreover, many who came to the United States as students (including myself) decided to become permanent residents when they finished their educations. The Korean population increased so rapidly that in 1980 Koreans in the United States ranked as the fourth largest Asian population in America. By the year 2000, Koreans will exceed one million people.[38] This phenomenal growth was primarily due to the revised immigration act in 1965. Today about 90 percent of all Koreans residing in the United States are immigrants who came after 1965.

Although 72 percent of Koreans held professional or managerial-level jobs in Korea, a majority could not find positions in America comparable to their qualifications. They became self-employed and started service-oriented businesses: hamburger stands, barbershops, grocery stores, food service, restaurants, maintenance companies, and others. Like the Chinese and Japanese, they created their communities, known as Koreatowns, in Los Angeles, Chicago, New York, and other large cities. Their priority was the education of their children. Most came to North America because of educational opportunities for their children.

The Many Faces of Marginality

Being relative newcomers and interested in their own political activities and religious life, Korean-Americans have suffered and been humiliated less than other Asians in America. They have, however, experienced the same harassment, discrimination, and rejection that the Chinese and Japanese in the U.S. have experienced. Usually to Caucasian-Americans, Asians are Asians. However, not being associated with the appropriate ethnic group still causes me pain. I offer an example: when I was the youth minister in a United Methodist Church in Toledo, Ohio, I was confronted by a ten-year-old boy in front of a shopping mall. Without any hesitation he shouted, "Hey, Chinaman!" and pointed his finger at me in front of many people. I felt humiliated publicly by a youngster. I wondered how to respond. First, I feared that some people from my church would see the incident. Then, I took courage and responded, kindly: "I am not a Chinese. I am a Korean." The boy replied, "Korean! It doesn't matter. You are a Chinaman to me."

Like this boy, most Americans are insensitive to the idea that I belong to a particular Asian ethnic group. This stereotypic image of Oriental-Americans hurts all of us, and is deep-seated in cultural and racial prejudice. Another example: May Ching, a Chinese girl, discusses subtle discrimination she's endured. "When you go into a store and want to buy something, they ignore you. When you ask questions about a different cut of meat, or something else, they make you feel like an idiot."[39] Asian-Americans note that such discrimination often prevents them from moving up professional ladders or attaining deserved promotions.

If the Asian experience of harassment, discrimination, humiliation, and rejection is based on cultural and racial bias, I suggest that other American ethnic minorities experience the same treatment. While Hispanic people are more closely related in terms of culture and race to Caucasian-Americans, they have suffered significant racial discrimination. Also non-blacks, like me, likely cannot comprehend the enormity of discrimination that African-Americans have borne through generations of dehumanization, rejection, and shame. Despite the struggle, begun in the 1960s, for black human rights, racial discrimination is prevalent today. The controversial verdict of Rodney King's case and the subsequent April 1992 Los Angeles riots seem to indicate a deep-seated racism. Also the 1969 Kerner Commission confirmed: "Our nation is moving toward two societies, one black, one white—separate and unequal."[40]

One of America's most neglected ethnic groups is Native Americans. In years of association with them in North Dakota, I admire their patience and tolerance in the face of still significant oppression. Their sacred lands stolen by foreigners and their people massacred almost to extinction, this people endure with a hospitable spirit. They are a truly marginal people in North America.

There are also many other ethnic groups in this country who have been rejected, shamed, and oppressed by the central group of our society. In this experience of marginality we find the common cord that gathers our ethnic and cultural differences into a mutual understanding, and can help to transform North America to be truly what it was meant to be: a nation of immigrants with freedom for the pursuit of happiness for all people.

2. IN-BETWEEN AND IN-BOTH

Defining Marginality

> If I cannot appreciate different colors,
> I want to be color blind.

Thinking from the Margin

In this chapter I will discuss both the negative and the positive perspectives on marginality. My aim is to lay the groundwork here for the next chapter, where I will describe and define a "new marginality" as a corrective for classical marginality, and to show what the implications of this definition are for the theological task. I have said my experiences as an Asian-American are supported by the experience of other Asian-Americans, especially Chinese-Americans, Korean-Americans, and Japanese-Americans, and they are the primary source of my definition of marginality.

Defining is often merely a process of categorization. Human knowledge is conveyed mostly in categories pre-established by social conventions. Our knowledge of marginality is no exception. Instead of using abstract categories pre-established by a dominant group, I will use a story which is commonly understood by marginal people. This story will become an important metaphor for the task of defining and applying marginality in this study.

About a mile from my residence is a small park where many people often stroll along a narrow path. One beautiful autumn afternoon, I decided to stop at a pond along the path. The calm water of the pond mirrored the beautiful autumn foliage. Sitting quietly on an old stump, I observed the peaceful pond. Suddenly a huge fish jumped up at the center of the pond, creating an enormous sound of water and powerful waves that spread all directions. The waves moved to the edge of the pond next to where I was sitting. The beautiful concentric circles of waves lapped endlessly toward the shore. When the waves finally reached the edge, however, they began to ebb back to the center from which they originated. Their backward movement was an amazing discovery for me, even though I should have expected it from my study of elementary physics. Perhaps I had always seen it, but had not paid attention. Why did I not pay attention to ebbs returning to the center, but noted only the waves coming out to the edge? Why was I interested only in something happening at and from the center? Why did I neglect what happened at and from the margin?

As I meditated on these questions at the small pond, I began to see myself as a victim of centrality. I had been taught that I should see and think from the center. That was why I had seen only the waves coming from the center. After noticing the ebb recede from the edge and grow toward the center, however, I learned to see and think from the margin as well. Whatever came from the center would eventually return to the center because of the margin. Thinking from the margin rather than from the center gives me a fresh perspective.

My careful observation of the pond helped me define marginality and the marginalized person. First of all, I noticed that marginality is defined only in relation to centrality. Without the center there is no margin; just as there is no center without the margin. They are mutually relative and co-existent. When we mention the margin, we acknowledge the center and vice versa. In this interdependent relationship, it is impossible to say which comes before the other. However, when we "think" of ourselves at center, the margin becomes secondary. Likewise, we can see the margin as primary if we "think" of ourselves at the margin.

Traditionally, we have learned to think from the perspective of centrality. We, therefore, think that the center defines the margin. When the rain fills the pond, the margin or the periphery expands; when the dry season comes, the margin of the pond contracts. Yet the center *seems* to be the same. Moreover, action takes place in the center. The margin *seems* to be receptive and appears to respond only to what happens at the center. The center is not only steady but is the origin of action. Thus, the center is attractive and seems to be a preferable location for us to be. For example, when we type, we set the margins. Here, we unconsciously put ourselves at the center and draw the peripheries. Since we think from the perspective of center, we have a tendency to put our house in the center of a lot or put our chair in the center of a room. In other words, we want to put ourselves at the center of everything. This inclination to be at the center seems to be an intrinsic human drive. In the history of civilization, the center attracted humanity more than any other thing in the world, for the center has been understood as the locus of power, wealth, and honor. This inclination has been and is a powerful drive in building civilizations, while it remains a destructive power in creating injustice. Many religious founders, such as Jesus, Lao-tzu, and Buddha, attempted to provide a means of freeing humanity from the idol of centrality, but the inclination to be at the center persists.

In this book I want to demonstrate how to see and think of ourselves from the "other" side, the side of the margin: to observe, to understand things from the perspective of marginality, and to see what role the margin plays in our understanding of the Christian faith. To approach this question, we need to look closely at marginality.

Marginality and centrality are so mutually inclusive and relative that it is imbalanced to stress one more than the other. If we stress marginality over centrality, are we not making the same mistake that centralists commit? No. Here, marginality is stressed because it has been neglected. By stressing marginality over centrality, we can restore the balance between the two poles. Such a balance, which creates harmony, finds a new center, the authentic center, which is no longer oppressive but liberative to the people located at the center or the margin. In this respect, stressing marginality in theology is not a mistake but the correct approach.

Returning to the story of the pond, let me also add that I saw other small fish jumping up here and there as the evening approached. I also saw leaves dropping from trees into the pond, creating ripples. The ripples caused many centers and margins that intersected and were confluent with one another. Ripples were created within ripples. Like the ripples in the pond, our lives are filled with many centers and margins. Centers are created within margins; margins are also created inside of centers.

A poor and oppressed male is often the central, the head, in his home, while he is marginal in the larger society. A woman belonging to the dominant group may be a marginal member in her home. The sense of being a marginal person is relative also to each individual. One may think of oneself as being at the margin, while others perceive that individual as situated at the center. For example, those who serve in the president's cabinet may see themselves as being at the margins of that core group in relation to their ability to influence the president, while they belong to the center of political authority from the perspective of ordinary citizens. The same idea is applicable to ethnic minority leaders who are marginal people in the larger American society, but are influential and, therefore, at the center within their ethnic group. It is difficult to draw a line between centrality and marginality. Both are dependent upon the perspectives of the subject and the object, and are relative to the contexts in which we define our status. Understanding the relativity of multiple centers and margins is important when we try to define ethnic minorities as marginal people.

I learned something else at the pond. The fish and leaves, which created waves, were determinants of various centers and margins, of centrality as well as marginality. As many things can create waves in the pond, so there are many determinants in our society.

Marginal people usually belong to subordinate groups, while those at the center usually belong to dominant groups. Marginal people are then the oppressed, the powerless, and the rejected. They are ethnic minorities, women, the unemployed, the poor, the illiterate, the homeless, the handicapped, the AIDS-infected, gays, lesbians, and so on. Those who are not part of the institutions that dominate can be regarded as marginal people. Racially, Caucasian-Americans belong to the dominant group and people of color to the subordinate group; but economically, not all Caucasians belong to the dominant group. If you are poor and unemployed, you may call yourself a marginal person even though you are Caucasian. If you are a Caucasian woman and belong to a highly professional group of people, you can consider yourself a marginal person if you take sexual oppression seriously. Also a person who works in a legal firm may feel a sense of marginality if he or she is not trained in the legal field. A friend of mine who has taught in a theological seminary for many years told me that she still feels marginal because she does not have a formal education in theology. Marginality has various understandings because of the variety of determinants. Particular determinants seem to affect the intensity and significance of the marginal experience more than others. Specifically, race, gender, economic status, politics, education, occupation, and age seem to be more important determinants than others. Moreover, these determinants are so interdependent that they influence each other. For example, if race determines your marginality, it also affects your economic, educational, and political status. If economic well-being is the determinant of your marginality, it also affects you in other areas of your life. Just as many centers and margins are interconnected and interrelated, so the determinants are interwoven.

It is impossible to discuss all types of marginality; however, all such forms and intensities of marginal experience share one thing in common: they allow the individual to know what it means to be at the edges of existence. From this experience of being at the margin of existence, I will explore from the context of my own perspective and that of other Asian-Americans.

Race, Culture, and Marginality

Ethnicity is the most important determinant of my marginality in the United States. My ethnicity includes my racial origin and my cultural preference.[1] As an Asian-American, all other determinants are relative to but of lesser significance than my racial origin and cultural difference. That is: as male, gender does not marginalize me; as teacher, my occupation does not determine my marginal status; as citizen, earning a medium income in North America, economic lack does not marginalize me. I must be faithful to who I am if I want my theology to be truly representative. Theology is autobiographical, so I reflect on my praxis and context.

While I do not have a marginal status in terms of gender, income, occupation, and education, this does not mean that I have not experienced marginality in these areas. As determinants of marginality are interconnected, it is difficult to isolate one from others. For example, if gender determines a woman's marginality, then gender is the prime factor of her marginal status. Therefore, other determinants of marginality—economic, racial—are primarily due to her gender categorization. However, her relationship to a woman of a different ethnic origin creates a new form of marginality for her. If she belongs to an ethnic minority, it is not only gender but also ethnicity that determines her marginality.[2] Being a male of an ethnic minority, gender is not the determinant of my marginality. For me, therefore, ethnicity is the primary determinant that creates my marginal status in this country. Because I am an ethnic minority, I experience marginality in political, economical, social, educational, and other areas. This is why, even though my marginality is based on ethnicity which includes my racial origin and a cultural difference, I am not free from other determinants of marginality.

Although a clear distinction between ethnicity and race has been made, they are often interchangeable in the experience of Asian-Americans. An ethnic group is a set of people who distinguish themselves socially from other groups primarily on the basis of cultural or national characteristics.[3] According to Manning Marable, race is a totally different dynamic and has its root in the structures of exploitation, power, and privilege. He said, "Race is an artificial social construction that was deliberately imposed on various subordinated groups of people at the outset of the expansion of European capitalism into the Western Hemisphere five centuries ago."[4] The earliest use of race in sixteenth- and seventeenth-century Europe was to designate the descendants of a common ancestor, emphasizing kinship linkage or generation. It was only in the late eighteenth century that the term *race* came to mean a distinct category of human beings with certain physical characteristics.[5] In the United States, race is an ideology based upon physical or biological traits, such as skin color, body structure, and facial features—the unchangeable physical characteristics that can be used to categorize people into inferior and superior groups.[6] Because ethnic minorities, such as Asian-Americans, African-Americans, Native Americans, and Hispanic-Americans, live as subordinate groups due to their biological and physical characteristics, for them ethnicity and race are inseparable. In fact, to be an Asian-American means to be yellow, just as to be an African-American means to be black. A clear distinction between ethnicity and race makes sense from the perspective of centrality, but it is not possible from the perspective of marginality. Race is inclusive of ethnicity, just as culture is. Both racial and cultural characteristics are included in the ethnicity of marginal people.

Knowing that the primary cause of my marginality is linked with race and culture, let me stress their importance. Race and culture were the criteria used by early sociologists to determine what marginality was. Marginality was recognized as a concept when it became clear that conflict occurred between groups of people because of varying race and culture. So racial and cultural determinants play the most important roles in the definition of marginality. Moreover, racism and cultural bias are primary issues for doing theology in a multiracial and multicultural society.

Race and culture are inseparable and mutually inclusive. However, the cultural determinant can be altered, while the racial determinant cannot. Culture is mutable, race is immutable. "Non-white immigrants may attain a high degree of cultural assimilation (adoption of American life-style), but structural assimilation (equal life-chances) is virtually impossible unless the immutable independent variable, 'race,' becomes mutable through miscegenation or cognitive mutation of the WASP."[7] For example, the second- or third-generation Asian-Americans are often easily acculturated, adopting the American lifestyle, but they can hardly be assimilated into American society on a equal basis because of their race. I believe, therefore, that the most fundamental determinant of marginality for Asian-Americans, as well as for African-Americans, Native Americans, and Hispanic-Americans, is race, even though cultural prejudice is directly related to it. Thus, it is necessary to take up the race-relations cycle as a means of understanding the process of marginalization in the United States.

The Process of Marginalization

Because we have inherited the word *marginality* from social scientists, it is important for us to learn from them how the process of marginalization works. One of those who conducted an extensive study in race relations and pioneered in understanding the process of marginalization was Robert E. Park, whose theory of the race-relations cycle became important in the study of racial assimilation in the United States.[8] If "failure of assimilation" is the cause of marginalization, as Park suggests, it is helpful for us to understand why the theory of assimilation of different races does not work in the United States.

The total assimilation of racial groups in this country has been depicted in the image of a melting pot, originally suggested by Israel Zangwill at the turn of the twentieth century.[9] This was a period when the dominant emphasis was on unification of the millions of immigrants who were pouring into the United States, primarily from Eastern and Southern Europe. Zangwill described his idea of the melting pot as follows:

There she lies, the great melting Pot—listen! Can't you hear the roaring
and the bubbling? There gapes her mouth—the harbor where a thousand feeders come from the ends of the world to pour in their human
freight. Ah, what a stirring and a seething! Celt and Latin, Slav and
Teuton, Greek and Syrian,—black and yellow— . . . East and West,
North and South, the palm and the pine, the pole and the equator, the
crescent and the cross—how the Great Alchemist melts and fuses them
with his purging flame! Here shall they all unite to build the Republic
of Man and the Kingdom of God. . . . Peace, peace, to all you unborn
millions, fated to fill this giant continent.[10]

The vision of America as a melting pot was taken seriously by early
sociologists. Park's adaptation of the theory of the melting pot became
sociological dogma. According to him, the race-relations cycle is
marked by stages of competition, conflict, and accommodation before
the eventual assimilation into the big melting pot.[11] Park named these
four stages: contact or encounter; competition, which includes conflict; accommodation, where conflict seems to disappear; and assimilation, where the fusion of races takes place as in a big melting pot. In
the final stage, marginality due to racial and cultural distance will disappear. In this theory, marginality is only a temporary condition and an
"in-between" stage of the assimilation process. As long as total assimilation does not take place, marginality persists. Current critiques suggest, however, that the persistence of marginality should indicate that
total assimilation is not possible.[12]

The melting-pot idea was only a vision, an ideal based on evolution-
alists' biases that were perpetuated in the mind of the dominant group.
Today most scholars disagree with Park's theory of the race-relations
cycle, and suggest that the eventual assimilation of all races and cultures is not possible or even desirable.[13] In their empirical studies of
ethnic people, particularly Native Americans, African-Americans, and
Asian-Americans, it was discovered that complete assimilation has not
occurred.[14] In those early theories, Asians, as well as other ethnic minorities in North America, have been the victims of racial prejudice and
discrimination. The banishment, after near genocide, of Native Americans onto reservations may be an extreme case. The pervasive pattern
of separating ethnic minorities from Caucasian society in education,
employment, and housing persists, in spite of the remarkable improvement in human rights and equal employment since the 1960s. The Los
Angeles riot after the Rodney King verdict seems to indicate that po-

larization of different races becomes more intense and racial prejudice increases even in our time.[15]

Park's theory of assimilation failed not only because it was based on premature data, but because it relied on the theoretical model of the melting-pot idea. He did not take racism seriously.[16] A two-category system, as Roy Sano pointed out, between white people and people of color operates at many crucial points in our lives.[17] Moreover, no single theory can be universalized; each situation in race relations must be viewed as distinctive. Generalizing is hazardous.[18] What is interesting, however, in Park's theory of the race-relations cycle is the pattern of race relations that occurs between the central group and the marginal groups in the United States. Therefore, even though I disagree with Park's notion of assimilation, he provides a model that helps us understand the importance of racial and cultural determinants in the process of marginalization.

We began with a common assumption that the failure of the melting-pot ideal in North America resulted in marginalization. This assumption, based on the mentality of central groups, must be viewed as wrong from the beginning. "Essentially," Lyman said, "the decision was made—but only gradually worked out in piecemeal fashion—that America was to be a white man's country."[19] The dream of the melting pot was for Europeans only. Hector St. John de Crevecoeur described the dream of the melting pot in America as follows:

> What then is the American, this new man? He is either a European, or the descendant of a European, hence that strange mixture of blood, which you will find in no other country. I could point out to you a family whose grandfather was an Englishman, whose wife was Dutch, whose son married a French woman, and whose present four sons now have four wives of different nations.[20]

The idea of total assimilation came to be a dream only for those of homogenous, national groups from the European continent, not for those who came from different shores. As Frank Ichishita put it, "It seems to me that the melting-pot concept was valid only if one was white. Blacks were kept out entirely and other nonwhites were invited in gingerly so as not to disturb the basic mix."[21] A seminal and definite work in this area was rendered by Ronald T. Takaki in his book *Iron Cages: Race and Culture in Nineteenth Century America.*[22]

Moreover, those who came from different continents never dreamed of becoming a part of the melting pot in total assimilation. The process of fusion by which different racial groups could be incorporated into the common cultural life was understood by them as unrealistic,[23] because of the pervasive racism and cultural bias of Caucasian-Americans. Their dream could not be of a melting pot, but rather a mosaic harmony of different racial and ethnic groups in the United States. If the vision of the central people was for unity for purposes of control, the vision of the marginal people was that of harmony for co-existence.

Let me illustrate that marginalization, not assimilation, is a useful key to the understanding of race relations in the United States. Since I have taken an autobiographical approach, I will reinterpret the race-relations cycle from my own experience and that of other Asians.

Following Park's race-relations cycle, the first stage is the initial contact or encounter between the central people who are white and the marginal people who are colored. This contact itself is an experience of marginality. As soon as we landed in America, we were marginalized. Leaving our homeland and coming to this country was a marginal experience. When I put my feet on American soil, I became a total stranger. The land, the water, and even the sky were foreign to me. The people were tall, and either white or dark. They spoke a language that I could not understand, and behaved in ways that embarrassed me.[24] I was out of place and knew that I was an alien. All immigrants from Asia, and people from other continents, probably had experiences similar to mine in their initial contact with America.

Another immediate dimension of marginalization was racism. I had never experienced racism before I came here; this is true for most Asians. However, in comparison to the experience of the first immigrants in this country, my own experience of racism was mild. Mary Paik Lee, who was five years old when she came to this country, vividly recalled her first day in America: "We landed in San Francisco on December 3, 1906. As we walked down the gangplank, a group of young white men . . . laughed at us and spit in our faces; one man kicked up my mother's skirt and called us names we couldn't understand. . . . I was so upset, I asked father why we came to a place where we were not wanted."[25] This experience of initial contact can hardly be called a reception. For Mary Paik Lee and her family, it was an experience of rejection.

About twenty years later another Korean woman recounted her experience of being associated with the Japanese. She said, "No matter where I appeared—whether in the library, on the street car, or down-town, I perceived that their [whites'] attention was fixed upon me and soon there followed a faint but audible whisper, 'Oh, she is a Jap!' "[26] Racism is experienced in many different forms by those who came. Because of ugly racism, the land of promise never became a reality and the initial reception given them signalled rejection. As in my story, just as the reception of a dandelion seed by the grass is followed by rejection, the first contact in the race-relations cycle was reception for the central group, but rejection for the marginal group.

The second stage in Park's race-relations cycle is competition, which comes after the initial contact. Competition is a process that marginalizes the vulnerable and the poor. From the perspective of centrality, the arrival of Asian laborers was regarded as competition. Caucasian workers thought that Asians came to take their jobs by providing cheap labor.[27] Under pressure from powerful labor unions, the Chinese Exclusion Act was passed to prevent further immigration of Chinese laborers. Let me quote again from a popular song, "Twelve Hundred More," published in 1877:

> O, California's coming down,
> As you can plainly see.
> They are hiring all the Chinamen
> And discharging you and me. . . .
> O, damn, "Twelve Hundred More!"
> They run their steamer in at night
> Upon our lovely bay;
> If 'twas a free and honest trade
> They'd land it in the day.
> They come here by the hundreds—
> The country is overrun—
> And go to work at any price—
> By them the labor's done.
> If you meet a workman in the street
> And look into his face,
> You'll see the signs of sorrow there—
> Oh, damn this long-tailed race!
> And men today are languishing
> Upon a prison floor,
> Because they've been supplanted by
> This vile "Twelve Hundred More!"[28]

From this song, it is clear that the Chinese people were seen only as competitors in a labor market. When they could no longer be competitive, they become further marginalized. But in a strict sense, they were not competitors. If they were competitors, why did they work for such low wages? How could they be curtailed from further emigration? Why were they harassed and ridiculed for their honest work? Why did they have to do the jobs considered the less desirable by Caucasian laborers? Could the dandelion really compete with grass in the green yard? As soon as it grew taller than the grass, it was taken away. Any fair competition presupposes equality. Even today in most cases Asian-Americans are disadvantaged in the resources, opportunities, and privileges necessary to compete fully with Caucasian-Americans. Racism placed Asians and other ethnic minorities in a subordinate category, the category of marginality. Numerous magazine and newspaper articles propagated the ideology that Asian-Americans are the "model minority," signifying that they have succeeded in their competition. This is a myth, however, created to preserve the oppressive system and blame other minorities for not "succeeding."[29]

As long as a two-category system exists in this country, fair competition is not possible. Perhaps conflict, tension, and strife were left behind, as minorities were oppressed and placed under unfair competition. They became more and more subdued after the initial reception. Their frustrations and periodic outbursts of violence subsided as they were controlled under the two-category system, the system of marginality. It is inappropriate to call the second stage competition. If it was indeed competition, it was clearly unfair, because it pitted white workers in a predominant white culture against newly arrived minority laborers for jobs. The particular conflict was based on race rather than class.[30] This stage is better characterized as control or exploitation, because after the first stage, the encounter, Asians began to find their place in society—on its margins.

The third stage is accommodation, where conflict between the central people and the marginal people disappears. Then marginal people are gradually ushered into total assimilation, the fourth and final stage of Park's race-relations cycle. Yet, as long as racism persists, total accommodation is not possible. Usually, second-generation Asian-Americans are fully acculturated through public education. To accommodate American lifestyles and value systems, the young often almost totally reject their ancestral roots. Racism prevents their full assimilation, however. The more they want to be assimilated, the more marginal they feel. As a result, the second generation of Asian-Americans experienced marginality more intensely than did the first generation. When they discovered that they would not be fully assimilated into the dominant group, they began to turn to their roots in search of their identity. Here the cycle of race relations occurs without assimilation.

Total accommodation to the lifestyles and values of centrality is possible. But total assimilation is not, because of persistent racism by central people. One important element of racism is the English language. English became the *lingua franca* and official dialect of Anglo-American people, and it, more than any other single element, promoted Anglo-conformity in the process of Americanization.[31] It was several years ago when a United Methodist minister told me with great surprise, "I couldn't believe that the one who answered the phone was your daughter." I asked him why, knowing what was on his mind. He said, "She speaks perfect English!" "Of course," I said. "She was born in Ohio and educated in a public school." "But, still I cannot believe it." Donna Dong, a Chinese-American, has said, "Someone, just because they saw my skin color, would detect an accent. Someone would always correct me."[32] It is odd, therefore, to hear nearly perfect English from the colored or non-Anglo-Americans.

David, a second-generation Korean-American, told me this story. During a service at Yale chapel, everyone was asked to greet the persons around him or her. He turned around to shake hands with the one behind him. When the woman saw his face, she was troubled and hesitated to shake his hand. He said, "It was not the color of my skin but the face, the face of oriental man, that scared her." It is, then, the face as well as the color of the Mongolian race that becomes an immutable variable marginalizing Asian-Americans.

As the cycle of race relations repeats without total assimilation, the marginalization of Asian-Americans, as well as other ethnic minorities, continues. Our examination of the race-relations cycle shows how Asians as well as other ethnic minorities in this country have been marginalized through persistent racism and cultural bias. After generations of these experiences of racism and cultural bias, many Asian-Americans are no longer interested in assimilating themselves into the Caucasian society. Instead they seek a unique place of their own, and in this way their marginality may help transform American society into a mosaic of various ethnic and cultural groups.

The process of marginalization provides us with enough background to begin our task of formally defining the meaning of marginality from the perspective of racial and cultural determinants. We will begin with a classical definition of marginality, which will be supplemented by a contemporary self-affirming definition of it. The former comes out of the perspective of centrality, while the latter is based on a marginal viewpoint. In the next chapter, both definitions are joined to provide a holistic understanding of marginality. Then that definition will be applied to our theological task.

"In-between": The Classical Definition

Although the word *marginality* can be defined from various perspectives, I focus on its racial and cultural determinants. I choose these precisely because social scientists coined the technical term *marginality* or *marginal person* as they examined the problem of racial and cultural conflicts. Clearly, the classical definition of marginality which is usually regarded as normative by the centralist group is its understanding of the nation's ethnic minorities. So, how the word *marginality* is understood by the majority influences how that group acts its bias. Racial and cultural components of marginality are more fundamental than other determinants. Since this classical definition deals with the personality orientation of those from different racial and cultural backgrounds, let me begin with a description of an old Chinese laundryman, depicted by L. C. Tsung in his 1963 book *The Marginal Man.* It captures a vivid picture of a marginal person in a classical sense:

> The neon sign of a Chinese hand laundry reminded Charles of the several shirts he had not yet picked up. . . . He entered the shop and saw the old man still hard at work behind the counter, ironing under a naked electric bulb, although it was already ten o'clock at night. . . . "How many years have you been in the States?" Charles asked out of curiosity as he paid the man. "Forty years," the old man answered in Cantonese, and raised his four fingers again. No expression showed on his face.
> "Did you have a family?"
> "Big family. A woman, many sons and grandsons. All back home in Tangshan."
> "Have you ever gone back since you came out here?"
> "No. I only send money," replied the old man. From underneath the counter he brought out a photograph and showed it to Charles. In the center sat a white-haired old woman, surrounded by some fifteen or twenty men, women and children, of various ages. . . . The whole clan, with contented expressions on their faces, were the off-spring of this emaciated old man, who supported not only himself but all of them by

his two shaking, bony hands. They seemed to represent the flow of a great river of life, originating from a tiny stream. The stream may dry up some day, but the river flows on. The old man put on his glasses again and identified each person in the picture to Charles Lin. A toothless smile came to his expressionless face. Charles Lin realized that this picture was the old man's only comfort and relaxation. He had toiled like a beast of a burden for forty years to support a large family which was his aim of existence, the sole meaning of his life. The picture to him was like a diploma, a *summa cum laude* to an honor student. Behind the facade of sadness and resignation there was the inner satisfaction which made this old man's life bearable and meaningful.[33]

Although the graphic depiction of this old man seems to be an image of the distant past, it profoundly affects the ethos of Asian-Americans. Our situation today is quite different from his, yet we share in the sense of marginality which expresses itself in different levels of intensities and forms. He is a classical symbol of marginality—a mirror that reflects the inner conflict it causes.

In defining marginality or a marginal person, Robert E. Park and Everett Stonequist borrowed insights from George Simmel and Werner Sombert and employed them to describe the individual who lives in two societies or two cultures and is a member of neither.[34] According to Robert Park, marginality is a type of personality that arises out of the conflict of races and cultures.[35] Everett Stonequist describes the marginal person as follows:

> One who is poised in psychological uncertainty between two (or more) social worlds, reflecting in his soul the discords and harmonies, repulsions and attractions of these worlds; one of which is often "dominant" over the other; within which membership is implicitly based upon birth or ancestry (race or nationality); and cohere exclusion removes the individual from a system of group relations.[36]

Stonequist's classical definition of marginality describes my predicament in this country. I am situated ambivalently between two worlds— America and Asia—and I absorb the repulsions and attractions or the rejection and acceptance of each. The marginal person has to live in these two worlds, which are not only different but often antagonistic to each other. From these two worlds, I chose membership in the dominant society, but it rejects me because of my root in the other world. Hence, I want to be accepted by the world of my ancestry, but it also rejects me. I am unwanted by both worlds, yet I live in them. That is why I am an absurd creature. I am supposed to be a part of this Caucasian-American society, but I do not really belong to it because of the way I look, speak, and behave. The more closely I identify myself with my Caucasian friends, the more I feel alienated from them.[37] I go back to my ancestral land, which has changed in its own way, and it has become a strange place. Moreover, I have changed by adopting the American lifestyle, and this exacerbates my reception back into the Korean culture in Asia. I am a part of two worlds without wholly belonging to either.

Other Asian-Americans are marginal people for the same reason. They are Asians in North America but are Americans in Asia. They are Asians in North America because they have their own racial and cultural roots in Asia; they are Americans in Asia because they are naturalized American citizens. They belong neither to the people of their lineage nor to the people of their residence. They are strangers who do not belong anywhere. A ten-year-old Korean girl, Sun Yong Pak, won the first prize in a speech contest sponsored by the Korean Lions Club in Orange County, California. The theme was "Who am I?" The essence of her speech was, "I feel strange in America and I would also feel strange if I returned to Korea."[38] She is a marginal person whose identity is lost between two conflicting worlds. Most second-generation Asian-Americans are alien not only to Americans and Asians, but also to their parents. That makes them a lost generation. Culturally, they are Americans because of assimilation through public education; racially, they are Asian and unassimilated because of their immutable physical Mongolian appearance in the Caucasian dominated world.[39] Joanne Miyamoto, a Japanese-American, beautifully illustrates the sense of her marginality in the following poem:

> when I was young
> kids used to ask me
> what are you?
> I'd tell them what my mom told me
> I'm an American
> chin chin Chinaman
> you're a Jap!
> flashing hot inside
> I'd go home
> my mom would say
> don't worry
> he who walks alone
> walks faster.[40]

Asian-Americans are a people whose fate is to live "in-between."
This fate does not belong exclusively to Asian-Americans. Ada María
Isasi-Díaz, a Hispanic-American, shares her experience of living in-between: "I am caught between two worlds, neither of which is fully
mine, both of which are partially mine. I do not belong in the Cuba of
today; I do not belong in the States."[41] The experience is, perhaps,
more intensely realized by African-Americans and Native Americans.

As marginality is relative to centrality, everyone tends to seek his or
her center at the center which belongs to the dominant group. So
ethnic minorities as marginal people also want to be at the center, even
if not as part of the group that claims to be central. Yet the more the
minority group seeks to be part of the majority group at center, the
more they feel marginalized.[42] This seems to indicate that highly acculturated Asian-Americans can experience more intense marginality than
those who are less acculturated. Furthermore, the intensity of marginal
experience is proportionate to the height of the conflict between or
among groups because of cultural and racial difference. The broader
the cultural and racial distance is, the more marginality is experienced.

Also a distinction exists between marginal experience and marginal
status. Marginality is experienced only by those who are in a marginal
status, but not all those who belong to marginal status are fully conscious of their marginality. Many Asian-Americans who stay within their
ethnic enclaves, for example, may not want to confront their marginality. Because they do not seek to be part of the dominant group, they
do not have to endure that rejection, even though they have been rejected, ultimately, because of their Asian-ness. Therefore, even those
strict traditionalists who adhere to the norms, values, and identity of
their ancestors still share the collective sense of marginality.[43] No marginal group is free from marginal experience, even though some members of the group try to avoid it.

To be in-between two worlds means to be fully in neither. The marginal person who is placed between this two-world boundary feels like
a non-being. This existential *nothingness* caused by the perspective of
two (or more) dominant worlds is a root of dehumanization. Donna
said, "I was Chinese-American, whatever that meant. That I was not an
individual, not [even] a human being."[44] One of my friends once told
me, "I hate to join in a social gathering in this country." I asked him,
"Why?" He said, "For them [the white people], I don't exist. They
completely dismiss me. I am less than their dogs or pictures on the
wall. They pay attention to dogs and are aware of the existence of pic-

tures, but I don't exist to their mind. They see me but act and think as if I don't exist." His experience as an Asian-American is not unique. I am sure many other ethnic minorities experience the same. Such a sense of non-existence can create self-alienation and undesirable personality development.

Such self-alienation of marginal people is due to their external alienation by dominant societies. The self is split in two when they are torn between two worlds. As Everett Stonequist said, "The duality of cultures produces a duality of personality—a divided self."[45] The marginal person is then a cultural schizophrenic. A Chinese-American puts it this way: he feels as if he is playing a kind of ping-pong game. "Now I'm Chinese, now I'm American." The Chinese elements play against the American elements of his personality. The formation of this double consciousness or dual personality is also vividly evident in the experience of African-Americans. Nearly a century ago, black writer W. E. B. Dubois observed that African-Americans possess two souls, two thought processes, and two unreconciled drives. This duality is at the core of their ethnic consciousness, forming the fundamental matrix for all expressions of African-American music, art, language patterns, folklore, religious rituals, and belief systems.[46] The duality of self can be illustrated through two mirrors. When two mirrors reflect a self simultaneously, each shows a different side of self. Such diversity of image gives rise to a dual self-consciousness.[47] Just as marginality arises out of two conflicting worlds, self-alienation results from two conflicting selves in a personality. As with the old Chinese laundryman, split between China and America, he suffers cultural schizophrenia—a byproduct of marginalization.

According to the classical definition of marginality, other negative personal traits appear because of schizophrenic maladjustment. Serious effects of marginality are excessive self-consciousness and race-consciousness. A marginal person becomes hypersensitive about his or her racial origins and develops an inferiority complex. Stonequist illustrated this in a life story of a marginal person: "I have always been more or less possessed of what writers call an *inferiority complex*. It has affected my every waking moment so that my life has seemed meaningless and without purpose."[48] Other symptoms such as ambivalence, excessive self-consciousness, restlessness, irritability, moodiness, lack of self-confidence, pessimism, sentimentalism and dreaming are byproducts of marginal situations. Because the dominant social norm was the basis for defining marginality, what it determined was that negative traits in a minority group were emphasized in the broad culture and affected personality formation in the minority. Such a description of minority traits might be accurate for the dominant group, but inaccurate to the minority being depicted. What is negative to the dominant group does not have to be understood as negative by the marginal group, just as what is positive to the former does not have to be positive to the latter. The value judgment of each group can be different. Also the characteristics that marginal people display are not seen only as negative but as inferior. Such value judgment by the dominant group—stereotypes—must be tested by marginal people to assess its accuracy. One positive characteristic that the classical definition attributes to the marginal group is that it has the potential to be an acute and able critic of the dominant group and its culture.[49]

In-between boundaries form a marginal condition. Marginality, therefore, is more than a boundary itself; it is many boundaries encompassing two or multiple worlds. In marginality, the two or multiple worlds are brought together and depart from each other or others. Neither world is independent, but exists in relation to the other and opposite—it is "*in*-between." In other words, marginality has no separate existence of its own. It is always relational, for it relates worlds that oppose one another. So marginality is best understood as a nexus, where two or three worlds are interconnected. It is also like a symbol, which does not exist by itself but exists only in relation to others. It is never closed. It is an open-ended and unfolding horizon where the others come to meet and go away. It can be compared to the growing edge of a tree, which opens up for new buds to develop. That is why marginality is a condition that offers opportunity for creativity.

The idea of interconnectedness "*in*-between" leads us to a positive and self-affirming understanding of marginality "*in*-both" worlds. This new self-affirming definition *complements* the earlier self-negating definition, or the classical definition of the dominant group.

"In-both": The Contemporary Definition

The contemporary self-affirming definition of marginality which I propose does *not replace* the classical definition. What has been said of the classical definition is the experience of ethnic minorities. But that definition is the dominant group's, one-sided, and incomplete. It needs balance from a self-affirming definition of contemporary Asian-Americans and other ethnic minorities in a genuinely pluralistic society in the making.

A new definition has developed because of a renewed interest in ethnic roots in a more pluralistically aware America and because marginal people demanded a balance to the demeaning definition of the central group. The classical definition of marginality is fifty years old. Ethnic-minority populations have swelled, society is less centered around the norms of Euro-Anglo culture, and Asian-Americans' influence on the American way of life is significant. Times have changed.

While anti-Asian, particularly anti-Japanese, sentiment has grown recently, such bias can no longer dismiss the importance of Asians or any minorities from U.S. economic, scientific, cultural, and political arenas. Being a country of immigrants, America is a microcosm of the globe. With renewed ethnic pride and with economic and political independence, many people in third-world countries no longer consider themselves subordinate to European and American Caucasians. Moreover, the traditional definition of a so-called third-world country is no longer meaningful, and most so-called second-world countries have become corrupted by the central or dominant forces and become even worse off politically, economically, and culturally than many third-world countries. Many Asian nations, such as Japan, South Korea, Taiwan, and Singapore, often competitively surpass many white nations in technology or trade.

The power structure established along racial lines must be redrawn or abolished, and the idea of a melting-pot society based on Caucasian supremacy must be replaced by a broader pluralistic thrust. In this new age, we, ethnic minorities, take pride in our roots and take seriously our potential to determine our destinies. We don't want to be told by the central group who we are or who we should be. As marginal people, we will define ourselves. This is the beginning of our contemporary self-understanding of marginality.

My children, who were born and grew up in this country, used to say to me: "You always tell us who we are, but you never want to hear who we think we are." They are now grown up. I am ready to hear what they say about themselves. Likewise, we ethnic minorities have matured. We want to say who we think we are. I am willing to listen to what other minorities and the dominant group say about me, but also I want them to listen to me discuss my perceptions as a marginal person.

I have been taught that I am in-between, between two antagonistic worlds without belonging to either. I don't deny it, but what I want to stress is my positive perspective of myself as a marginal person. I am in-both, in both the world of my ancestors and the world of my residence. In other words, I am both an Asian and an American. The contemporary self-affirming definition of marginality emphasizes the idea of in-both rather than in-between. "In-both" complements and balances "in-between."[50]

To stress in-bothness, we have to affirm our roots and our branches. To affirm our roots, first of all we should affirm our color, yellow, which is distinctive of who we are.[51] Yellow is no longer a dirty word, as racial colors go. The affirmation of our own skin color comes from the appreciation of our racial origin. For Asians yellow is beautiful and bright. As Francis Oka, a Japanese-American man, has said:

> Yellow is the color of the sun
>   and daffodil,
> a lemon grown ripe,
>   a stream of yellow water paint
> spreading across my canvas
>   a color I know and can relate to.[52]

For him, yellow, the color of her skin, represents the power and vitality of her life. Genny Lim, a Chinese-American woman, also expresses her liberation from the label of the once so-called disgraceful color. She recalls her childhood love of yellow:

> I never painted myself yellow
> the way I colored the sun when I was five.
> The way I colored whitefolks with the "fresh" crayola.
> Yellow pages adults thumbed through for restaurants,
> taxis, airlines, plumbers . . .
> The color of summer squash, corn, eggyolk, innocence and
>   tapioca.[53]

Many people hate the dandelion, a yellow flower. It is a beautiful flower, but is treated as a weed. I love it, because I identify with it. It is a golden yellow, a symbol of the rising sun. As the story of my life, the parable of the dandelion is a positive and an affirmative expression of an Asian-American image.[54] I am delighted to know that Robert Fulghum, a non-yellow person, also likes dandelions. I see myself and other Asian-Americans in his story of dandelions.

> Now I happen to like dandelions a lot. They cover my yard each spring
> with fine yellow flowers, with no help from me at all. They mind their
> business and I mind mine. The young leaves make a spicy salad. The
> flowers add fine flavor and elegant color to a classic light wine. Toast
> the roots, grind and brew, and you have a palatable coffee. The tender-
> est shoots make a tonic tea. The dried mature leaves are high in iron,
> vitamin A and C, and make a good laxative. Bees favor dandelions, and
> the cooperative result is high class honey. . . . If dandelions were rare
> and fragile, people would knock themselves out to pay $14.95 a plant,
> raise them by hand in greenhouses, and form dandelion societies and
> all that. But they are everywhere and don't need us and kind of do what
> they please. So we call them "weeds," and murder them at every op-
> portunity. Well, I say they are flowers, by God, and pretty damn fine
> flowers at that. And I am honored to have them in my yard, where I
> want them.[55]

I am more strongly convinced than ever that the dandelion is a fine
symbol of my marginality, not only because of its yellowness but also
because of what it is. It is known as a useless and dispensable weed,
but it is known to the marginal person as a useful and beautiful flower.
What the contemporary self-affirming definition of marginality attempts to do is to affirm the wholesomeness of its nature and shape a
new creative image from the old image of disgrace and shame. This is
what Fulghum's story of dandelions did for me.[56]

There is a danger of ethnocentricity when minorities are exclusively
preoccupied with their own roots and identities. We have a tendency
to think our ethnicity is better than another's when we attempt to
boost our racial pride. A story illustrates the danger of ethnocentricity.
According to this story from Asian folklore, God molded a human being
with clay and baked it in an oven. The first one was not baked enough,
so it turned out to be white. The second one was baked too much, so
it turned out to be black. Finally, God baked the third one just right, so
it turned out to be yellow.

The genuine appreciation of our racial and cultural heritage should
not preclude an appreciation of others. We, marginal people, cannot
be exclusivists. We are called to live in the margin where worlds
emerge. We are, by our very nature as marginal, inclusive and open to
all centers. We are pluralistic because we live in-both or in-all. An exclusivist approach is unacceptable to in-both marginal people. Such a
contemporary self-affirming definition of marginality is possible when
we appreciate other origins. Likewise, appreciation of our own skin

color has to be accompanied by our appreciation of other skin colors as well. If we cannot appreciate the colors of other races, we cannot affirm our color. From the marginal point of view, there is no sharp distinction between white skin and colored skin. Likewise, white is a color in the view of colored people. When a white flower is painted on a yellow canvas, the white is distinctive, as is yellow on a white canvas. Perspective is the point. Mutual appreciation of skin color is a way of affirming our solidarity as marginal people.

Being in-both Asians and Americans, the affirmation of Asian-ness is also the affirmation of American-ness. It is not easy, however, to affirm categorically that we are Asians and Americans simultaneously. Diana Chang, a Chinese-American girl, illustrates this difficulty:

> Are you Chinese?
> "Yes."
> American?
> "Yes."
> Really Chinese?
> "No, . . . not quite."
> Really American?
> "Well, actually, you see . . . "
> But I would rather say
> Yes.
>
> Not neither-nor,
> not maybe,
> but both, and not only.
> The home I've had,
> the ways I am
> I'd rather say it
> twice,
> yes.[57]

In every yes there is no, just as in every no there is yes. It is not possible to affirm or deny categorically. In our affirmation of both heritages there is also our negation of each of them. Any absolute affirmation is, then, as evil as an absolute negation of our past. The positive definition of marginality must include the negative definition.

It is quite clear that discovering our identity means more than discovering our roots. It certainly begins with our acceptance of the fundamental determinant of our make-up—race. That permanent, physical characteristic; that immutable variable that separates us from all other races. Once we appreciate our yellowness, we can begin to appreciate all the other aspects of our origins.

Culture, as a "total process of human activity," includes languages, habits, beliefs, customs, social organizations, mores, and values. No Asian-Americans are expected to know all the cultural components of their ancestors, just as Asians in Asia do not. What is expected is that they appreciate the culture and identify with the basic ethos of Asian people. Then Asian-Americans can speak of being a true Asian and a true North American.

To be Asian-Americans in a contemporary pluralistic society means to strive to be simultaneously true Asians and true Americans. In a genuinely pluralistic society, Anglo-Americans will be regarded only as one of many ethnic groups; likewise to be an authentic American does not mean to be a white person. True Americans in the pluralistic world are more than white, more than black, more than red, and more than yellow. To be genuinely American means to be part of the whole, an indispensable section of a beautiful mosaic, or a vital ingredient that makes a tossed salad tasty. We must aim for that indispensable portion of the whole that helps our nation evolve to a full pluralism of ethnic Americans. If we, as Asian-Americans, are asked to be like the Caucasian-Americans who reject us, we cannot be true Americans. We will become aliens placed in-between. However, if we don't have to become like the historically dominant group who rejects us, it is possible for us to be both Americans and Asians at the same time. From the perspective of an expanding cultural and racial pluralism, the white center will not be the norm of the North America to be. This is already a reality globally. The dream of equality, dignity, and freedom for all Americans, as it was eloquently spoken of by Martin Luther King, Jr.[58]

To me the dream is now a reality unfolding on the global stage and appearing on the horizon. Because I believe and affirm that the American dream is to be realized in a genuinely pluralistic society,[59] we Asian-Americans can become genuine and authentic North Americans without accepting the norm of dominant groups. In fact, we should deny and resist, if necessary, the power of centrality, in order to become such. What makes Asian-Americans true citizens of this nation is their full participation in making America a free, just nation of immigrants and former immigrants. To become Americans for Asian-Americans means to become truly Asian-Americans, rather than to become Anglo-Americans, African-Americans, Hispanic-Americans, or Native Americans. From the perspective of the margin, every American brings his or her ethnicity, whether from a majority or minority perspective, to the whole; this alone is the norm of real America. So, every American is a marginal person who lives in both or multiple worlds by simply being a part of this pluralistic society. Therefore, marginality imposes a new reality that transcends marginalization, for it means to be truly in both or in all worlds.

3. IN-BEYOND

New Marginality and Theology

> " . . . that is, in Christ God was reconciling the world to
> himself, not counting their trespasses against them, and
> entrusting the message of reconciliation to us."
>
> *(2 Cor 5:19)*

I have now faced the difficult task of laying bare two contradicting or
even opposing definitions of marginality. I have juxtaposed the negative (classical) and the positive (contemporary) definitions without denying either of them.[1] I can now examine how, historically, these
contrasting definitions have developed before we attempt to solve the
problem of bringing them together in a holistic definition of marginality.

In-Beyond: A Holistic Definition

The classical definition of marginality, with its negative outlook on the
marginal person, is the perspective of the dominant, Caucasian-American group. This perspective has been the norm of North-American civilization. It represents centrality from which marginality is conceived
and defined. From the perspective of centrality, ethnic minorities,
particularly we, Asian-Americans, are marginal people, who live in-
between our Asian past and North American-ethnic present. Being in-
between, we belong to neither. We are alienated not only from these

dominant worlds but from ourselves. In this we are pulled toward several identities and deprived of a singular self-image. Our souls are split because of the pervasive power of the dominant, central group's perspective regarding centrality. This reality causes the marginal to become powerless and invisible people.

In this contemporary, self-affirming definition, however, the norm of marginality shifts from the center to the margin, the norm is from the outside to the inside, or from the other to the self. Such shift of the norm for defining marginality is historically inevitable. As I wrote in the previous chapter, this transition is accompanied by changing economic, technological, political, cultural, and religious global structures. Also this shift has been influenced by a heightening new sense of freedom in third-world countries, where most marginal people originate before emigrating to North America.

One example of the economic change is that the share of East Asian gross world product has more than doubled during the last twenty years. Thirty-seven percent of all U.S. trade is with East Asia. Japan's economy is already the second largest in the world. Hong Kong, Singapore, Taiwan, and South Korea have per-capita incomes above those of many Western European countries. Malaysia and Thailand are rapidly closing that same gap. In 1986-87, sixteen percent of America's foreign capital came from Japan. Japan has accumulated some three-quarters of a trillion dollars in foreign assets, and by the end of the century, Japan will be a mature creditor, investor, technological leader, and macroeconomic policy-maker. Japan will be living off her investments. In contrast, the United States is now the world's largest debtor. If our trade deficit is not decreased, the external debt will soon reach twenty-five percent of the Gross National Product—we will owe the world more than the value of the sum of buildings, machinery, factories, and equipment from America's manufacturing industries.[2] The technological and economic expansion of East Asians in the world is an important factor that boosts Asian-American pride, confidence, identity, and self-esteem.

Another gauge is population. The rapid demographical growth of U.S. ethnic minorities and their inability to assimilate into the dominant group also has facilitated this change. Specifically, the Asian-American population has drastically increased.[3] Some of these international and domestic changes have ushered in a new age of pluralism and a growing consciousness among ethnic minorities of the need and wish to affirm their place in North America. In a pluralistic society, the image and power of North America can no longer be identified exclusively with one dominant group. When Caucasian-Americans are regarded as only one of many ethnic groups and the American image is understood as multi-ethnic, then Asian-Americans and other minorities will find their legitimate place. During this transitional period, Asian-Americans affirm themselves through ethnic pride. This ability to affirm self makes the contemporary definition of marginality possible.

As illustrated in the diagrams, the configuration of cultural and ethnic locations is changing from a Caucasian-centric America to a pluralistic nation.

Diagram 1 **In-Between** (society dominated by the Anglo-American): classical self-negating definition of marginality

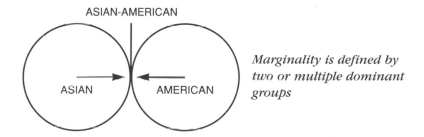

Marginality is defined by two or multiple dominant groups

Diagram 2 **In-Both** (the emergence of a pluralistic society): contemporary self-affirming definition of marginality

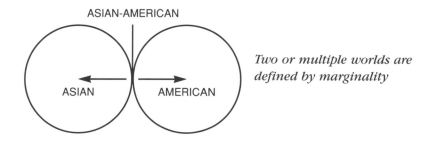

Two or multiple worlds are defined by marginality

The classical definition of marginality maintains a strict, structural separation between dominant and subordinate groups in the United States,[4] while the contemporary self-affirming definition presupposes an emergence of the new configuration, a genuinely pluralistic society. In a pluralistic society, the norm for marginality is no longer imposed on the outsider but is born within it. So a group of ethnic minorities, such as

Asian-American people, seeks its identity, claims its rightful place, and
is regarded as one of many ethnicities in the new social, political, and
cultural configuration of North America. This search is expressed in the
new definition of marginality. Thus, my vision of a genuinely pluralistic
society is not illusion, but reality unfolding. As this vision begins to be
fully realized in our practical life situations, we marginal people affirm
our identity and assert our right to be co-equal with all other ethnicities
in this country. The contemporary understanding of marginality is positive and ever-evolving. On the other hand, the classical understanding
of marginality is negative and losing its significance.

The distinction between these two different definitions of marginality can be understood as historical process. But it is more than historical process; it is existential reality: both definitions are real to marginal
people. I have experienced each. The sense of alienation, of not belonging wholly to this world or that world, is the most common experience of marginal people. Marginal people live in-between two or
multiple worlds. This means that they don't yet fully share the power,
privilege, or resources of the dominant group. Although North America
has changed drastically in recent years, we are still in-between. Moreover, we will never completely overcome being in-between as long as
we are among many ethnic groups in a pluralistic society. Ideally ethnic
minorities would overcome the negative experience of in-between if
we were allowed to assimilate into the melting pot. But total assimilation is unrealistic and undesirable. The resurgence of ethnic consciousness and indigenous cultural values challenges the dominant paradigm
of assimilation.[5]

Let me also affirm the reality of the positive experience of marginality provided by a contemporary self-affirming definition. For me,
the contemporary definition is as realistic and meaningful as the classical definition. Those who don't recognize the emerging pluralistic
America, however, may continue to be victims of the negative definition. Those who recognize America's growth and act on the conviction
of the new definition of marginality see it as a balance to the other definition of marginality. The contemporary self-affirming definition means
a marginal person is in-both worlds without giving up either one. *I am
more than an Asian because I am an American, and I am more than
an American because I am an Asian.* This positive self-affirmation
helps me accept that the contemporary self-affirming definition is as
realistic and meaningful as the classical self-negating definition. In
other words, *to be in-both is as authentic as to be in-between.*

To accept the negative and positive definitions as valid seems to be illogical from the centralist way of thinking. If the logic of centrality is based on the exclusive way of thinking, it is certainly supported by the Aristotelian logic of the exclusive middle. From the centralist perspective, it is, then, irrational to affirm the negative and positive definitions at the same time. In fact, the idea of in-between or in-both cannot be dealt with in the centralist logic of the excluded middle, for it belongs to a marginal experience of the middle. Here, Abraham Maslow's idea will help to illustrate what I write. He said: "*A* is *A* and everything else is *AB* in Aristotelian logic, and never the twain shall meet. But self-actualizing people see that *A* and not-*A* interpenetrate and are one, that any person can be simultaneously good and bad, male and female, adult and child."[6] Because the negative and positive elements coexist in our personal experience, denial of the one is the denial of the other. To assign the negative experience to a certain group of marginal people and the positive experience to a different group merely justifies the validity of centralist thinking; that is, to think in terms of the logic of the excluded middle. I would like to believe that every marginal person experiences the negative and the positive traits of marginality.[7] Because both elements always coexist in marginality, it is neither necessary to justify by the norm of centrality nor to prove by the logic of the exclusive middle. My task is to explain the reality of this paradox in a comprehensive definition of marginality.

In order to include both definitions in this new and comprehensive definition of marginality, let me explain that the negative experience of being in-between is also the positive experience of being in-both. They are two different aspects of one reality. Let me illustrate by returning to the story of the pond. I regard a frog in the pond as a marginal creature. It lives at the periphery of the pond, which connects the land and water, and the air and water. When the frog floats on the pond, it touches water and air, and certainly is in between the water and air. At the same time, it is in both of them. To be in between is to be in both simultaneously. I also saw the inseparability of in-between and in-both at the merger of two or more circles of waves created by small fish in the pond. The ripples created from their centers spread outward and converged with one another to create margins. As we see in the diagram, at the margin the in-between and the in-both are identical, for the margin does not exist by itself or have an independent existence.

Diagram 3 **In-Beyond** (new marginality): holistic definition of marginality

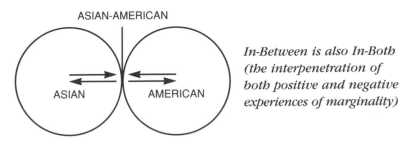

ASIAN-AMERICAN

ASIAN   AMERICAN

In-Between is also In-Both (the interpenetration of both positive and negative experiences of marginality)

Thus, I disagree with those who think that marginal people are outside of the two different worlds. They cannot have an independent existence as the third category of people. They are, in spite of their alienation from two worlds, part of them. Marginality is being at the margin that connects both worlds. That is why marginal people have no independent place or existence as such. Their transcendence is possible only in their immanence. In other words, to be in-beyond means to be in-between *and* in-both.

Just as in-between and in-both are one in-beyond, the margin and creative core are inseparable in new marginality. The margin is the locus—a focal point, a new and creative core—where two (or multiple) worlds emerge. As we see in Diagram 1, the margin remains.

In the classical definition of marginality, the margin is defined by two or multiple centers of dominant worlds. Thus, the margin remains as the margin defined in terms of centrality. However, in Diagram 2, a creative core is formed at the margin. In the contemporary self-affirming definition, the creative core is the margin where two or multiple worlds merge. This creative core, however, does not replace the old centers—the centers of centrality—because it is at the margin of marginality. Although the creative core and the center of centrality are different, they are related to each other. Just as the contemporary self-affirming definition and the classical self-negating definition are inseparable in the holistic understanding of marginality, the creative core is connected to the margin in the making of a new marginality. As we see in Diagram 3, the core or new center is also the margin at the same time. However, in new marginality, the margin is no longer the margin of centrality, the margin defined by dominant groups, but the new margin, the margin of marginality. Thus, in new marginality, the creative core is also the margin. In this margin of marginality, the conflict between the margin and the center disappears, and a reconciliation between marginality and centrality takes place.

The holistic definition of marginality is, therefore, close to how Charles W. Willie attempted to define the new concept of the marginal person. He wrote, the new concept of the marginal person is "the one who rises above two social or cultural groups, freeing the different groups to work together."[8] Although I agree with him in spirit, I have some difficulty accepting what he discussed as "freeing the different groups." New marginal persons like Moses, Martin Buber, or Martin Luther King, Jr., were each part of two worlds. If they were not in-between and in-both worlds, they would not have been marginal persons. According to Willie, Martin Luther King, Jr., was "one who found his identity neither among blacks nor among whites, but in the synthesis of these two races."[9] To think of him as the synthesis of two races (the black and white) is not only misleading but a misunderstanding of marginality. Martin Luther King, Jr., as a marginal individual, was not a person of a new race, not a hybrid of the black and the white, but an authentic black American. He was in the world of neither black nor white Americans because he was truly in both simultaneously. To be in-beyond such two worlds, one must be in-both worlds but also in-between them at the same time.

Explaining the paradox of coexistence of in-between and in-both will help us understand the meaning of "in-beyond." In-between, as I said, focuses on the negative characteristics of marginality, while in-both stresses the positive characteristics of it. In an exclusive way of thinking, the negative characteristics must be either eliminated or nullified through the positive characteristics, so that marginality is overcome. Therefore, with the classical definition of marginality, one can say that the person who is in-both worlds is no longer regarded as a marginal person. This kind of thinking is common among Asian-American writers. According to them, those Asian-Americans who have discovered their identity are transformed into new Asian-Americans, who are no longer regarded as marginal people.[10] I think these writers delude themselves and accept the centralist perspective that advocates exclusive thinking. However firmly new Asian-Americans establish their self-esteem and discover their identity as Asians or as Americans, and however assertive they might be, as long as a dominant group exists and classifies them as a subordinate American group, they cannot be free of marginality. For example, no matter how much Sen.

Daniel Inouye has been assertive and strengthened his esteem, he is
not free of marginality. In 1987 when he was co-chairing the committee investigating the Iran-Contra scandal, some of the telegrams and
phone calls received by the committee told the senator that he should
"go home to Japan where he belonged."[11] Despite that he was born in
America and had received a Distinguished Service Cross as an American soldier during World War II, he is a marginal Asian-American. Thus,
he is a marginal person, in the perspective of the dominant group, as
long as he is an Asian-American, while he is a dominant person in the
perspective of the marginal group. He is always a person of "and" or
"both."[12]

As a hyphenated person, an Asian-American symbolizes the middle
which is joined by two worlds. As Harry Kitano has said, "The middleman by definition will fare no better or worse at the top or the
bottom—you are the middle of that sandwich whether the wheat
bread goes on top or the white bread goes on top. So in some way a
permanent middleman position is maybe what the Asian in the United
States has to look forward to."[13] The hyphenated minority or the
minority of "and" is *extrinsically* in-between because of societal
pressure, but is *intrinsically* in-both.[14] The latter belongs to the contemporary self-definition which affirms the inherent value of one's
marginality, while the former belongs to the classical or other-directed
definition which negates it. Thus the concepts, in-between and in-
both, are needed to formulate a comprehensive definition of marginality. As David Ng has written, "Pacific Asian Americans are not either/or
types of persons, but live in an in-between state which is both/and."[15]
Both/and complement each other and make a whole. The condition of
in-between and in-both must be harmonized for one to become *a new
marginal person who overcomes marginality without ceasing to be a
marginal person.*

The holistic understanding of a marginal person is, therefore, a new
marginal person, or a person living in-beyond. The essence of being
in-beyond is not a by-product of being in-between and being in-both;
rather, it embodies a state of being *in both of them without either
being blended.* Because being in-between and being in-both coexist
in the new marginal person, the person in-beyond reflects a holistic
or comprehensive understanding of marginality. This new marginal
person has the ability to be continuously creative. Creativity is a process of transformation from being to non-being, and from non-being to
being, simultaneously: that is, the process of change from being in-be-

tween to being in-both, and from being in-both to being in-between at the same time. In such creativity, the mutual transformation between being in-between and being in-both takes place without ceasing to be each. As we see from Diagram 3, new marginality is dependent neither on the dominant group nor on the marginal group, but on both. In other words, the norm of new marginality is the harmony of difference. Through harmony, not union, new marginal persons can transcend and live in-beyond. *To transcend or to live in-beyond does not mean to be free of the two different worlds in which persons exist, but to live in both of them without being bound by either of them.* The new marginal person is a liberated person, a person who is truly free, because each is a whole person and able to be fully present in the world. Because the new marginal person is whole, he or she reconciles two opposing worlds unto the self. The new marginal person is a reconciler and a wounded healer to the two-category system. To become a genuine Asian-American, ethnic minority member, or Anglo-American, each must become a new marginal person—a symbol of a creative nexus that connects different, often antagonistic worlds together, and a catalyst who inspires the creation of a beautiful mosaic of colorful people in this nation.

Now come back to the pond. I like to think of the pond as a microcosm of North America. The pond would be peaceful and mirror-like if fish did not jump up and create splashes. How peaceful our world would be if none of us wanted to dominate another, show off, or be selfish. Yet to expect no splashes or ripples is unrealistic. The world is filled with centers and margins, and tension between them is a constant. We want to create our own centers, stronger and more powerful than others. The more we want to create our own centers, the more we create margins in the world. As I gazed at the ripples from the waves created by the fish and the leaves, I saw that the many centers and margins are created by different variables. Gender, class, and religion are determinants of marginality as much as race and culture are. It does not matter which determinants define marginality, rather it is the common phenomenon that marginal people endure rejection, self-affirmation, and accommodation with each determinant. All marginal people experience living in-between and in-both worlds.

Let me take an example from a gender perspective. Women who work in predominantly male occupations stand in-between two worlds; the world of those men who reject them in the occupation because of their gender, and the world of those women who don't accept them because of their liberation from traditional women's roles. Such women are alienated from the two worlds without wholly belonging to either of them. Asian-American women are doubly burdened when they gain employment in such a situation, because they are women and Asian-American. With the women's rights movement and the new consciousness of pluralism, however, women in America have secured a place in both worlds. Now most occupations are no longer clearly defined according to gender. Many women enter into professions, such as medicine, law, and theology, which have traditionally been regarded as male dominant. The positive self-affirmation of women is beginning to be realized by more women choosing the occupations as careers. As long as men dominate, however, women are marginal. Likewise, men who enter into occupations which have traditionally been female-dominated experience marginality. For example, fathers who request child custody from the court or seek paternity leave from unwilling employers marginalize themselves.

Is it possible for women or men to perfect the positive experience only by eliminating the negative experience? It is not possible or even desirable for people to be free from the negative experience of being in-between.[16] They will feel alienation and have a negative experience of marginality as long as they are in two worlds. The women and men are physiologically, socially, and psychologically different. As long as these distinctions exist between men and women, neither will have only a positive experience. As a finite creature, no one is free of negative experience. Mark C. Taylor said, "Finitude and contingency include within themselves their opposites as indispensable presuppositions, necessary constituents, and the essential ground of their being."[17] The new marginal woman, therefore, possesses the negative and positive experience of marginality. She is not a hybrid of male and female, but a genuine woman authentically participating in two worlds without being bound by either. Likewise, a man will become a new marginal person if he participates authentically in both worlds. Thus, a new marginal person, whether male or female, whether white, black, yellow, or red, should bring a creative harmony to these negative and positive experiences, living in-beyond both worlds that marginalize them.

Neither/nor and Both/and

Marginality has implications for theology. Traditionally, marginal people have not played an important role in the interpretation of Scriptures or in understanding the tradition of the church, since they have been outside of the dominant group of scholars and church officials. No important official church doctrines have been developed from the marginal perspective. In recent years, while liberation theologies have contributed greatly to the removal of dominant group theological monopoly, in general such schools of thought still operate under the auspices of the dominant groups who define and control the center. As long as the third-world liberation theologians attempt to validate their theological interpretation by the work of European-American scholars who have dominated racial and ethnic minorities, they will never be free of the hermeneutics of centrality and will never produce an authentic theology that represents their own perspective. The more closely marginal people want to identify themselves with central people, the more intensely they experience alienation. Likewise, the more marginal scholars want to validate their work through the scholars of centrality, the more their work is less authentic. Marginal people, therefore, need to think and validate their work through their experience and perspective. The norm that validates their theology is not that of dominant-group people but of new marginal people who live in-beyond. The new norm that validates the theology of marginality is then the holistic experience of marginality itself, the experience of being in-beyond, which includes in-between and in-both simultaneously. Because the experience of being in-beyond includes negative and positive experiences, it is never exclusive. Marginal thinking is an inclusive, open-ended, and creative nexus, which becomes the point where various views and interpretations meet. In this respect, even though a marginal approach to theology is different from traditional and official approaches of theology, it is open to the contributions of the traditional and official approaches to reinterpreting theological themes. This inclusive approach to theology is certainly different from that of most liberation theologies which are rather exclusive and confrontational, and create a sharp dichotomy between the oppressed and the oppressor.

Understanding the method of interpretation, we must study the way of thinking. In the past many different schools of thought arose and provided centralist people with different methods of interpretation. However, in the theological world few schools of thought have attempted to go beyond the Hellenistic way of thinking, which is deeply enshrined in the Aristotelian logic of the excluded middle.[18] Such exclusivist logic has been used as an intellectual tool to maintain strict categorical distinctions regarding all issues and as a separatist tool to marginalize those who are different. It has been used also by the church as means to control its theological interpretations. If a theology of marginality can present something new and offer a new interpretation of the Christian faith, it must use a way of thinking indigenous to the experience of marginality and thus be distinctive from traditional Western church thought. That is why we want to begin our hermeneutical method from a marginal thought process.

How we think is ultimately conditioned by who we are. Thinking is more than the activity of our rational faculty. It is a process that involves the mind, heart, and body.[19] It reflects the whole person. Paul explained it simply when he said: "When I was a child, I spoke like a child, I thought like a child, I reasoned like a child; when I became an adult, I put an end to childish ways" (1 Cor 13:11). Following Paul's insight, I, therefore, speak like an Asian-American, I think like an Asian-American, and I reason like an Asian-American. If I don't do this, I deceive myself and my thought is not genuine. When a marginal person speaks, thinks, and reasons like a centralist person, he or she is other-directed and a negatively defined marginal person whose identity is derived from the dominant group. It is important to speak, think, and reason like a marginal person if I am a marginal person. Since I defined a new marginal person as one who seeks a comprehensive and holistic understanding of marginality, let me offer an authentic and marginal thought process for such a person.

I defined a new marginal people as those who are in-between and in-both worlds and think from these two viewpoints. So it is necessary to understand both ways of thinking before defining a way of thinking for new marginal people.

In-between people are of neither this nor that world. If they see life from the locus of being in-between, they must think in terms of neither/nor. This way of thinking is based on the negative understanding of marginality influenced by the centralist perspective.

In-both people define themselves by affirming their existence in both worlds. They are self-directed and possess a positive self-image based on their conviction that a genuinely pluralistic society is in the making. Because they act on this conviction, they affirm this and that world simultaneously, and think in terms of both/and. Their affirmation of both worlds is unrealistic in practice, however, because the genuinely multiethnic society which they envision is not yet realized. Thus, new marginality, defined as a comprehensive understanding of marginality, includes not only the affirmation of both/and but also its negation—neither/nor. The new marginal people should think in terms of a neither/nor and both/and, for they are people of in-between and in-both.

Thinking in terms of neither/nor and both/and seems complicated, for new marginal people are not easily categorized. Because they are alienated by both worlds, they are doubly denied. That is why they think in terms of the neither/nor viewpoint. Moreover, they derive their self-affirmation from both worlds. Such self-affirmation is expressed in terms of the both/and viewpoint. Since new marginal people live in and reconcile these two different worlds, they think from neither/nor and both/and perspectives. They think in simultaneous double negations and double affirmations, because they are in-between two worlds and in-both worlds at the same time. This reasoning is best understood as a simultaneous total negation and affirmation. It is a paradox; the total exclusion (negation) coexists with the total inclusion (affirmation) in this way of thinking.

The relationship between a neither/nor (total negation) and a both/and (total affirmation) is similar to the relationship between in-between and in-both. The neither/nor and both/and are opposite but complementary. In other words, the total negation and total affirmation harmoniously coexist in the way of thinking of new marginal people. Such paradoxical reasoning is close to a mystic mind-set. In a complementary relationship, negation is not a rejection of affirmation but an indispensable part of it. Likewise, affirmation always presupposes negation to be affirmative. Thus negation has to be understood as the background of affirmation, and affirmation as the foreground of negation. It is, therefore, possible to affirm and negate simultaneously. Affirmation is necessary for negation, and negation is, likewise, necessary for affirmation. Neither exists without the other. In this respect, losing self is gaining self, and gaining self is losing self. In order that we become all things to one another, we must first become nothing at all.

I will delineate neither/nor thinking further. Marginal people are forced to be in-between two worlds; the decision has already been made by the dominant group. Thus, the neither/nor thinking based on being in-between is a passive form of negation. Neither/nor thinking is not the total negation of self but rather the self totally negated by others. When it is applied to our thought processes, it means "non-thinking"; neither/nor thinking is non-thinking.

Marginal people are, therefore, expected to think nothing and say nothing. In Maxine Hong Kingston's *China Men*, Bak Goong was told by a foreman that laborers were not permitted talk while working. "If I knew I had to take a vow of silence, I would have shaved off my hair and become a monk," said Bak Goong. In the cane field, he heard the boss shouting: "Shut up, Go work. Chinaman, go work. You stay, go work. Shut up." He was not even supposed to scream when he felt the sting of the whip on his shoulder.[20] Like Bak Goong, marginal persons are expected to say and think nothing. Silence and non-thinking are expressed in terms of the neither/nor way of thinking. Neither/nor thinking, however, is more profound than this concept. Such thinking comes from the experience of nothingness, the existential nothingness of marginal people. Neither/nor thinking means the total and unconditional negation of all things. Yet, for Asian-Americans, the idea of non-being or non-thinking has profound meaning in their cultural roots. According to Asian wisdom, nothing is the source of all things, and non-thinking is the origin of all thinking processes.[21] By being completely negated, one can reach the depth of his or her being. The neither/nor way of thinking for marginal people does not negate or deny the existence of others, but rather is a receptive thought process that encompasses the condition of nothingness. As receptive expression, the neither/nor way of thinking serves as the counterpoint of the both/and way of thinking.

In contrast to the neither/nor, passive way of thinking, the both/and thought process is an active form of self-expression. It affirms both worlds in spite of their denial. The both/and thinkers do not wait until the worlds offer acceptance. This self-assertion is the inner strength of new marginal people. The more negated they are, the more affirmative they become. Like the dandelion's root, the more it is pulled out, the more it penetrates into the ground. Both/and is expressed in unconditional affirmation despite neither/nor's unconditional negation.

This was illustrated by Japanese-Americans during World War II. One-hundred and twenty thousand Japanese-Americans were incarcerated in concentration camps. Few resisted internment. No one even protested against Civilian Exclusion Order No. 27.[22] They yielded completely, their existence as Americans was negated. In spite of this, the second generation of Japanese-Americans, the nisei, affirmed their total and unconditional loyalty to the country that totally and unconditionally abrogated their right of citizenship, and volunteered to join the 442nd unit, an all-Japanese American Regiment. That unit was "probably the most decorated in United States military history."[23] These citizens earned 18,143 individual decorations, including one Congressional Medal of Honor, forty-seven Distinguished Service Crosses, 350 Silver

Stars, 810 Bronze Stars, and more than 3,600 Purple Hearts. They gave life and limb to prove their loyalty to a nation and people that rejected them.[24]

Because the marginal way of both/and thinking is an unconditional affirmation of that which negates it, such thinking also affirms and includes the centralist way of either/or thinking. The either/or thought process has its foundation in dualism that excludes the middle and is closely related to the experience of central-group people. Those at the center want to exclude their competitors. Based on exclusivist either/or thinking, an analytical and critical method of reasoning is embraced by the dominant group. Marginal people, however, think in terms of an inclusive both/and, which complements the neither/nor thinking. This is a holistic and open-ended thought process.[25] The either/or and both/and ways of thinking are not contradictory from the perspective of marginality, even though they are so from the perspective of centrality. In other words, *exclusivist thinking excludes inclusivist thinking, but inclusivist thinking includes exclusivist thinking.* That is, either/or thinking excludes both/and thinking, but the latter includes the former, because the former already presupposes the latter. It cannot be both/and unless the thought process presupposes two distinctive perspectives. In both/and thinking, the two forms are complementary and form a harmonious whole, while in either/or thinking, they are in conflict. Both/and thought does not eliminate opposites but complements them. In other words, in both/and thinking the opposites are not in conflict but in harmony.

In a genuinely pluralistic society either/or thinking loses its claim and becomes relative to the holistic way of both/and thinking. When central-group people no longer think absolutely and exclusively, the marginal people who think inclusively find their rightful place in a pluralistic society.

Let us look at marginal thinking from *both* a neither/nor *and* a both/and perspective. The simultaneous double negations and double affirmations imply a total negation and a total affirmation at the same time. However, total negation does not exclude total affirmation, and vice versa. To explain it simply, yes is yes but also no, and no is no but also yes, because yes contains no and no contains yes. This kind of totally inclusive thinking includes a distinction between yes and no, but the distinction is always relative to the inclusion of the whole. It is rather natural for Asian-Americans to think yes and no simultaneously.

Julie Matsui-Estrella, a Japanese-American, who works at the Pacific Asian Center for Theology and Strategies at the Graduate Theological Union in Berkeley, Calif., told me how she usually responds when an Asian-American offers her, for example, a piece of candy. "I would say no before accepting it," she said. "Do you say no just once before saying yes?" I asked. She said, "Two or three times, or even more. They know that no doesn't always mean no; it also means yes. But when I deal with white Americans, I never do that. If I say no, they will instantly take it away."[26] No is in yes because, even though we want the candy, we also do not want to accept it.

Being in-between and in-both worlds, total negation (in-between) and total affirmation (in-both) always coexist in new marginal people. Because these ideas coexist, they are not only the most inclusive but also the most relational form of thinking. It is relational because yes exists always in relation to no, just as no can exist in relation to yes. Neither/nor and both/and ways of thinking de-absolutize the "either/or" way of thinking.

The way of expressing marginal thinking is also distinctive. As the Apostle Paul said, children not only think and reason like children but also speak like children. Marginal people must also speak like marginal people. If inclusivity is a key to marginal thinking, the words or symbols we use also must be inclusive. We have begun to use gender-inclusive language, but it is not enough. Race, culture, and class particularities must be expressed inclusively. In a pluralistic society where no people dominate, ethnic groups must be allowed to speak and to write in diverse ways to express their specific life situation. No single language standard should be imposed on marginal people. Diversity should be encouraged in language usages. The inclusive way of marginal thinking should also allow us to express ourselves in all forms—stories, parables, poems, narratives, and metaphysical discourses. Such diverse expression becomes a mosaic harmony, and such creativity should not be mistaken for ignorance. Unlike their stereotypes, not all marginal people speak and write like the poor and the uneducated. An educated marginal person speaks and writes like an educated marginal person. A Korean-American speaks and writes like a Korean-American. As I am an educated Korean-American, I must speak and write like an educated Korean-American. I will not necessarily write like an educated Japanese-American. No uniformity is possible in expression. Nevertheless, the underlying harmony of all expression is found in the experience of marginality.

Theology of Marginality

Can the perspective of marginality be the perspective of Christianity? Can the marginal way of thinking be a Christian way of thinking? We defined the marginal way of thinking in terms of a neither/nor and a both/and viewpoint. Can this also be regarded as a paradigm of Christian thinking? In order to answer these questions, let me state: the Christian way of thinking is ultimately to think like Jesus Christ. To think like Jesus Christ means to have the mind of Jesus Christ. Following Paul's teaching, let me reiterate that to become a Christian means to speak, think, and reason like Jesus Christ. Thus, the hermeneutical principle of Christianity is fundamentally grounded in Jesus Christ himself. As Gustavo Gutiérrez said, "The great hermeneutical principle of faith, and hence the basis and foundation of all theological reasoning, is Jesus Christ."[27] The question is, then, whether or not Jesus was a new marginal person. If he was a new marginal person, to have the mind of Jesus Christ means to have the mind of marginal people. If the mind of new marginal people operates through the neither/nor and both/and way of thinking, this way of thinking is regarded as the hermeneutical principle of the Christian faith.

As I will explain in detail in the next chapter, Jesus Christ was a new marginal person *par excellence*. Countless witnesses in the Bible justify this claim. He was a stranger to his own people. According to the author of the Letter to the Hebrews, "Therefore Jesus also suffered outside the city gate in order to sanctify the people by his own blood. Let us then go to him outside the camp and bear the abuse he endured" (Heb 13:12-13). Being outside the camp (or the house of Israel), Jesus became a friend of marginalized people: outcasts, tax collectors, Gentiles, women, the poor, and the oppressed. According to John's Gospel, "He came to what was his own, and his own people did not accept him" (John 1:11). He was not accepted by the dominant groups of his day. The Pharisees, scribes, Sadducees, and Romans rejected him. He was accepted by marginal people because he was a marginal person. He was an outsider, one who lived in-between. On the cross, he was rejected not only by his own people but also by his own Father. He was certainly a man in-between two different worlds without fully belonging to either. He was homeless. "Foxes have holes, and birds of the air have nests; but the Son of Man has nowhere to lay his head" (Matt 8:20). He was human and divine; therefore, he lived in-both worlds.

Although he was rejected, he was a reconciler who broke down walls between Jews and Gentiles, between men and women, between the law and grace. He was a Jew by birth and lineage, but also a man of whole humanity by his act of love. Thus, he was truly the new marginal person who was not only in-between but also in-both worlds. He was the man who lived in-beyond racial, cultural, gender, and class divisions, but was also the man of the whole world. He was, therefore, the new marginal person *par excellence.*

If Jesus Christ was the new marginal person who lived in-between and in-both, to have the mind of Jesus Christ means to think in terms of neither/nor and both/and. Likewise, to be a Christian means to be in the world but not of the world. To be "in the world but not of the world" is marginal thinking, which utilizes simultaneously the total affirmation and the total negation of the world.

The central events of Christ's life that express the marginal way of thinking are his death and resurrection. Death represents the absolute negation of life, expressible in the neither/nor. Resurrection represents the absolute affirmation of life, expressible in both/and. Death and resurrection belong together, just as neither/nor and both/and do. Without death, there is no resurrection; without resurrection, death has no meaning. Likewise, the simultaneous transcendence and immanence of God is expressible in the marginal way of thinking. God is totally transcendent (neither/nor) and totally immanent (both/and).[28] Thus, the marginal way of *both* neither/nor *and* both/and thinking is also the Christian way of thinking.

Marginal thinking has special meaning to Christian life. Such inclusive thinking can apply to Christian love. The way of Jesus Christ is to love one another as he loved us. This love denies all and accepts all. Love denies our selfishness in order to accept others; love accepts others in order to deny our selfishness. The neither/nor negates our selfishness, but the both/and accepts all. In love the total negation and total acceptance take place simultaneously. Love is thus inclusive enough to accept everyone, even enemies. By giving up self, one becomes all things to all people. Love is not exclusive but always inclusive, just as marginal thinking is. Love does not insist on its way but is always receptive to others. It yields to others, allowing them to change and grow in their way. Love never dominates others; thus it does not belong to any "dominant" person but is the way of marginality.[29] The love of God is the marginalization of God.

I recall the margin of the small pond. The margin was receptive to all kinds of ripples coming from their respective centers. Its receptivity was the both/and way, the way of unconditional acceptance of all. Some ripples were strong and some were weak, but the margin was always there to receive them. What made the margin powerful was not its reaction but inaction. By inaction, it activated waves. In other words, it was the neither/nor, the denial of selfishness, which gave it power. The act of reception empowered the margin. A theology of marginality uses reception rather than dominance to change the world.

In this respect a theology of marginality is different from most liberation theologies, which seek only to liberate the poor and the oppressed through reaction. According to a theology of marginality, the liberation of marginal people is not possible without the liberation of central-group people from their exclusive thinking. Liberation is, then, a mutual process. The goal of marginal people, however, is more than liberation from central-group people, rather it is a harmonious coexistence of all people in a genuinely pluralistic society. In this respect, a theology of marginality is holistic, the whole is inseparable from the parts.

The power of new marginality is love, which is willing to suffer redemptively by accepting others unconditionally as Jesus did on the cross. If justice is more important than love in liberation theology, love is more important than justice in marginal theology. Justice reacts to injustice but love responds to it; justice often demands revenge but love forgives; justice is often given by the law, while law is fulfilled by love. Justice and love are inseparable, for love includes justice. Likewise, marginality and liberation belong together. Because reconciliation includes liberation, reconciliation is not possible without liberation. New marginal people liberate themselves by sacrificing themselves (neither/nor) to reconcile and to heal the wound of the whole (both/and).

A theology of marginality does not use correlation. It does not begin with human questions and end with divine answers. Nor does it begin with identifying existential needs and asking God's fulfillment. Correlation between a question and an answer or a need and a fulfillment presupposes they are separate. According to marginal theology, the answer and question are not separate. Correlation is not needed if the answer is found inside the question. In a theology of marginality, the answer is in the question and question in the answer. According to the simultaneous neither/nor and both/and viewpoints, negation and affirmation, no and yes, or question and answer coexist and complement one another. Correlation is based on dualistic thinking in the minds of central-group people. New marginal people think inclusively, and look for an answer in the question, because the answer is a different form of the question. As Francis of Assisi said, "What you are looking for is what is looking."[30] Our approach to marginal theology then is not correlational but co-inherent and meditative. It seeks an answer from within rather than outside itself.

The new marginal theology is always open-ended and never finished. As we are limited, so we will never be able to put the final word on our theology. Those who have written dogmatics and systematic theology in the past have presumed that a theology is complete. Such presumption exists in everyone who wants to put self at the center.

Even the work of Christ is not finished. It continues until all things are summed up in him. If creation is open-ended for Christ, then our understanding of Christ is incomplete, and so, our marginal way of thinking must include all possibilities.[31] Marginal theology is a catalyst that helps others to construct their own theologies out of their contexts, and thus, build a beautiful mosaic of theological expression in the world.

A theology of marginality is also a theology of emigration. The history of the Hebrew people is none other than the history of emigration. It began with the journey of Abraham, who immigrated to Canaan in response to God's call. Later his descendants became immigrants in Egypt. After years of marginalized life in Egypt, they emigrated to Palestine. Again they were exiled to Babylon. Then the Diaspora took the Jews to various nations of the world. When the new Israel was born after World War II, many Jews returned to their homeland. The history of the people of Israel is the history of emigration and marginalization.

North America is also the land of immigrants. Asians, Africans, Hispanics, Caucasians, and other ethnics came as immigrants and all were or are, in some way, marginalized and alienated. In a genuinely pluralistic society every one has come as an immigrant. If North America is the continent of immigrants, a theology of marginality is also North American.

Finally, a theology of marginality is multidimensional. It is interested not only in economic, social, and political injustice but also in psychological, spiritual, racial, and cultural issues of alienation and self-identity. While traditional Western theology began from above, that is, from the Word of God as a universal truth for all people regardless of their context, contemporary liberation theology approaches from below or from the praxis of the poor and the oppressed. Unlike these, a marginal theology approaches from the margin, and connects above and below, and left, right, and center. A marginal perspective also includes a central perspective. A theology of marginality, therefore, deals with both the central perspective of marginality (neither/nor) and the self-affirming perspective of marginality (both/and). This inclusive approach makes a marginal theology holistic and appropriate for a multicultural society.

Reconciling Worlds

Marginality, which has been defined in terms of centrality, has a variety of nuances and implications for different people. Because marginality is a dynamic word, it cannot be fixed upon a certain category of people. Even so-called successful people, even white middle-class people, can experience marginality. People are marginalized economically, politically, socially, physically, racially, culturally, sexually, or educationally. There are many determinants of marginality. I focused on racial and cultural determinants to define marginality and used my experience, and that of other Northeast Asian-Americans, to illustrate marginality. I examined the processes that marginalize Asian-Americans and used the classical definition of marginality as a starting point for my definition of marginality. The classical definition, I think, is one-sided, because it is seen from a centralist perspective. Therefore, I suggested a contemporary self-affirming definition to complement the classical definition. These combined definitions provide a comprehensive definition of marginality. They imply also a new marginal person who lives in-beyond to reconcile and to harmonize both worlds.[32]

The new marginal person, who represents the ideal of all marginal people, experiences both in-between and in-both simultaneously. The experience of being in-between expresses itself in alienation and existential nothingness. In-between is categorized as neither/nor. On the other hand, the experience of being in-both worlds with a renewed identity is categorized as both/and. Since the new marginal person includes experiences of being in-between and in-both, he or she thinks simultaneously in neither/nor and both/and ways. Such marginal thinking is also a Christian way of thinking, because Jesus was the new marginal person *par excellence*. As the new marginal person, Jesus was in-beyond without being free of the worlds that marginalized him. He was transcendent with immanence and immanent with transcendence. Thus, God was in Jesus Christ to reconcile the worlds to self.

My further task in this book is to apply marginal thinking to the reinterpretation of Jesus Christ and other theological themes in the following chapters. I hope to read the Scriptures anew with the perspective of new marginality and to re-examine traditional doctrines for fresh insights from the marginal viewpoint. My interest is not in a centralist approach to critical exegesis but rather toward a creative interpretation of the Christian faith from the new marginal perspective.

4. JESUS-CHRIST

The Margin of Marginality

> Therefore Jesus also suffered outside the city gate in order
> to sanctify the people by his own blood. Let us then go
> to him outside the camp and bear the abuse he endured.
> *(Heb 13:12-13)*

"Who do you think that I am?" is a question that Jesus still asks us today. Peter's reply was affirmative. "You are the Messiah, the Son of the living God." In Matthew's account, Jesus was satisfied with his answer, but, although Peter did not realize it, Jesus knew that Peter's answer did not truly come from himself. "Flesh and blood has not revealed this to you, but my Father in heaven" (Matt 16:15-17). Peter, like other human beings, was interested in the center. He misunderstood Jesus, because he perceived Jesus from his own perspective of centrality. From Peter's point of view, the son of the living God must be at the center of centrality: the king of kings and ruler of rulers. Peter, no doubt, wanted to share the power and domain of Christ over the twelve tribes of Israel. He misunderstood Jesus' goals because they did not come from his own centralist position. Right after Peter answered Jesus' question, "Jesus began to show his disciples that he must go to Jerusalem and undergo great suffering at the hands of the elders and chief priests and scribes, and be killed, and on the third day be raised" (16:21). Hearing this Peter began to rebuke him and said, "God forbid it, Lord! This must never happen to you" (16:22). Jesus said to Peter, "Get behind me, Satan! You are a stumbling block to me, for

you are setting your mind not on divine things but on human things"
(Matt 16:23). From what has been recorded in Matthew, we can easily see
that Peter did not understand Jesus because Peter thought of him from a
human perspective. Humans naturally seek the center, the position of power.

Nevertheless, in the history of Christianity the same mistakes have
been made again and again. Jesus was understood from the perspective
of centrality. He was regarded as the center of centrality, and his followers wanted to be a part of the central authority to rule and dominate the world. In the name of Jesus, papal authority enjoyed power
over European nations for many centuries, and the exclusiveness of
Christ was affirmed by the early councils, confining Christ within doc-
trinal guidelines. Christians became increasingly interested in the
power and majesty of Christ and forgot that it was his weakness that
made him powerful, and his humility that raised him to be the Lord of
lords. They were more interested in his lordship than his servanthood,
and more interested in his resurrection than his death. Jesus became
the subject of metaphysical speculation by scholars of central groups
and the center of glorification by privileged church officials. Still, we
want Jesus to be at the center that we seek, but the center we seek is
not the real center. It is an egotistic one that seeks power and dominance.
That is why Jesus said to Peter, "Satan, your thought comes from man."

Today Jesus still asks: "Who do you think that I am?" I answer: you
are Jesus-Christ, the Son of the living God. I use a hyphenated "Jesus-
Christ" because Jesus is the Christ, while the Christ is also Jesus. In
other words, Jesus as the Christ is not enough.[1] He is also the Christ as
Jesus. Just as "Asian-American" means an Asian and an American.
Whenever I say Jesus, I mean Jesus-Christ; whenever I say Christ, I
mean Christ-Jesus. They are inseparable, two facets of one existence.
Also I understand the "Son of the living God" phrase differently from
Peter. To be the Son of the living God does not mean to be at the center
of centrality. It means to be at the margin of marginality, the servant of
all servants. I will provide sufficient evidence of Jesus' birth, life, death
and resurrection to support the notion that Jesus was, and is, the
margin of marginality rather than the center of centrality.

Incarnation as Divine Marginalization

Jesus was born as a marginal person. Conceived by an unwed woman,
born far from his hometown, sheltered in a manger, visited by Eastern

wise men rather than by the elite of his nation, and flight into Egypt: these are all inklings of what would be his life-long marginality.

One of the most common mistakes made by central-group people is to study the idea of incarnation in the Gospel of John and Philippians without considering the Gospel accounts' background of Jesus' birth.[2] When these passages are examined without the stories of Jesus' birth, they are easily misunderstood metaphysically. In light of the historical background of Jesus' birth, however, we can understand Jesus from a new perspective.

The determinants of Jesus' marginality, class, economic, political, social, and ethnic orientations, made him the marginal person *par excellence*, so the stories of incarnation ought to be interpreted from the perspective of marginality. In the prologue of John, we see that Jesus-Christ was not only a marginal person in his country but also in the cosmos: he was rejected by his people and by the world created through him. "He was in the world, and the world came into being through him; yet the world did not know him. He came to what was his own, and his own people did not accept him" (John 1:10-11). Jesus-Christ became a marginal person by emptying himself to become a servant of people (Phil 2:5-11). Thus the stories of Jesus' birth and incarnation are stories of divine marginalization. During the incarnation, God was marginalized in Jesus-Christ.

Let us further discuss why Jesus was born to be a marginal person. He was conceived by Mary when she was unwed. Even though the story describes Jesus' conception to a virgin as a divine act that emancipated Mary from mortal and social sanctions, Mary was deeply troubled by her situation. According to the account in Luke, Mary's conception before a formal wedding was divine and glorified by the angel. Nevertheless, Mary was terrified. She told the angel, "How can this be, since I am a virgin?" (Luke 1:34). It is important to note the moral and ethical perceptions of Jewish society at that time. According to its mores, it was a disgrace to be an unmarried, pregnant woman and to be a child born to such a woman. According to Matthew, Joseph was a righteous person, "and unwilling to expose her to public disgrace, [so] planned to dismiss her quietly" (Matt 1:19). Thus, while the birth of Jesus to Mary was divinely justified, it was nevertheless socially condemned. Jesus, as well as his parents, was marginalized from the time of his conception.[3]

Another "marginal" episode took place in Bethlehem in Judea. According to Luke, Mary went with Joseph from Nazareth in Galilee to the city of David, for Joseph was a descendant of David (Luke 2:1-5). While they were in a Bethlehem stable, Mary gave birth to her son, Jesus, and wrapped him in cloth and laid him in a manger (2:6, 7). We do not know how accurate this story is.[4] What is intriguing, however, is the symbolic significance of the manger. Laying the tender baby, just thrust from the warm protection of the womb, into the roughly carved wooden manger has amazing symbolic meaning to marginality.

Because I grew up on a farm and raised a cow, I know how unsanitary the inside of a stall is. If the centralist group accepts the story at face value, it will likely be romanticized because they, as centralist people, are removed from marginal experience, and often want to romanticize Jesus' divine birth rather than consider the less glamorous reality. The placement of Jesus in the manger perfectly symbolizes his marginality.

Centralist people of the city of David rejected Jesus from birth. No one offered a single room to his family. John narrated it this way: "He came to what was his own, and his own people did not accept him" (John 1:11). The essence of the Christmas story is, then, Jesus' divine marginalization: God marginalized his Son to save the world.

Now let me examine the story of the incarnation (or the story of Jesus' divine birth in the world) in the Fourth Gospel. The prologue of John (1:1-18) describes the process of divine marginalization. As I have already indicated, instead of metaphysical speculations of a logos doctrine or a critical analysis of the story as centralists have done, I am re-examining the story of the incarnation in light of the story of Jesus' birth (or the Christmas story), and understand it from a marginal perspective.

John's prologue discusses the incarnation from a divine perspective. It relates Jesus' birth from God's perspective (above), while the Synoptic Gospels tell of Jesus' birth from human perspective (below). The prologue complements the Christmas story. It deals with the other side of the Christmas story.

In the prologue, divine marginalization is initiated in creation. The prologue begins with the assumption of the coequality and coexistence of Christ, the Word, with God (John 1:1-2), and continues with a description of the creation of the world through Christ (1:3-4). If creation, here, is regarded as an act of divine immanence extended through a creative presence of Christ, creation then is a process by which Christ marginalizes himself from the divine center. By fully participating in the creative process as the agent of creation, Christ affirms

the world as his own, despite that his people ignore and reject him.
"He was in the world, and the world came into being through him; yet
the world did not know him. He came to what was his own, and his
own people did not accept him" (1:10-11). The process of divine marginalization begins with creation and *is actualized through Christ's
rejection by his creation.* Christ becomes a marginal person in the
cosmos. John's prologue tells the story of divine marginalization on a
cosmic scale.

Another well-known story of incarnation is found in Philippians. The
text is a song by which Paul illustrates Christ's humility.[5] It has been
the topic of much metaphysical speculation by Christian and Buddhist
scholars. It is no coincidence that the Christian idea of *kenosis* (self-
emptying) has attracted the attention of Buddhists with their notion of
sunyata.[6] I do not agree that the intent of the song describes emptiness
as divine nature. Rather, the song attempts to show emptiness as a process in which the divine nature becomes human, and takes on the form
of the servant. In this respect, God *becomes* empty, rather than God is
empty in essence or in originality. Emptiness is not an original nature
but rather a consequent nature of God.[7] It is consequential to God, because it means *giving up* divine nature to become a servant. Emptiness, in Philippians, therefore describes the process of God's transition
from the nature of God to the nature of a servant:

> . . . who, though he was in the form of God, did not regard equality
> with God as something to be exploited, but emptied himself, taking
> the form of a slave, being born in human likeness. And being found in
> human form, he humbled himself and became obedient to the point of
> death—even death on a cross (Phil 2:6-8).[8]

In other words, the self-emptying process signifies the transition from
divinity to humanity. It serves as a means of divine incarnation in the
world. God became human through emptying the divine nature.

What is interesting here is that Christ became an ordinary human
being, and further, took on what is considered the lowest kind of
occupation—a servant. The incarnation, the transition from divine
nature to human nature, was divine marginalization. However, when
divinity takes on human form and lowly human occupation, it becomes
the margin of marginality. Christ became the margin of marginality by
giving up everything he had.

Becoming a servant often means to become nothing, to become a non-human being. Unless you have been a servant, you may not understand what servanthood means. Early African-Americans and Asian-Americans undoubtedly know what servitude means. Let me tell a story about servitude from my life. I was fortunate enough to serve an old master for a few months. I was the extension of his hands and legs, and did exactly what my master told me to do. No matter how much I disagreed with him or how unhappy I was with my work, I could never reject or deny his demands. I was practically his possession. I had no rights of my own. I lived in fear and uncertainty. My master demanded absolute obedience of me.[9] To be a servant means to have no personal worth, no innate value.

As a servant, Jesus "humbled himself and became obedient to the point of death—even death on a cross" (Phil 2:8). Servants do not belong to the dominant group. They are outsiders, alienated from the world in which they live. To take on the nature of servitude after having had the nature of God, therefore, means to become the precise margin of marginality.

According to this passage in Philippians, the self-emptying process seems to be an essential point of the incarnation. Christ became as nothing. Thus, as servant, Christ was alienated from and placed in-between two worlds without belonging to either. He entered a neither/nor category. This kind of total negation was necessary for Jesus-Christ to make a total affirmation of himself in-both worlds:

> Therefore God also highly exalted him and gave him the name that is above every name, so that at the name of Jesus every knee should bend, in heaven and on earth and under the earth, and every tongue should confess that Jesus Christ is Lord, to the glory of God the Father. (Phil 2:9-11)[10]

Only because he took the lowest position was he raised to the highest position. Likewise, because he was nothing through the emptying process, he was the one who could live in-beyond all things in heaven, on earth, and in the world below. This scriptural passage, therefore, is a magnificent song that captures the process of divine marginalization. What is important to know, however, is that the act of self-emptying takes place simultaneously with the act of self-fulfillment, that is, the humiliation of Christ simultaneously accompanies his exaltation. In the same manner, Christ is still the servant of the world at the margin of marginality, and Lord of all lords. He is this *because* he was the servant of all servants. Although they are inseparable, Christ's marginality precedes his lordship. The emphasis is placed on marginality or servanthood rather than on centrality or lordship. If Christ is present in the world, the self-emptying process continues. It is a mistake to stress the lordship of Christ alone, and neglect his servanthood, as if it were only a historical phase of who he is.

As we have seen, a holistic understanding of the incarnation is not possible unless it is seen from the narrative of Jesus' birth as related in Scripture. Moreover, John's prologue symbolically retells the Christmas story on a cosmic scale and provides a description of Christ's cosmic marginalization. The process of divine marginalization occurs from above, while in the Christmas story divine marginalization occurs from below. Thus, they complement each other. In Philippians the total negation (in-between) and total affirmation (in-both) of two or multiple worlds were possible through the self-emptying process. Thus Jesus-Christ is identified as a new marginal person who lives in-beyond by totally affirming the worlds that negate him.

The incarnation can also be compared to divine immigration, in which God emigrated from a heavenly place to this world. As an immigrant in the new world, Christ, like the Asian-American, experienced rejection, harassment, and humiliation. Many Asians, prominent in their countries, gave up everything to come to America. Where they once held professional-level positions in their native land, here, they started as janitors, launderers, cooks, and other marginal workers. The similarity ends there. God's divine emigration was intended to save the world, while human emigration is to save the immigrant; also God moves from eternity to temporality, while the human being merely moves from place to place. It is crucial to understand that the analogy between humanity and divinity is limited.

The Life of Jesus as a Paradigm of New Marginality

The life of Jesus was a life of marginality, according to the Gospel accounts. The infant Jesus was marginalized again when Herod, frightened by predictions of the infant's influence, sought to kill him and ordered the slaughter of all children two or fewer years old (Matt 2:16). Jesus and his parents escaped to Egypt, where they remained until Herod died (2:13-15).[11] Jesus' childhood exposed him to double marginalization: political from Roman authority, and cultural and ethnic by living in a foreign land.

Although we know almost nothing about his life in Nazareth, it must have been humble. If, as is probable, Joseph died at an early age, Jesus undoubtedly, as an elder son, took over his carpentry trade and likely experienced early the toils and conflicts of adult life.[12] Humbleness is even expressed by the town in which he grew up—Nazareth. Nathanael, when asked by Philip to come to see Jesus, sneeringly dismissed Jesus, saying, "Can anything good come out of Nazareth?" (John 1:46). I used to live in North Dakota. When I took a trip, people looked at my car license plate and said, "Oh, North Dakota!" and sneered at me. They wanted to humiliate and marginalize me, but I was used to it. Nazareth must have been Israel's equivalent of a North Dakota town. It is, therefore, likely that Jesus' life as a Nazarene marginalized him in the eyes of the larger community.

Baptism had a profound implication for Jesus' ministry. It began his ministry and ended it—for the cross symbolized his dedication of his ministry. In other words, Jesus dedicated his life through his baptism in the river Jordan. Repentance also had a profound implication for Jesus' baptism. Repentance was the primary act which led John the Baptist to baptize people (Matt 3:1-12).[13] From my reading of the Scripture, it is clear that John the Baptist was not simply interested in short-term repentance for personal sins but in repentance to prepare for the coming of the kingdom of God (3:2). He was concerned about the transformation of people's outlooks. Repentance involved the radical change of the social, political, economic, religious, and racial orientations which marginalized people. Repentance, therefore, dealt with justice, peace, compassion, and harmony among all people. Because he, too, was committed to this kind of repentance, Jesus wanted to be baptized. This radical transformation involved a total detachment (or emptying process) from past situations that marginalized him. By immersing himself in the Jordan, Jesus was symbolically placed in-between the worlds, belonging neither to heaven nor earth. He no longer belonged to heaven because he left there, and he did not belong to the world because through baptism he renounced his ways. Baptism was, then, a clear expression of Jesus' experience in the neither/nor—in the total negation—symbolized in death. However, baptism did not end with his immersion in water but ended with his rise from the water, symbolizing his total affirmation. Jesus' affirmation was confirmed by the vision and voice of the Spirit (Matt 3:16-17; Mark 1:10-12; Luke 3:21-22). It is important to remember that Jesus was not adopted as the Son of God by baptism but confirmed to that by the Spirit of God at his baptism.[14] In other words, the self-affirmation of Jesus as the Christ upon his rise from the water was confirmed by the Spirit. Jesus was Christ at his incarnation but was denied by the world. At baptism, he reaffirmed his true nature and the Spirit confirmed his reaffirmation. By his total affirmation to be in-both worlds, he became a person of both/and—Jesus and Christ, simultaneously. His affirmation and heavenly confirmation did not remove his marginal status as long as the whole world was not ready to accept him as the Son of God. In this respect, Jesus became a new marginal person *par excellence* through baptism, a person who lives in-beyond by integrating and harmonizing both the total negation (neither/nor) and the total affirmation (both/and) of two different worlds into himself through death and resurrection.

If I look at the temptation of Christ in the wilderness from a perspective of marginality, I see a new insight on Jesus-Christ's marginality. I am not interested in reinterpreting traditional beliefs of the central group. Rather, I hope to show an alternative interpretation of Jesus' temptation. From the marginal perspective, the devil is a personification of the self-centering force which acts as the center of centrality.[15] People seek the center because of this force, which manifests itself in three different forms: wealth, glory, and dominance.[16] The first temptation deals with wealth symbolized by bread (Matt 4:2-4). Bread can mean very little in our time, but it does symbolize a basic element for human survival. The lack of *bread* represents an economic element which marginalizes the poor and hungry. Jesus overcame the temptation of wealth by transcending his physical needs. Another force that marginalizes people is the desire for glorification. When Jesus was placed on the pinnacle of the temple, where he would be seen by the crowds in Jerusalem, he was asked to throw himself from it (4:5-7) to prove his faith in God.[17] This temptation to receive glorification from others naturally arose from his power to perform miracles that impressed ordinary people. It is identical with a pride and self-glorification that condescends to others who have a different ethnic and cultural background. Jesus overcame the temptation for glorification from others by defending his divine integrity. Finally, the third force that marginalizes people is the desire for dominance. The power to rule all the kingdoms of the world (4:8) is an ambitious goal that has tempted human beings throughout history. Power is manifested in the political systems of dominant groups and is a direct means of marginalizing the weak and powerless. Jesus overcame that temptation by serving and worshipping God alone (4:10).

The significance of the temptations proved Jesus' commitment and reaffirmation at his baptism to a new marginality. He did not yield to temptations that could have given him centrality in the kingdoms of the world. By resisting temptations, he became a new marginal person, aligned with marginal people.

Jesus' public ministry may best be characterized as a life of marginality. He was a homeless man with a group of homeless people around him. He associated with marginal people, although he never closed the door to central-group people. He taught, acted, suffered, and died as a marginal man. He rose from the dead to help us live in-beyond.

The people Jesus called to be his disciples were marginal people. None came from the religious political establishment; they were not elders, high priests, or Judaic-law teachers. Most were fishermen, except for a tax collector and a clerk, Judas, who betrayed Jesus. His other associations were primarily with the poor, weak, outcast, foreigners, and prostitutes.

His ministry was divided into two categories: healing ministry and teaching/preaching ministry. It is a centralist tendency to stress Jesus' prodigious healing power. Such thinking may arise from today's highly professionalized medicine. The often impersonal relationship between patients and doctors and the highly technological aspects of medicine can give us the impression that Jesus' healing was attributed to him alone. We must remember, however, that the healed were more than patients or mere objects to be healed. Jesus remarked frequently to his patients that it was their faith that healed them: ". . . your faith has made you well" (Mark 5:34, 10:52). Faith has a dimension of personal relationship between the healer and the healed. No doubt, therefore, Jesus' patients were or became closely related to him, and some of them must have continued their association with him even after their healing. In this respect, those who had been healed by Jesus' ministry also became his followers. Thus the people with whom Jesus associated: the sick (Matt 8:14-17; Mark 1:29-34; Luke 4:38-41), the blind (Matt 9:27-31, 20:29-34), the mute (Matt 9:32-34), the deaf (Mark 7:31-37), the crippled (Matt 15:29-31; Luke 13:10-17), women (Matt 15:21-28; Mark 7:24-30; Luke 8:1-3, 10:38-42), the paralyzed (Matt 9:1-8, 14; Mark 3:1-6; Luke 5:17-26, 6:6-11; Mark 2:1-12), the possessed (Matt 8:28-34; Mark 5:1-20; Luke 8:26-39) prostitutes (John 8:1-11), Gentiles (John 4:1-42; Mark 7:24-30), and the crowds of poor and weak who followed him (Mark 3:7-12; Matt 15:32-39; Mark 8:1-10) were marginalized from the larger society because of what they lacked. Jesus was a friend to these, but he did not associate exclusively with marginalized people. He was available to anyone willing to approach him, such as the Roman officer (Matt 8:5-13; Luke 7:1-10), a local synagogue official (Matt 9:18-26; Mark 5:21-43; Luke 8:40-56), the rich young man (Matt 19:16-30; Mark 10:17-31; Luke 18:18-30), a lawyer (Luke 10:25-28), Pharisees (John 3:1-21; Luke 7:36-50), and a council member (Matt 27:57-61; Mark 15:42-47; Luke 23:50-56; John 19:38-42). His presence to all was to help each fulfill an individual need for wholeness. He healed the sick, restored sight to the blind, gave hearing to the dumb and speech to the deaf, straightened the bones of the crippled, helped the paralyzed to walk, drove demons from the possessed, empathized with prostitutes, offered fellowship to women and Gentiles, fed the poor, strengthened the weak, and taught all persons to follow the way of love. As healer and reconciler, he pioneered the new marginality.

Jesus was a homeless man. "Foxes have holes, and birds of the air have nests; but the Son of Man has nowhere to lay his head" (Matt 8:20). It is easy for us to forget the homeless aspect of his life, because his healing and preaching are emphasized. But it's likely his personal life was not much different from that of the beggar or the homeless in New York City or San Francisco. I often go to the University of California at Berkeley campus, where I see a talented, homeless man who performs an extraordinary act. People come to see him and often applaud his performances. Some of them drop a dollar bill or a few coins into his collection box before walking away. After his performance, he is once again homeless, wandering here and there, seeking a place to rest. He wears the same clothing for months and has not bathed for a long time. That is what life is like for the homeless of the world. Was Jesus' life much different from, or even worse than, this homeless man's? The crowds came to see Jesus' prodigious performances, then went away. They were more interested in the miracles and signs than they were in Jesus.[18]

Thus, behind the miracle stories and wonderful teachings was the lonely figure of a homeless man, rejected in his hometown (Matt 14:53-58; Mark 6:1-6) and misunderstood by his disciples, who were more interested in moving toward centrality than in staying at the margin.

The homeless are also the poorest of the poor. All they own is what they can carry. They live each day at the mercy of those who donate something. Jesus was one of the poorest and lowliest. That was why he said, ". . . just as you did it to one of the least of these who are members of my family, you did it to me" (Matt 25:40). This seems to imply that the true presence of Christ is found among the poor.

A Korean-American grocer who operates a fruit stand in New York City told me that he gets up at four o'clock every morning and goes to the market. He said, "If I live today, I hope to live another day. The place I work is like a war-zone. I used to carry a gun, but I don't carry it anymore, since I became a Christian. Christ is stronger than the gun, stronger than the bullet, and stronger than the police. He is always with me and protects me." As he spoke, I looked at him; the expressionless face of this poor and helpless man reminded me of the face of Jesus. Was Christ present in this man? Was he the Christ who is reflected in the poor, the humble, and the helpless? A long time ago, East Indian Rabindranath Tagore wrote a beautiful poem that seems to depict Jesus:

> Here is thy footstool and there rest thy feet where live the poorest, and lowliest, and lost. When I try to bow to thee, my obeisance cannot reach down to the depth where thy feet rest among the poorest, lowliest, and lost. Pride can never approach to where thou walkest in the clothes of the humble among the poorest, and lowliest, and the lost. My heart can never find its way to where thou keepest company with the companionless among the poorest, the lowliest, and the lost.[19]

The homeless person is also a beggar. Being a homeless man, Jesus was a beggar, and his followers were beggars also. When he sent them out on a mission, two-by-two, he said, "Carry no purse, no bag, no sandals; and greet no one on the road" (Luke 10:4). Being beggars, Jesus and his disciples no doubt carried beggar's bags when they were on the road. Being a homeless man, Jesus went around "as a beggar among beggars, as an outcast among the outcast."[20] He was, however, more than a beggar, because he became the servant among servants to save the world. In this respect, tracing my roots in Asian culture, I can compare him with Kuan-yen, Bodhisattva, who often appears as a beggar or a poor old woman to assist others in need.[21] Being a servant and a beggar, Jesus did not have to serve an earthly master. He was free but suffered and was despised like the servant whom Isaiah described:

> He was despised and rejected by others; a man of suffering and acquainted with infirmity; and as one from whom others hide their faces, he was despised, and we held him of no account. . . . But he was wounded for our transgressions, crushed for our iniquities; upon him

> was the punishment that made us whole, and by his bruise we are
> healed. . . . He was oppressed, and he was afflicted, yet he did not
> open his mouth; like a lamb that is led to the slaughter, and like a
> sheep that before its shearers is silent, so he did not open his mouth.
> (Isa 53:3-7)

Because Jesus was a servant, he suffered for the transgressions of the
world; because he was a beggar, he was despised and rejected by
others. As servant, he was in the world at the margin of marginality; as
beggar, he was free from the world's dominance that marginalized him.
Jesus was in the world but not of it.[22] He negated the world as a beggar
but affirmed it as a servant. Thus he lived in-beyond and was in-between and in-both simultaneously.

The teaching of Jesus also reflects his life. I will discuss the Sermon
on the Mount, what I consider the essence of his teaching (Luke 6:12-49;
Matt 5:3—7:27). I will examine it from the perspective of marginality.

In Luke's beatitudes, we notice that Jesus was speaking to marginal
people; it was they who came to hear his sermon. Jesus said, blessed
are the poor (Luke 6:20),[23] the hungry (6:21), those who weep now
(6:21), and those who are hated, excluded, and cast out (6:22-23). It
was they who were economically, politically, and socially marginalized.
They are blessed because they will receive what they presently lack:
they will receive the kingdom of God, food, joy, and reward in heaven.
On the contrary, Jesus warned those who were rich, full, laughing, and
accepted (6:24-26). They were dominant-group people. Their fate will
be reversed. They will be poor, hungry, woeful and will mourn. Jesus,
as the new marginal person, thinks inclusively and complementarily.
Centrality and marginality are defined in relationship to each other;
they are inseparable and complementary. The loss of one is the gain of
the other. Jesus, therefore, said, "So the last will be first, and the first
will be last" (Matt 20:16). "For those who want to save their life will lose
it, and those who lose their life for my sake will find it" (16:25). Negation presupposes affirmation, and affirmation presupposes negation.

Because Jesus was the marginal person *par excellence,* he thought
marginally, in terms of neither/nor and both/and. It is this inclusive and
complementary thinking that causes marginal people to yield positively rather than react against opposites. By yielding they will eventually overcome their marginality, and the centralist perspective will give
way to marginality. The law of love is based on this principle of reversal.[24]

Let us examine Jesus' ideas on love which follow the beatitudes. Love is the supreme principle of life. The whole of Jesus' teachings and life can be summed up in love. Jesus said, "But I say to you that listen, Love your enemies, do good to those who hate you" (Luke 6:27). "But I say to you" contrasts against what central-group people taught. In other words, Jesus' love represented a marginal perspective. Central-group people, including Pharisees, Sadducees, scribes, and other Jewish rulers, taught their people to love those who loved them, to hate the enemy and to do good to those who were good. Their way of life was based on justice and the law, so justice and the law became the instruments of the dominant groups to control and to exclude the weak, the poor and the powerless rather than to restore order and equality to all. But Jesus' life was based on love and grace. Love and grace are all inclusive. Such a life approach is key to understanding Jesus. While justice and the law force people to live in-between, love invites them to live in-both. Also love does not exclude the law, but includes and fulfills it. Jesus said he came not to abolish the law but to fulfill it (Matt 5:17). Life in-between is included in life in-both. As love encompassed his being, it colored his judgments. His denunciation of Pharisees, Sadducees, lawyers, and other central-group people must be understood within the law of love, which is the norm of new marginality.

The Loneliness of Jesus-Christ

After his baptism everything Jesus did led to death and resurrection. They were inseparable. One automatically implied the other; death and resurrection mutually complement and complete Jesus' life. This idea was expressed in the last supper, a sacred event, because it was the final meal together for this marginal group. The meal became a rite of death and life (or new life); it became sacred because it exemplified the most dangerous margin: the margin of marginality that connects both death and life.

The entirety of Jesus' ministry led toward this rite. It was not an accident that Judas Iscariot was included in his discipleship. The seed of death was planted with the start of Jesus' ministry, grew in his conflicts with central groups, and bloomed at the supper. The plot for arrest became obvious with Jesus' entry into Jerusalem. This move intensified the polarities of centrality and marginality (Mark 11:1-11). It is not appropriate to call Jesus' entry into Jerusalem triumphant. Rather it was a humble entry of marginality. The colt which Jesus was riding symbolized marginality, while the horse which the Roman rulers rode symbolized centrality and triumph. The entry was the symbolic penetration of marginality into the center of centrality. This created alarm, and the center had to act to eliminate the alien element—marginality.[25]

Returning to the supper rite, we know it commemorated the Jewish Passover. Its very simplicity emphasized marginality.[26] It used the bread and wine, the common symbols of food and drink for marginal people. According to Mark, whose Gospel identified with marginality, no sayings related to "forgiveness of sins" or "remembrance of me" were said by Jesus. Nevertheless, forgiveness of sins has become more important than participation in the rite.

During a communion service at a Korean-American church, where I pastored for several years, a Korean-American lady came forward to a rail but could not take the bread because her hand was shaking violently. I decided to put the host in her mouth after dipping it in the grape juice. After the service I asked her why her hand was shaking so violently. She said, "It was so holy that the sinner like me could not take it." I said to her, "It is not as holy as you think, and you are not as sinful as you think you are." Why do we often make the rite so holy and perceive ourselves as so sinful? Isn't it a way to elevate those who administer the rite? Hasn't it been a way for priests to put themselves at the center rather than at the margin? Clearly the rite is a simple act of eating bread and drinking wine with Jesus (Mark 14:22-26). Instead of making it too holy and too sacred, we must try to find in it the profound symbolic meaning of life and death. Because the bread and wine represent the blood and body of Jesus who died on the cross, they are symbols of death as well. Therefore, they have dual meanings: the meaning of life and meaning of death simultaneously. In other words, the bread and wine are symbols of death and resurrection. To live is to die, and to die is to re-live. The inseparable connection between negation and affirmation or between neither/nor and both/and is the new symbolic significance of this ritual. That is why I call it the rite of death and life. Everyone who eats and drinks will live and die, but everyone who participates in this symbolic act with Christ will die like Jesus died, and will again regain life like Jesus did. That is why the last supper is different from other suppers.

Dying like Jesus died expresses the epitome of negative marginality. There are two experiences which need consideration as related to

Jesus' death: his suffering with humiliation and his loneliness by rejection. Suffering and loneliness are mutually inclusive. Moreover, suffering, humiliation, loneliness, and rejection are elements of marginality.

Loneliness is basic to Jesus' life because he was rejected by his world. Loneliness marginalizes people. Because rejection and loneliness exist in a cause and effect relationship for Jesus, loneliness deepens as death approaches, and he is released from rejection when he dies. When loneliness and rejection reach to their maximums, marginality has expanded to that also. So Jesus-Christ is the margin of marginality at death and because of his death.

Jesus epitomized rejection. It was that which killed him on the cross. As Isaiah said, "He was despised and rejected by others; a man of suffering and acquainted with infirmity; and as one from whom others hide their faces[,] he was despised, and we held him of no account" (Isa 53:3). This rejection is a mark of marginality. An Asian-American is also rejected and despised by central-group people in North America. The following description of an Asian-American woman by her white husband depicts the similar predicament of Jesus in 2 Isaiah:

> I hate my wife for her flat yellow face and her fat cucumber legs, but mostly for her lack of elegance and lack of intelligence compared to judith gluck . . .
>
> She's like a stupid water buffalo from the old country, slowly plodding between muddy furrows, and that's all she knows of love beneath my curses and sometimes blows . . .
>
> So I hate my gentle wife for her flat yellow face and her soft cucumber legs bearing the burden of the love she has borne for centuries, centuries before anglicans and dylans, playmates and rock before me or judith gluck.[27]

The rejection of Jesus intensified as his ministry climaxed. The more people followed Jesus, the more rejection he faced. The more he was rejected, the more he suffered loneliness. Especially, the betrayal by Judas caused him unbearable pain and isolation. Following Judas, Jesus was rejected by his other disciples in the garden and as he approached the cross: "You will all become deserters; for it is written, 'I will strike the shepherd, and the sheep will be scattered' " (Mark 14:27). Even Peter could not keep his promise, and denied Jesus three times. With frequent and heightening rejection, his pain escalated and death came closer. "I am deeply grieved, even unto death" (Mark 14:34). It became a time of prayer. Often, prayer becomes genuine in loneliness. God is present in loneliness, which alone touches the depth of human existence. In loneliness, Jesus was freed from the power that sought the center of the world and remained at the margin of marginality where God was present.

With arrest, Jesus stood isolated, alone before the council. He was accused of blasphemy and judged "deserving [of] death" (Mark 14:64). They spat on him, blindfolded him, slapped him. Pilate avoided his responsibility and asked the crowd to decide Jesus' fate. They shouted, "Crucify him!" (Mark 15:14). He was now rejected by his marginal followers. The soldiers ridiculed, robed, and crowned him. They beat, spat on, and bowed before him, just before his trek to the cross (Mark 15:16-20). This extreme humiliation reminds me of lesser ones endured by an early Chinese immigrant whose queue was cut off as a form of public mockery; Mary Paik Lee, a Korean-American woman, who was laughed at, spat upon, and kicked by white, young men;[28] and a Japanese-American who was led like a sacrificial lamb to a relocation center during World War II. People can experience such humiliation only when they are at the margin of marginality.

Jesus' final rejection was from his Father. Sick with despair, he cried, *"Eloi, Eloi, lema sabachthani?,"* which means "My God, my God, why have you forsaken me?" (Mark 15:34). He could endure no more; his loneliness was cosmic. He hung in-between belonging to neither heaven nor earth. He was completely negated. Only divinity could endure such, and Jesus-Christ was unique and distinctive in that. At that moment he reached and tolerated the nadir of everything.[29] Such unfathomable depth cannot be comprehended in the human experience; its depth is divine. By being present in the bottomless abyss, Jesus-Christ is divine and human at the same time. Yet, paradoxically, the total negation is always complemented by the total affirmation; likewise, total detachment is possible because of the total attachment. In the depth of depth, therefore, both a negation and an affirmation are two different expressions of one, just as death and resurrection are inseparable.

Loneliness and suffering are intensely relational, but different. Loneliness is a suffering expressed in detachment, while suffering is a pain expressed in attachment. That is why they coexist. When Jesus experienced cosmic loneliness, he also experienced cosmic suffering. Just as his

loneliness was so great that it resonated through the earth, so his suffering was so intense that the cosmos felt it. Luke described it this way:

> It was now about noon and darkness came over the whole land until
> three in the afternoon, while the sun's light failed; and the curtain of
> the temple was torn in two. Then Jesus, crying with a loud voice said,
> "Father, into your hands I commend my spirit." Having said this, he
> breathed his last. (Luke 23:44-46)

Let us look to the garden again to consider Jesus as sufferer. As the
final hour there approached, Jesus prayed, "Abba, Father, for you all
things are possible; remove this cup from me; yet, not what I want, but
what you want" (Mark 14:36). From his ministry's beginning, he knew
he had to bear the cross. Yet, when he confronted it, it was too much
for him. He was a human being, like all of us, and wanted to avoid pain
and suffering. He never, however, responded to suffering with violence. That was his greatness, and evidence of true marginality. His
suffering was an act of love. That is why he endured the crucifixion
without resistance. Although suffering seems to be a negative experience, it always contains a positive element of creativity because of its
embracing love. If there was no love to embrace the world, suffering
would be a destructive force. Jesus' suffering was redemptive because
it was love that healed and embraced that which caused suffering. For
love to embrace and affirm all, it suffers. Love without suffering is unrealistic and has no redemptive value. Love is redemptive because of
suffering. That is why we cannot talk about God's love without the
cross. It is the cross where love becomes truly redemptive. This is perhaps why Jesus said, "If any want to become my followers, let them
deny themselves and take up their cross and follow me" (Matt 16:24).
Only when we participate in his suffering with our suffering does our
pain become redemptive. A faith without suffering is empty and ro-
mantic and without redemptive value. Such is the faith of some central-
group people who want to minimize suffering in life. For them the cross is
a decoration, love is romance, and faith is to hide a lack of belief. But for
marginalized people, *suffering is the way of life, the cross is harnessed as
an unremovable sign of struggle, and faith is a praxis itself.* Crucifixion
was not a way of death for central people. Romans, Sanhedrin members, and dominant-group members did not die on a cross. Crucifixion
was for marginal people—criminals and outcasts. The cross was for
those who were in-between. It is, then, the symbol of marginality. On

the cross rejection, loneliness, humiliation, and suffering are met. Marginal people bear the cross; central-group people put the cross on marginal peoples' shoulders. When both groups join on the cross, reconciliation takes place and new marginality is possible.

Death symbolizes tragedy, failure, disappointment, and darkness: utter negation. It is the denial of human all, a definitive "No." It is the assertion of a neither/nor. It is the abyss of abysses that separates this from that world. Everything stops in death: cosmic loneliness, immeasurable suffering, unbearable humiliation, and divine rejection. Yet, paradoxically, all things come from it. Death is the end of the old but the beginning of the new.

Paul attempts to explain the relationship between the dead and resurrection in terms of a physical body and a spiritual body. He said, "It is sown a physical body, it is raised a spiritual body" (1 Cor 15:44). He explains this complementary relationship through the analogy of a seed: "But someone will ask, 'How are the dead raised? With what kind of body do they come?' Fool! What you sow does not come to life unless it dies" (15:35-36). Death and life, and negation and affirmation, are interconnected. It is the margin of marginality again where all is negated and affirmed. In it the neither/nor is the beginning of the both/and. That is why death is necessary for resurrection, and resurrection is possible because of death. On the cross death and resurrection join.

Resurrection symbolizes hope, joy, and life renewal. It represents the dawning of the day; in it we can glimpse divinity. It is ultimate affirmation; the fulfillment of all life's hopes; a definitive "Yes" to humanity. It is the assertion of both/and. Everything begins anew because Christ's resurrection had cosmic dimensions. He became limitless, beyond space and time. Still his cosmic presence permeates the universal. The risen Christ is a universal spirit present in each individual.

With resurrection, Christ transcended all marginality. He broke the bonds of every cultural, racial, religious, sexual, economic, social, or regional bias that marginalized him and eventually led him to the cross. With resurrection Jesus-Christ is a new humanity, a new marginal person, who lives in-beyond by affirming both worlds. Resurrection is based on faith. It cannot be proved. As Paul wrote, ". . . and if Christ has not been raised, your proclamation has been in vain" (1 Cor 15:14). The ultimate test for the validity of resurrection is faith. In the same manner, the affirmation of new marginality comes from the conviction that a genuine pluralistic society is dawning.

The cross symbolizes death and resurrection. It was once filled and now is empty. The cross means that death presupposes resurrection, and resurrection is possible because of death. Marginal people relate to Jesus' humiliation, loneliness, suffering, and death, and are reminded of each when they see a representation of the cross in a crucifix. This powerful memory gives marginal people comfort and determination to continue their struggle in life. On the other hand, the empty cross represents triumph, joy, and hope. It reminds marginal people that they can have a space—an empty space—to live authentically without dominion from the central-group. In this empty space, they can paint with their favorite colors, plant their favorite flowers, eat their favorite foods, play their favorite games, and invite others to celebrate their joy in freedom and peace. The cross, thus, gives us memory and hope. The memory inspires us, and the hope encourages us to walk with Jesus-Christ, the pioneer of new marginality.

The Creative Core: The Margin of Marginality

The resurrection of Christ-Jesus marks the beginning of a new age. It offers us a glimpse of the reign of God, where all people live in harmony and peace as children of God. The emergence of this new vision was clearly evident when Christ-Jesus appeared to his disciples in his resurrection. The same Christ-Jesus appeared in a different form—a new and powerful person who drew people to himself. He, a new center or a creative core, emerged among marginalized people. The scattered disciples were drawn together at the news that their leader was resurrected from the dead (Matt 28:16-20; Luke 24:36-49). This time Christ-Jesus appeared to them as the Lord: "So the other disciples told him, 'We have seen the Lord' " (John 20:25). Thomas also confessed and said to him, "My Lord and my God!" (20:28). The lordship of Christ-Jesus became the creative core of marginalized people.

Christ-Jesus' power centered with the coming of the Spirit on Pentecost (Acts 2:1-13). The new core was the Spirit. People from every nation found a common core and understanding without a common language. Peter witnessed this powerful center in the name of Christ-Jesus (2:14-42), and a new life was formed around him (2:43-47). Eventually, a new community of believers was born and its head was Christ-Jesus himself (1 Cor 12:12-26).

This creative core is where the Son, Spirit, and Father are present. In this core the Son meets Father and Spirit, just as Father meets Son and Spirit.[30] This creative core is often expressed in the Scripture by a single proposition "in." ". . . I am in the Father and the Father is in me" (John 14:11). The Spirit is also sent *in* his name (14:26). God is also known to us *in* Christ-Jesus' name (16:23). In this "in" or core, all become one. In Jesus' prayer he said, "As you, Father, are in me and I am in you, may they also be in us" (17:21). This core is the unifying force of the divine trinity as well as the world. To be in this core is to be with God. It is the holy of holies, the sacred core, where God said to Moses, "I AM WHO I AM" (Exod 3:14). This core is as undefinable and incomprehensible as God is, although we are in it.

This creative core is, then, different from the center that people seek. The center they seek is the center of centrality, a false center. It does not exist. We seek the center because we think it is the source of existence, the locus of dominance, and the place of security. My experience during the Korean War is helpful to illustrate the human struggle to find the center of existence. When more than 100 refugees were attacked by enemy artillery, every one of us wanted to be at the center of the group. We felt subconsciously that the center was the best and safest place to be. No one wanted to be on the periphery. When we found ourselves pushed out to it, we started to move back into the center. When we thought that we were secure in the center, we were pushed out again to the margin. This struggle was relentless. No one secured the center because it changed constantly. Everything seems to revolve around a center that does not exist. *The center we seek is the center of our creation.* It is not real. Like the center of a wheel is hollow, so the one we create is incomprehensible and unreachable. The creative core, which is the new center, seeks the people, while the false center is sought by them. That is why the creative core or the new center cannot be found by people who seek it. Jesus illustrated, "Those who try to make their life secure will lose it, but those who lose their life will keep it" (Luke 17:33). Therefore, *God is not central to those who seek the center, but God is center to those who seek marginality, because the real center is the creative core, the margin of marginality.*

So it is with Christ-Jesus. The creative core is connected with his resurrection and new life, while the margin of marginality is connected with his ministry and death. So the creative core and the margin of marginality are one. Both are in-between, negated, empty.[31] The creative core is the place of neither/nor thinking, and the nexus of all margins.

The creative core is in-both, and the place of both/and thinking, as explained in Diagram 4.

Diagram 4:
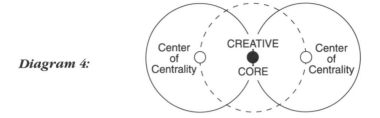

As we see in Diagram 4, the creative core or the new center marginalizes the center of centrality and brings the marginals toward the creative core. Previous centers become margins, and margins cores (the new centers). The new, transforming core will never replace the center of centrality, for it is also the margin of marginality. It is a dynamic, creative, transforming core, because it does not dominate but harmonizes margins with coexistence. In this dynamic process everyone moves toward the margin of marginality, the real center; there marginality is overcome by marginality. When the former marginality is overcome by the new marginality, a creative core is formed again. In this way countless cores of new marginality are formed because Christ-Jesus, each core, is present.

The creative core invites reconciliation. As Paul said, God was in Christ-Jesus to reconcile the world to self (2 Cor 5:19). A new marginal person is a reconciler of two different or, even, antagonistic worlds. Being between these two margins, an individual reconciles each and lives in-beyond the two. He or she is at the creative core. Wherever there is an event of reconciliation, there is a new marginality. Wherever there is a new marginality, there is a creative core where Christ-Jesus is present. Until the whole world is reconciled, the process continues, and Christ-Jesus will remain the margin of marginality.

What makes Christ-Jesus different from the centers of other new marginalities? He is the new marginal person *par excellence,* because in him every marginal determinant is nullified, and every one can overcome his or her marginality. In the creative core of Christ-Jesus, racism is overcome, sexism is no longer in practice, the poor become self-sufficient, the weak find strength. All people live in harmony and peace. The creative core of Christ-Jesus includes all things. It is the authentic center where God reigns over the world. To recognize this creative core means we put our center in God, who is none other than the margin of marginality. When we are there at the margin of marginality, we glimpse the divine presence and become the agent of reconciliation.

Pioneering New Marginality

Christ-Jesus was the marginal man *par excellence*. He was a man of sorrow and grief and love. He lived and died in love. He taught people to love. Those who lived solely by law and order did not know him; often his disciples did not understand him. This human lack led to Jesus' rejection and ridicule. Human misunderstanding and prejudice led to his crucifixion. On the cross he became free and the new marginal person at resurrection. Jesus was transformed from servant to Lord at his resurrection. Christ-Jesus is the pioneer of new marginality and the exemplar of all marginal people. In him is the creative core where God is present, and we are joined in that core by the virtue of our marginality. It is at this core where God seeks us all, and draws us to the new marginality. At this core God reigns with genuine pluralism. Although we will never be free from marginality on earth, a pluralistic world is my vision of God's reign that I seek as a marginalized person in the United States. My prayer in the name of Christ-Jesus is: "May your kingdom come on earth."

5. TRUE DISCIPLESHIP

The New Marginal People of God

> If any want to become my followers, let them deny
> themselves and take up their cross and follow me.
> For those who want to save their life will lose it,
> and those who lose their life for my sake,
> and for the sake of the gospel, will save it.
> *(Mark 8:34-35)*

If Jesus-Christ is the self-emptying God who pioneered a new marginal people, we who follow Jesus-Christ are called to be the new marginal people of God. What does it mean to become the new marginal people of God? Are we not called as the children of God and thus liberated from marginality? In fact, our state as children of God does not mean that we are equal with God. The children of God is a familial symbol describing our relation to God. From a Christian perspective, our relation to God is based on Jesus-Christ, the Son of God, margin of our marginality. Because we are the children of God through Jesus-Christ, we are also joined with him in the family of the divine Trinity. Jesus-Christ represents us before God. Through our representation by him who is the pioneer of our marginality, we become the marginal people of God.

What does it mean to be liberated from marginality? In reality we will never be free from marginality. As the followers of Christ, we will always be marginal people. Liberation from the margin does not mean to be at the center that dominates the margin. Liberation means to transfer one form of marginality to another form of marginality, that is, to transfer from the marginality of human centrality to the new marginality of divine presence in the world. As long as we are the followers of Jesus-Christ, we can never be free from marginality, for Jesus-Christ himself is marginal. In this respect, the liberation of marginality does not liberate us from marginality itself.

If we cannot be free from marginality in this world, we must have been created to be marginal. Let us, therefore, examine the creation story in Genesis, in order to understand that marginality is an intrinsic aspect of creation. We can then understand that the marginal condition of the present day is none other than human marginalization of marginality. Finally, let us discuss the possibility of returning to the original marginality as the followers of Jesus-Christ.

Creation and Marginalization

According to John 1, the Word, through which the world was made, became flesh and dwelt among us. Therefore, creation and incarnation are united in the Word. Creation is an external process manifested in divine marginality, while incarnation is the internal process by which divine marginality manifests itself. In this respect, marginality is a key to understanding creation and incarnation. Because God is marginalized in incarnation, creation takes place at the margin.

Traditionally, creation was attributed to God, while redemption was attributed to the Son. In the trinitarian Godhead, designations are to a Creator, Savior, and Sustainer. This kind of trinitarian symbolism seems to be based on human conceptualization of the division of labor. Trinity paradoxically means "three is one" and "one is three." In this trinitarian formula, Creator and Savior are not only inseparable, but their functions are united—creation is inseparable from redemption. Thus, instead of thinking of creation from the perspective of Creator, let us think of it from the perspective of Savior, Jesus-Christ, who is known as the agent of creation rather than partner in creation. The hermeneutical advantages of understanding divine creativity from the Son's perspective are that the unity of Old Testament and New Testament concepts of creation is possible; the dualistic interpretation of creation and redemption is easily overcome; and it is apparent that the people whom God created are the marginal people of God.

I bring Old Testament and New Testament passages regarding creation together to clarify that the marginal people of God were intended by God in creation. Specifically, I examine Genesis in the Old

Testament, and the Gospel of John and the Epistle to the Colossians in the New Testament. In both testaments, it is clear that Jesus-Christ, the Word and creative core of marginality, is the agent of creation. When I say Christ or the Word as the agent, I do not simply mean Jesus-Christ as an instrument of creation, but Christ as the key and seal of creation. This means "all things came into being through him, and without him not one thing came into being" (John 1:3). Or "for in him all things in heaven and on earth were created, things visible and invisible, whether thrones or dominions or rulers or powers—all things have been created through him and for him. He himself is before all things, and in him all things hold together" (Col 1:16-17). Clearly, Christ is imprinted upon all creation. In this respect, Christ as the first-born and archetype is more than the instrument of creation. His very nature is imprinted in all creation. He is the seal on all. Christ is the creative core of marginality, the point where creativity and marginality join. Creation viewed from this perspective affirms primordial creativity in marginality.

The possible correlation between the Genesis creation story and John's is the Word as foundation of creativity. If creation means a transition from chaos to order, it is an act of the Word, the universal principle of order,[1] and the power of creativity.[2] In Genesis, God's creating comes from the Creator's word (as in, "God said") which seems to correspond to "the Word" in John 1.[3] In re-reading the Genesis creation story, I reaffirm that the ordering process from existing chaos is the essence of creation. In the beginning, "the earth was a formless void, and darkness covered the face of the deep" (Gen 1:2). The idea of *creatio ex nihilo* or creation out of nothing is not found in this text.[4] There was "darkness," which should not be regarded as nothing. It could be a symbol of chaos or the undifferentiated whole. Thus, creating began with dividing the light from the dark: " . . . God separated the light from the darkness" (1:4). "God called the light Day, and the darkness he called Night" (1:5). Separating the light from the darkness means that the light was in darkness before creation. Darkness and light coexisted before God said, let there be light. Next came the separation of waters: separating " . . . the waters that were under the dome from the waters that were above the dome" (1:7). Again, separation of the dry land from the seas takes place (1:9-10). Separation presupposes an existence before separation, so it cannot be understood in either/or terms but rather from only both/and. Moreover separation accompanies marginality, and is expressed as in-between and in-both. Marginal thinking seems to be imprinted deeply in the very order of creation.

Creation is then a process of separating what is united. Just as cells separate and create new cells in organisms, so by dividing light from darkness or dry land from water, the world was born. Because separating expresses differentiation, creation does this. Creation makes things *different.* In chaos things are indifferent, but in creation they change. Thus species originated. God said, "Let the earth put forth vegetation: plants . . . , of every kind on earth . . . " (1:11) and it happened. " . . . God created the great sea monsters and every living creature that moves . . . , with which the waters swarm, and every winged bird of every kind" (1:21). "God made the wild animals of the earth . . . , and the cattle of every kind, and everything that creeps upon the ground of every kind. And God saw that it was good" (1:25). As we notice, the repetition of "of every kind" suggests the importance of variety in the creative process. Difference is the key to understanding that separation in creation is its essential order.

With the same logic, let us look at humankind. God said, "Let us make humankind in our image, according to our likeness" (Gen 1:26). God specified that humanity align to a self-image rather than to his or her kind. Let me examine closely by analyzing another passage, which expresses it in a different way: "So God created humankind in his own image, in the image of God he created him; male and female he created them" (1:27). In this context each seems to be identical. The image of God is then understood as relationship, especially that between male and female.[5] It is, however, more than relationship, it also means gender difference.

Let me now make an exegetical jump. *If there is a continuity between the creation of humankind and other creatures in the world,* we can rephrase Gen 1:27 to read: God created humankind according to their own kinds (the image of God); in their own kind God created them as male and female. Likewise, we can restate Gen 1:26 as, Let us make humankind in every variety after our likeness. In this verse, the image of God as variety can mean racial and ethnic difference. The image of God in Gen 1:27 represents the immutable variable of gender, while in Gen 1:26 it can signify the immutable variable of race. So race and gender belong to the order of creation, and we were created to be different. Plurality is the essence of creative order and God's intention. Racial difference is the original design of God's creation. Because God is plurality, 1:26, "Let us . . .", implies the trinitarian nature. What is created must be plural in nature. We are created to be different, because we have inherited God's plurality.

Difference, which presupposes plurality, is expressed in every creation. Even an individual is plural because God created through a trinitarian plurality. Therefore, as I am created by God as self-image, I am a plural of that image.[6] I am a plural because I am created in "our" image—that of divine plurality.[7] As a plural self, what I am is also who we are.[8] I am yellow, but my yellow color also contains the colors of white, brown, red, and black. So racial difference is not something added to my existence but is intrinsic to it. Therefore, I cannot understand myself unless I understand others who are in me; I am included in them, as the reverse is true. This concept reminds me of Jesus' prayer: " . . . that they may all be one. As you, Father, are in me, and I am in you, may they also be in us" (John 17:21). This unity presupposes difference in plurality. The unity of difference is possible through harmony, and harmony is possible because of individual plurality. So we can affirm our global inclusiveness and claim our right to be different without losing our identity. Thus the harmonious coexistence of all kinds of people is possible.

Difference and plurality are essential aspects of creativity. They are mutually dependent and constitute interdependent variables in the creative process. This interdependent relationship seems to be a key to understanding dynamism and creativity in the Old Testament.[9] This plurality is the condition of marginality. If everything is the same and singular, marginality is not possible.

In the story of creation, pluralistic difference has two dimensions: vertical and horizontal. The vertical dimension pertains to hierarchical order, and the horizontal dimension pertains to egalitarian order. The vertical dimension is applicable between different species, but the horizontal dimension is designated within each species. For example, humanity occupies the center among all other creatures, who are thus marginal to it. When human beings are charged to be the stewards of God's creation, this idea of "responsibility" over other creatures is acceptable because of the hierarchical order of creation.[10] Humankind is the center of marginality, here, rather than the center of centrality.[11] In the same manner, God as the creator occupies the center of our marginality, for we are marginal to God.

Regarding egalitarian order among ourselves (the horizontal dimension), we are equal regardless of gender, race, or class. Our difference, *based on human equality,* should be the foundation of human society, whereas the hierarchical ideology of domination is perversive to the original order of creation. Because of the horizontal and vertical dimensions in creation, we are marginal without being marginalized: as creatures we are marginal in relation to God the Creator, but as equal human beings we should not be subject to human marginalization. Nevertheless, because we are created to be the marginal people of God, we can freely choose to be marginal to each other for the service of the whole. To be created means to be marginal, but to be creative means to be at the margin, the creative core, of marginality.

Because God is the creative core of marginality, those who seek the center of centrality distance themselves from their active participation in divine creativity. Being the marginal people of God, we can participate in this creative core. We are created to be marginal people, because marginality is creative. Marginality and creativity are inseparable: to be marginal means to be creative, and to be creative means to be at the margin. Thus, the center of centrality removes itself from the sphere of creativity and prevents its constant transformation, because the creative core is at the margin.

As with a plant, its growth takes place along its edges or margins. When a center is not in touch with its margins, it decays. When I go walking, I often see a huge tree which was damaged by a storm because its center was rotten. In spite of the rotting center, the edge of the tree is alive and firm. I see that creativity takes place at the edge or margin of the tree. When the center of the tree is no longer in touch with the margin, the tree eventually dies. Like the tree, many inner cities that are not in touch with their suburbs are decaying. The way to revitalize the inner city is to make it a margin again. The donut-shaped city eventually falls, just as the tree having a rotten inside can not stand. Thus, the center must become the margin to be creative.

Further, we are marginal because we are created to be creative. God, who is the source of creativity, is at the margin which is Jesus-Christ. God who is placed at the center of centrality is a dead God, who is like the rotten center of a tree and who remains only in our images and concepts. This dead God is the one of centrality, of the dominant group who re-marginalizes the creative God's marginal people. The marginalization of God's marginal people is a *second act*, an act of human marginalization in social, political, economic, and religious life. The *first act,* the act of divine marginalization in creation, is obscured by our selfish inclination to be at the center. This center is a false center based on an erroneous notion of sameness and singularity as the norm of truth.

Centrality and Sin

If racial and gender difference is the base of creative order, the denial of such difference is the most serious sin of humanity. This denial is an ontic sin, because it repudiates the very design of God's creation. No creature can change what has been created. Any attempt to deny what is becomes the foundation of all other sins humanity commits. Such sins—social injustice, crime, violence, adultery, and theft—are relative to ontic sin. Indifference, which I define as one's conscious attempt to deny difference, is the root of all sins. It is a subtle form of rebellion against the order of God's creation. It is also the cause of the human fall, this denial of difference between the creature and Creator: " . . . You will be like God" (Gen 3:5). Indifference causes human rebellion against God, human desire to take God's place, and other serious crimes. The ontic sin, therefore, is the root of oppression and marginalization in human society. When difference is not taken seriously, order disappears, injustice arises, and harmony is broken.

"Indifference" is the denial of God's creativity. Sameness and oneness cannot be creative. The same gender cannot be procreative, and single ethnicity cannot be novel. The concept of sameness and singularity, which is normative to the centralist approach, perishes, like the rotten center of the tree. Creation, therefore, is based on difference and plurality. Just as women are different from men, so black is different from white, and yellow is different from black and white. No matter how much a centralist might want to alter gender or race, he or she cannot. People are born to be different. The interdependent relationship among differences is possible because of margins. Differences make margins possible, but margins make differences creative. Margins are in-between and in-both differences. Because of difference's simultaneous negation (in-between) and affirmation (in-both), margins are creative. If there were no difference, there would be neither marginality nor creativity. Racial or ethnic differences, therefore, are the creative designs of God's marginal people.

When racial and ethnic differences are denied by dominant groups, such as Caucasians in North America, the harmonious coexistence of ethnic minorities is not possible. In fact, their right to exist at all is denied, like the dandelion in the parable. Difference cannot coexist when sameness dominates. Likewise, dominant people usually expect others to think and act as they do, because they dismiss difference and insist on homogeneity.[12] Their norm then becomes the norm of ethnic minorities. This single norm not only oppresses but marginalizes minorities whose norms are pluralistic. The imposition of sameness over difference and singularity over plurality is based on the centralist ideology of dominance; and it is responsible for a societal and alternative creation to the original order of creation. This is certainly a perversion of God's order which marginalizes God's marginal people.

The centralistic ideology of sameness and singularity, therefore, creates a double negation, the negation of God's creative order by negating the existence of difference. In other words, by denying the difference, powerless people are doubly marginalized. They have to live "in-between," in between the original order of creation (the first act of marginalization) and the perversion of the original order (the second act of marginalization). However, to live in-between also means to live in-both, for marginality is inclusive of both the negation and affirmation of existence. When people are marginalized by a centralist group, they are neither at the center of divine creativity nor at the center of human centrality. They, therefore, are in the position of a neither/nor. Nevertheless, they are at the margin of divine creativity and of human centrality. They are in the position of both/and.

The first act of marginalization began with the divine, and the second act of marginalization began with human social order. This double marginalization is due to our centralist inclination to seek our center, which is a revolt against original marginality in creation. The center that we seek is our creation; it is based on an idea of sameness and singularity. What is real is created by God, and what is created by God is not only different but also plural, for Godself is both different and plural in trinity. The denial of difference by those who seek the center excludes different people from their right to existence, their right to freedom, and their right to have their own space to make their own history and civilization. Moreover, the denial of difference repudiates equality. By embracing difference, we can learn to respect others and to endorse human equality. Moreover, affirming difference and equality is the foundation of a pluralistic society where all people, regardless of ethnic or gender differences, can coexist as God's people. Such a pluralistic society is a microcosm of God's creative order and the vision of God's reign in the world.

Mere recognition of difference is not enough. We must believe that plurality is God's creative order and irreducible to singularity. When singularity is prized above plurality, the result is the alienation of those who are different. For example, white Americans marginalize ethnic minorities because they value their singularity, whiteness, more than a broader plurality. This is white supremacy. The more similar to white, the more valued by the white.

Similar to white supremacy, ethnocentrists value singularity and sameness to plurality and difference. For them, their ethnicity becomes a centralist norm, which marginalizes those of different ethnic orientations. When the norm of a single ethnicity is affirmed, racism emerges and can become an ideology whose most extreme form is manifest in ethnic "cleansing."[13] By elevating a single ethnic group as an ultimate value, unity is stressed through uniformity. This is contrary to the creative order of plurality. The monolithic norm that the centralist upholds perishes, because it lacks creativity. Creativity is inherent to difference and plurality.

A centralist approach marginalizes God's marginal people. The centralist marginalizes by rejecting difference. This is caused by the centralist's failure or refusal to recognize that he or she, as all humankind, is marginal in creation. By seeking centrality, the individual rejects his or her original nature of marginality. By rejecting their original nature of marginality, they are also marginalized from it. Therefore, those who marginalize God's people also marginalize themselves. The more they seek the center, the more they are marginalized from the original order of creation. Thus, double marginalization occurs to all people, including the marginalizer and the marginalized. Those who seek the center of centrality marginalize themselves by rejecting their original nature of marginality, while those who are marginalized by the centralists are re-marginalized from their original marginalization in creation. The more people are marginalized by centralists, the more they become close to the original marginality. That is why those who are poor and marginalized are closer to the reign of God.

The story of creation is about difference and plurality. As Creator, God is plural and singular. We do not fully understand divine mystery in either.[14] One appropriate metaphor that helps is the parenthood of God. As mother and father, God helps all humankind understand unity and diversity in our world. Such an example of pluralistic parenthood provides a model for plurality in humankind. God's universal parenthood also implies a universal kinship.[15] Different tribes or ethnic groups are harmonized in the household of God. Such coexistence presupposes difference.

The Marginal People of God

From a marginal perspective, the history of Israel and of Christianity can be understood in light of God's call to be marginal people again. If we were created to be the marginal people of God, then salvation means to return to that original design. We can conceive that the tower of Babel was the symbol of our rebellion against God's original intent, for it was the symbol of centralization. The history of salvation begins with God's scattering us abroad; it is God's decentralization of all people. The history of the people of Israel began with the scattering of people—the removal of Abram, Sarah, and their family to a strange land (Gen 12:1-9). The history of Israel originated in their journey from Ur,[16] the symbol of Babel. In this respect, Abram and Sarah's journey represented the continuation of God's dispersal of people from Babel. Abram and Sarah's journey has a profound implication for understanding the divine will, for their departure from their homeland was based on *God's call:* "Go from your country and your kindred and your father's house to the land that I will show you" (12:1). This call made Abram and Sarah and their family marginal people. It was Abram and Sarah's faith that enabled them to accept God's call to be immigrants and marginalized. As is written in Hebrews, "By faith Abram obeyed when he was called to set out for a place that he was to receive as an inheritance; and he set out, not knowing where he was going" (Heb 11:8). Faith at this deep level arrives from the conviction that one is in conformity with God's original design.

From the story of Abram and Sarah, it is possible to conceive that emigration or sojourning in a strange land is one of the initial steps to becoming a marginal person. "Israel's faith is essentially a journeying in and out of a land, and its faith can be organized around these focuses."[17] Immigration is the most vivid and profound symbol of marginality for us. Through immigration we are completely detached from a country that had protected and nurtured us. Immigration also estranges us from a centrality that previously protected us. We become displaced and must readjust our lives.

Those who are immigrants in America have experienced what Abraham experienced in his journey to a strange land. Especially those who come from Asian countries have experienced a drastic change in their lives in North America. As I said in chapter 1, Asians who first came to this country were truly marginalized, because they were placed in an entirely new environment. This was also true for the first pilgrims in

America. Thousands and thousands of people are emigrating into this country. They had sold all they had and brought only a few things with them. They still come by air and by ship. Because of our immigration experience, we can understand Abram and Sarah's.

This Old Testament story focuses primarily on Abram and Sarah's faith and their blessings.[18] While their alienation and suffering in a new land was not of central concern to biblical narrators, it is to this discussion. Like any immigrants, Abram and Sarah no doubt had feelings of repulsion and attraction for the new land, Canaan. They were in-between the two worlds. Certainly, immigration is a marginalizing experience.[19] Abram and Sarah were marginal pioneers and the perfect symbol of sojourners. If Abram and Sarah's lives symbolized Israel's faith, then faith demands scattering to strange places and a marginal existence. God's scattering decentralizes and immigration marginalizes the central-group people, so they experience God in their midst.

As North America is a land of immigrants, it can be a promised land where all can become the marginal people of God. By building an altar as Abraham did (Gen 12:7, 13:4), America could become "the city set *under* the hill," the symbol of the *New* Jerusalem for its immigrants. In the old Jerusalem (the city set *on* the hill), God was placed in the center of centrality; but, in the new Jerusalem, God becomes the margin of marginality, which is the creative core of existence.

While the Hebrew Bible was usually written with a centralist bias, there is clear evidence to support the notion that faith is a *second act*, and God's call to be marginal people is the *first act*. The *third act* is the promise which includes receiving land, becoming a powerful nation, and making a great name (Gen 12:1-9). These three acts are inseparable. The first and third acts seem to contradict each other, but they are connected in the second act. The order of these acts cannot be reversed. When the third act becomes the first, the result is the creation of the tower of Babel, the human centralization of power and domination. Tragedies in the history of Judaism and Christianity were due to the reversal of this order. The same tragic mistakes have been repeated again and again in human history. God's call to be marginal people comes first, and the fulfillment of this request determines the outcome of the first act. They are one and coexist in the second act—the human response to God's call. This paradoxical unity is experienced in marginality. The coexistence of *both* marginality (the first act) *and* centrality (the third act) is possible in faith (the second act), the connecting principle. Without the second act, the relationship between the first and third acts breaks down and becomes a dialectical relationship, the relationship of *either* the first *or* the second acts. In the either/or relationship, the first act is no longer the call to be the marginal people of God but the call to be the marginal people of centrality, who are no longer the people of faith. When the connecting principle of faith is lost, the third act, the promise of greatness, becomes the sole aim of human existence, and the first act is forgotten. When the promise was fulfilled in the Davidic kingdom, people forgot that they were God's marginal people. The Davidic kingdom became a new symbol of homogeneity, like Babel. Thus God scattered the Hebrew people as he did Abram and Sarah. In this way history repeated itself. The lives of Abram and Sarah represent a microcosm of Jewish history. This microcosm was manifest in Moses' life and in the Exodus. The Exodus was God's act of liberating the Hebrew people from Egyptian slavery and initiating their emigration to Canaan.

Since the descendants of Abraham lived in Egypt more than four hundred years, they were permanent Egyptian settlers. Joseph's rise in power gave the Hebrew people favorable status. Even after the death of Joseph, "the Israelites were fruitful and prolific; they multiplied and grew exceedingly strong, so that the land was filled with them" (Exod 1:7). The Hebrew people were no longer sojourners in Egypt, but permanent residents and likely citizens. Egypt was their nation. They could be compared, however, to sixth-generation and seventh-generation Asian-Americans who would no doubt identify themselves as North Americans, but are not always accepted as such. Thus, the Hebrew people likely considered themselves Egyptians, even though they were not accepted as natives because of their Hebrew roots.

The oppression of the Hebrew people and the genocide of their newborns began because they had become strong enough to occupy a position of centrality in Egypt after Joseph's rise in power. As the new king said, "Look, the Israelite people are more numerous and more powerful than we" (Exod 1:8). It was then the ethnicity of the Hebrew people that prevented them from being one of the dominant groups of Egypt. Their ethnicity caused their marginalization. They lived in-between, without wholly belonging to Egypt where they had resided for centuries, or to the land that was promised to them.

From a marginal perspective, the Exodus can be interpreted as God's call to turn from marginalization in Egypt to God. The Exodus shifted the focus from human marginalization to divine marginalization. While liberated from Egyptian rule, they were not freed from marginality.

They were destined to be marginal people of God for the service of the world. Pharaoh's servants became God's servants through the Exodus and Moses.

Moses was a new marginal person. Born into the Levi tribe, he grew up in Pharaoh's palace as an Egyptian prince. He was a man in between the worlds. His natural parents were Hebrew, but his adopted parents were Egyptian rulers. He was not a Hebrew because he was reared a prince of Egypt; he was not an Egyptian because he was born of Hebrews. Thus, he was neither/nor and both/and. He was a perfect model of a marginal person, in-between and in-both. Moses' marginality was a sign of God's calling and a mark of his election as God's servant.[20]

God's call is closely related to the discovery of one's identity as a marginal person. Many second-generation and third-generation Asian-Americans lose their identity as Asians when they grow up in a white Anglo-American community. However, in later life they begin to rediscover and appreciate their ethnic and cultural heritages. Likewise, Moses, who grew up in a palace, must have been thoroughly inculturated by Egyptian culture, although he refused to be called a son of Pharaoh's daughter (Heb 11:24). Ultimately, he intensely identified himself as a Hebrew and defended his people when he saw their suffering and mistreatment by Egyptian rulers (Exod 2:11-12, 14). The public demonstration of his Hebrew identity marked the beginning of God's call to Moses to become a marginal person. Moses fled to the Midianites, distant blood-relatives of Israel.

Becoming a refugee in the land of Midian, Moses must have experienced the loneliness and alienation which are the very characteristics of a marginal person. He became a simple shepherd after marrying Reuel's first daughter, Zipporah. His life in Midian contrasted greatly with his previous life. From centrality, he moved to marginality. In this simple and primitive marginal life, he encountered God and was asked to rescue the Hebrew people from Egypt. This call was the *first act*, and came with the theophany of the burning bush (Exod 3:1-6). Unlike Abram, Moses wanted to know who this God was before accepting the call. God declined to name self, but convinced Moses that the God of his people spoke (3:13-16). The *second act* was Moses' response in faith to God's call. Moses was more reluctant than Abram, knowing how difficult it would be to rescue the Hebrews from Pharaoh. But God convinced him and provided Aaron as his aide. The *third act* was God's promise to be with him to perform wonders for circumventing Pharaoh's stubbornness. Thus, the paradigm of the three acts, which evolved from Abram and Sarah, was re-enacted in Moses. Moses, as the man of faith, became a new marginal person, a servant of God, and a rescuer of his marginal people.

The crossing of the Red Sea by the Hebrew people reminds me of crossing the thirty-eighth parallel dividing North and South Korea during the Korean War. I was one of thousands and thousands of refugees who wanted freedom from Communist rule in North Korea. Taking whatever we could carry, we journeyed through unknown roads for many days and nights. Avoiding the enemy's artillery, we followed the crowd south toward liberation. This was our redemptive emigration. Likewise, guided by the pillar of cloud and of fire, the Hebrew people journeyed to the land of freedom. The Red Sea was the axis that changed the Hebrew people from the margin of centrality to the margin of marginality.

The life of wandering in the wilderness for forty years was an experience of in-between. The Hebrews were in neither Egypt nor the promised land. They were uprooted without belonging anywhere. Because the experience of wilderness was difficult for them to endure, they even wanted to return to captivity in Egypt. It is often easier to suffer oppression than to endure marginality. Their suffering, alienation, powerlessness, hunger, and thirst were meant to make them yield to their dependence on the power of human centrality or to place their dependence on God. The wilderness experience clarified for them their need to shift their focus on marginality from centrality to God. Marginality was, then, the potentiality of becoming God's people. The more marginalized they were, the closer they came to God, the margin of marginality.

In the covenant between God and these desert Hebrews, the three acts were consummated. God's call to be his marginal people (the first act) was accepted by the Hebrew people (the second act) in front of God on Mount Sinai. Moses acted as the covenant mediator who represented God to the people and the people before God (Exod 20:19; 24:1-2, 9-11). The first and most important commandment demands their pledge to serve God alone: "I am the Lord your God . . . you shall have no other gods before me" (20:2-3). Serving other gods, the idols of centrality, was unacceptable. God alone is the Lord to whom they were pledged to serve. This pledge meant they would become the marginal people of God. The reward for fulfilling their pledge, the Ten Commandments, was the third act, which fulfilled God's promise to Abram and Sarah. At the covenant ceremony, the Hebrew people were officially chosen to be the new marginal people for the world. In other words, they were chosen to be servants of God for the fulfillment of God's kingdom on earth. They were not chosen to be rulers nor to be at the center of centrality. When they put the third act (the promise of blessings) before the first act (divine marginalization), they had to break the first commandment.

Tragedies in Hebrew history resulted from transposition of acts. They wanted to be at the center of centrality rather than at the margin of marginality. God blessed them, however, when they were at the margin rather than the center, because God was and is at the margin of marginality. When God was their leader, they won the battle. God was with David and gave him victory over the Philistines when he was a marginal figure (1 Sam 17:38-54). However, when David occupied the center of centrality in his kingdom, people came under the yoke of his centralized power. Consequently, they were marginalized by the power of centrality. They were bound by the political, economic, and social situation rather than by the covenant. The kingdom of David represented the center of centrality.[21] Like the rotten center, David's household was corrupted by lust and murder. Because people put the third act before the first act, David became the symbol of hope for a Messiah.[22] The Kingdom of David began to break down and division took place. Finally, the kingdom fell and scattering began.

As spokespersons of God, many prophets warned against the centralization of Hebrew power.[23] Amos's indictment of Israel and his judgment against the luxurious excesses of its rulers seem to represent the voice of marginality. "Therefore thus says the Lord: 'Your wife shall become a prostitute in the city, and your sons and your daughters will fall by the sword, and your land shall be parceled out by line; you yourself shall die in an unclean land, and Israel shall surely go into exile away from its land' " (Amos 7:17). Hosea depicts God as the husband of the adulteress, the symbol of marginality. According to Hosea, God will make those who occupy the center by acquiring wealth and power live again in tents as in the wilderness during the Exodus: "Ah, I am rich, I have gained wealth for myself; in all of my gain. . . . I am the Lord your God from the land of Egypt; I will make you live in tents again, as in the days of the appointed festival" (Hos 12:8-9). It was Jeremiah who insisted that God wanted the Hebrew people to live in exile, rather than clinging to their land:

Build houses and live in them; plant gardens and eat what they produce. Take wives and have sons and daughters; take wives for your sons, and give your daughters in marriage, that they may bear sons and daughters; multiply there, and do not decrease. But seek the welfare of the city where I have sent you into exile, and pray to the Lord on its behalf, for in its welfare you will find your welfare. (Jer 29:5-7)

Again, repentance occurs with decentralization. Diaspora decentralized and made the Hebrews marginal people of God again.

In this respect, the kingdom of David represents the city of Babel, and the Babylonian captivity represents the scattering of people. This scattering was necessary for detachment from centrality and for attachment to the margin of marginality. Through the edict of Cyrus, the new exodus began with the return of the Hebrew people to their homeland. This was the new beginning. The first act again was responded to by the second act and fulfilled in the third act. This time the people of Israel became the servants and the marginal people of God again. As is described in 2 Isaiah, the remnant people of Israel as the servants of God were the new marginal people, who became the symbol of the true Messiah, as opposed to the Davidic messiah of centrality. Because most Hebrew Bible narrators represented the center of centrality, David became the symbol of the hoped-for Messiah. From the marginal perspective, however, the Suffering Servant became the symbol of the true Messiah, which was fully and perfectly manifested in Jesus-Christ, the archetype of new marginality.

True Disciples of Jesus-Christ

The New Testament as a whole approaches Jesus-Christ from the centralist perspective. Especially, the Gospel according to Matthew stresses Jesus-Christ as the descendant of King David, tracing him from that lineage in genealogy.[24] It is not a question of whether Jesus was a descendant of David or not, but rather a question of emphasis on the kingdom of David as the cumulative representation of God's favor and blessings. In other words, the Gospel emphasizes the third act (blessings) without considering the first act (God's call) and the second act (faith), which deal with God's original order of creation and the human response to becoming God's marginal people. If we examine the Gospels from the perspective of marginality, however, we realize that

Jesus-Christ is not the fulfillment of David but the fulfillment of the Suffering Servant, who is the true symbol of God's marginal people. As the suffering servant, Jesus-Christ fulfilled the expectation of Judaic history and the history of salvation. As I have indicated in chapter 4, Jesus-Christ is the margin of marginality, the perfect symbol of the Messiah. He was not the center of centrality that the Hebrew people, including his disciples, wanted and thought him to be. Therefore, to be the followers or the disciples of Jesus-Christ means to recover the original order of creation, that is, to become the marginal people of God.

Central-group people need to become marginal before becoming the marginal people of God. The rich young ruler, representing the central-group person, could not become God's marginal person, because he had to give up the centralist position inherent in his wealth (Luke 18:18-30; Matt 19:16-30; Mark 10:17-31). He could have become a marginal person, given up his wealth, and followed as a disciple of Jesus-Christ. In this respect, marginality is a precondition for entering the new marginality, that is, becoming the disciple of Jesus-Christ. It is not possible for centralists to become new marginal people unless they become marginalized people first. To become disciples, they must be marginalized by either the centralist group or by God through dispersion. So, decentralization, marginalization, and new marginalization are the way to discipleship. Therefore, the marginalized are close to the kingdom of God. Thus Jesus said, "Blessed are you who are poor, for yours is the Kingdom of God" (Luke 6:20).

Jesus-Christ made a preferential option for the poor, the weak, the powerless, and other marginalized people who were victims of a centralist group. Jesus-Christ preferred them, because he was a marginal Jew apart from the centralist perspective of Jewish history.[25] Being marginal, Jesus could identify with the marginal people. He was a new marginal person and as such he could help transform others' marginality into new marginality. By doing this, marginal people consciously identified themselves as his disciples. This transition is possible when they shift the axis of dependence from the center of centrality to the margin of marginality. From the perspective of new marginal people, the margin of marginality becomes their center, and the center of centrality becomes their margin. How is it possible for us to make this shift to become new marginal people from marginal people?

Shifting the axis means to move the norm from the negative to the positive or from the denial to the affirmation of marginality. The negative aspects coexist with the positive aspects of this state. This absurdity exists because marginal people live in the world dominated by centralist groups. Thus, the norm based on self-affirmation of marginality has to coexist with the norm of centrality that negates marginality. This paradoxical experience of positive and negative is inevitable. Both of these, however, are overcome in new marginality. So new marginal people live the coexistence of negative and positive aspects of marginality and the simultaneous transcendence of them. This is precisely why the new marginality can be expressed in terms on in-beyond, including neither/nor and both/and.

Let us examine the disciples of Jesus-Christ, including Paul. All those called to discipleship were marginal people. They were fishermen and tax collectors, eschewed by central-group people. No rulers or centralists were designated as called by Jesus-Christ as disciples. Even though persons like Cornelius, the centurion (Matt 8:5-8), and Nicodemus, a ruler of the Jews (John 7:50), came to Jesus, they never became disciples, because they did not give up their centrality. In Paul's case, he gave up his centralist position when he became a disciple of Jesus-Christ. Thus, we cannot become disciples unless we give up our power. Although marginality and discipleship are inseparable, marginality is not discipleship because the former is a condition of the latter. On the other hand, discipleship is always marginal. Because marginality is a condition of discipleship, God chose the foolish, weak, and humble (1 Cor 1:27-28), or he chose the poor who were rich in faith (Jas 2:5).

Being marginal people, the disciples dealt with the ambiguity of the negative and positive characteristics of marginality. They were the victims of oppressive groups but discovered their identity as servants of God. Their preoccupation with the centralist norm became clear when they regarded Jesus-Christ as a centralist messiah intended to restore the Davidic kingdom for the Hebrew tribes. They were ambitious to be rulers of the twelve tribes when Jesus-Christ was elevated to messianic king. They judged themselves by the norm of centrality and wanted to overcome their marginality through centrality. This negative characteristic persisted throughout their discipleship. When Jesus-Christ was betrayed and tried, Peter denied him three times. Nevertheless, behind the denial was his affirmation of himself as a disciple of Jesus-Christ. Peter knew that he was different from others, and affirmed his identity with a definite yes. Yet, this yes was not powerful enough to overcome no, the negative image of marginality by which they were attracted to centrality. This paradox of denial and affirmation held Peter and other disciples in its grip. They were, therefore, in-between two norms that created a paradoxical experience of repulsion and attraction, denial and affirmation, fear and fascination.

The disciples certainly were marginal, but their total participation in the death and resurrection of Jesus-Christ was what made them true disciples. The cross of Jesus-Christ represented the dual dimensions of death and resurrection. Death cut off the power of centrality, while resurrection gives rise to new marginality. The cross represented both, and was the cause of radical human transformation. That is why Jesus-Christ said, "If any want to become my followers, let them deny themselves and take up their cross and follow me. For those who want to save their life will lose it, and those who lose their life for my sake, and for the sake of the gospel, will save it" (Mark 8:34-35).

The experience of death and resurrection is symbolized in the rite of baptism, the initiation ceremony of Christianity. Baptized Christians are the bearers of the cross, the symbol of death and resurrection. Death renews life. In the cross of Jesus-Christ, we become a new creation (2 Cor 5:17), and help restore the original order of it. When we are restored to the original order, we become God's marginal people, true disciples of Jesus-Christ, the Son of God, who is the creative core, the margin of marginality. Our participation in the creative core of marginality makes us creative agents of reconciliation. The center of centrality is transformed into the margin of the creative core and becomes creative again. In this way creativity continues through margins until the reign of God becomes reality on earth as it is in heaven.

Pseudo-Christianity

How can we become true disciples of Jesus-Christ in the world of centrality? Is it possible to become followers of Jesus-Christ without becoming marginal people? As I said, becoming marginal people is the condition for becoming disciples of Jesus-Christ. We cannot be disciples unless we are marginal. The church today, however, seeks centrality rather than marginality. How can we become marginal when the church is interested in centrality? Can we be Christians without the church? Do we have to be outside the church to become true disciples of Jesus-Christ?

Briefly, Christians in early days were marginal people, oppressed by Romans and rejected by various religious and cultic groups. Later, and through the efforts of the Emperor Constantine, Christianity became the state religion. Although Constantine was converted at the Battle of the Milvian Bridge, he remained outside of true discipleship; he lacked marginality. If he had given up his centrality, as Paul renounced his, he certainly would have been a true disciple of Jesus-Christ.

With Constantine, a new form of Christianity, a pseudo-Christianity, which is based on centrality, developed. During the Middle Ages, powerful popes dominated secular kings. The rise of secular power did not diminish the church's greed for power and control. Even the Protestant Reformation did not break the church's centralist tendency, although exception should be made for some radical reformers. During World War II, many Christians allied themselves with the Nazi regime, seeking to share centrality's power. In spite of this tragic history of pseudo-Christianity, we are still promoting the central ideology of dominance in church today. This pseudo-Christianity has become a partner with the capitalist society. Pseudo-Christianity became the handmaid of early European colonial policy and penetrated deeply into the third-world countries.

How can we become true disciples when the church is seeking its place in centrality? My answer is the cross. Jesus said, "If any want to become my followers, let them deny themselves and take up their cross and follow me" (Mark 8:34). Christians are bearers of the cross, and the church is a community called into being by our crucified God.[26] We must die with our church so that a new church will rise again. The death of our centralist inclinations will give rise to marginality, and our resurrection will create a community of new marginality. Pseudo-Christianity must die, so that in its ashes true Christianity will rise again.

6. Authentic Church

The Community of New Marginality

For where two or three are gathered in my name,
I am there among them.
(Matt 18:20)

The church is the community of God's marginal people. The church is different from other communities of marginal people, because it is conscious of the presence of Jesus-Christ as the margin of marginality. This consciousness of Christ's presence in their midst is the essence of the church. Because Jesus-Christ is the margin of marginality, he is actively present at the margin; his presence is necessarily eclipsed in the center of centrality. Those who occupy the center of centrality unconsciously avoid the presence of Christ by distancing themselves from the margin. Thus it is difficult for centralist people to experience the genuine presence of Christ. But those who are poor, powerless, and at society's margin are easily and naturally conscious of Christ's presence as the margin of marginality. Those marginal people who have experienced the presence of Christ become *new* marginal people. Therefore, the church is a community of new marginal people, where the genuine fellowship of brotherhood/sisterhood is experienced, and where the original order of creation is restored.

Consciousness of Christ's presence is inseparable from any gathering of marginal people. Christ is present when marginal people are gathered, just as marginal people are brought together in Christ's presence. Although the two are inseparable, theologically the presence of Christ precedes the gathering of marginal people. Because of the presence of Christ as the margin of marginality, marginal people come together. When they realize his presence among them, they become the church; when they are unconscious of it, they are not the church. Thus, consciousness of the margin of marginality makes the church different from a mere gathering of marginal people. Through this consciousness, the church is the community of new marginality.

If Christ is the marginal one, he is removed from the center of centrality, which was symbolized by the power of Caesar. That, perhaps, is why Jesus said, "Give to the emperor the things that are the emperor's, and to God the things that are God's" (Mark 12:17). Since the centralist ideology of domination is a perversive act, contrary to the order of creation, those who uphold centralist ideologies remove themselves from the margin where Christ is present. The community of centralists necessarily and by definition excludes the presence of Jesus-Christ, the margin of marginality. Thus, in the churches of dominant groups who support any centralist ideology, Christ is excluded. Those churches are without the active presence of Christ. His presence is eclipsed because he is placed at the center of centrality which oppresses him, humiliates him, and finally crucifies him. The ills of today's church are fundamentally due to the seduction of a centralist inclination which does not perceive the actual presence of Jesus-Christ at the margin.

Present Situation of the Church

As I indicated previously, my approach in this book is initially autobiographical. My assessment of the church is based on my experience. As an ordained parish minister who has worked in white and Korean-American congregations of mainline churches, especially the United Methodist Church, my assessment of today's church is limited. Although countless studies of today's church have been conducted, most of them were done from a centralist perspective. So, my observation of today's church from the eye of marginality may provide a new perspective not readily perceivable to centralists. My evaluation of the church can be useful to others who may share similar experiences.

Before I became aware of my marginality, I thought the church I served was normative. I did not question the authority of the church nor the values for which the church stood. Although I was occasionally critical, I never seriously challenged its orthodox tradition, institutional hierarchy, or liturgies. Now, I see the situation differently. For me, marginality is a key to understanding the life and teaching of Jesus Christ and the life and teaching of the church today—the institutional church.[1] I will consider the church from two viewpoints: the ideal church and the practicing church. With this distinction I will critique the practicing church on the basis of the ideal church, in which I see the life and teaching of Jesus Christ.

I can summarize the church's condition in one word: *centrality.* The church is deeply embedded in centralist motivation. Most are based on a centralist ideology and a hierarchical structure of belief, which both exclude and control the poor, minorities, and the powerless. This is contrary to the essence of Jesus Christ's intent. As Jesus Christ was a marginal person, the norm of the church should be marginality. A church based on the norm of centrality contradicts the church of Jesus Christ. A centralist inclination is the cardinal sin of humankind; thus, a church built on a centralist inclination cannot be the church of Jesus Christ. As long as the church consists of sinful human beings, it is not possible to eliminate entirely its centralist motivation. Nevertheless, the ideal church that I envision will move away from centrality and return to the marginality from which it sprang. The contemporary church, based on centralist motives, is the fundamental Christian problem needing resolution.

The centralist motive is clearly expressed in most churches—Roman Catholic, Protestant, Evangelical, or liberal. One motive that drives people to succeed in the secular or sacred spheres is to belong to the dominant group, and as such, to dominate others. The success of ministry is often judged by the centralist values of dominant society rather than by the marginal values of Jesus Christ. It is unfortunate that even many liberation theologians—including Latin American, feminist, and various third-world theologians—use the centralist system of values as the norm of their theological process for liberation. The marginal approach cannot accept centralist values as a Christian value, because the marginal approach stresses the practice of marginal values as the norm of theology for the liberation of the whole.

Since centralist ideology predominates, its obvious characteristics are personal power, wealth, and glory. Each appeared in demonic forms at Jesus' temptation in the wilderness (Matt 4:1-11).[2] These values are enshrined in the institutions, traditions, and mores of dominant groups. On the other hand, the marginal values are love, humility, and service.

During the Constantinian era, as we have seen, the church became a dominant group and acquired centralist values. Imitating the practice and structure of the empire, the church became a pyramidal, hierarchical, and male-dominated institution.[3] Church membership grew because of the empire's power to crush diverse religious belief to establish its orthodoxy. Historians often judge the greatness of a church by the power, wealth, and glory it wields over states and various sociopolitical orders. For example, Gregory the Great was often regarded as the great pope because of his enormous influence on worldly affairs. It was not love and service but hegemony—its wealth, cathedrals, lands—that made the church important and able to support the poor and needy. Glorified as it was, it had long since overshadowed secular institutions, and developed its hierarchical order: pope, cardinals, archbishops, bishops, priests, deacons, and laity. The ideology of domination within and without the church was built on hierarchical structures.

Following the legacies of the past, today's mainline churches are interested in the status quo, identifying themselves as centralist rather than marginal. The dynamic that motivates churches to succeed today is neither love nor service, but power and wealth, the opposite of Jesus Christ's intent. The practicing church is little different from political institutions, and its seminaries are often more authoritarian in practice and structure than many secular learning institutions.[4] Despite Christ's example of humility, we are often more interested in authority; and despite his ideal of service, we often want to identify with the powerful who expect service.

In this church, power belongs to those who acquire high positions. Within the United Methodist church, for example, enormous power is granted to the bishopric. Because of the link between the centralist power and hierarchy, we cannot know how many clergy seek higher office because of a desire to serve or mere attraction to its prestige. Once the ideal of servanthood loses its marginal focus, power becomes a motive for seeking office. Despite our vow to serve, living in a centralist paradigm almost guarantees a tendency to want to be served. Ministers are no less driven in this regard, and institutional ministry sets up conditions for the servers to become the served.

This centralist ideology of power and dominance is supported by dogmas, traditions, and theological training. Dogma is a church's "correct belief system." It is seldom questioned, and often used to defend centralist ideology against heresies. Dogma helps secure control. It does not recognize multiple shades of truth, as it is based on an ideology of dominance that either excludes or suppresses diverse interpretations. As "the" truth, dogma excludes and marginalizes those who hold different views. I hope that churches will move away from a dogmatic stand and be willing to accept various theological interpretations that reflect contemporary life. Reinterpretation of dogma is not enough. From the perspective of marginality, the reinterpretation tends to perpetuate its control rather than eradicate its roots. Without consistent reformulation of our faith and open-ended dialogue, we cannot eliminate this centralist tendency. As diversity and difference were the basis of God's creative order, the church should not force one absolute system of belief upon everyone, especially to those of different cultural, racial, or historical backgrounds.

Most church traditions support a centralist ideology of dominance and oppress marginal people. Usually Western, Christian church traditions are alien and inappropriate for Eastern people, especially Asian-Americans. As a United Methodist, I accept the Wesleyan tradition which has English roots and which was formalized by dominant-group Caucasian-Americans. As an Asian-American, however, it is difficult for me to accept this tradition. Because of my cultural, historical, and ethnic background, I am marginalized in the United Methodist Church. When I try to belong to that tradition, I experience a sense of being "in-between." Because I cannot be part of the Methodist tradition without rejecting my cultural and ethnic tradition, I am a marginalized Methodist. I am also a marginalized Asian because I am a United Methodist. Other Asian-Americans, African-Americans, or Native Americans in Christian congregations may feel this way. All denominations, whether Roman Catholic or Protestant, are oppressive because they are based on the principle of exclusivity. Denominations and their traditions are essentially religious categories that include the similar and exclude the different.

The church's tradition is visibly expressed in the rites we perform every Sunday. Before awareness of my marginality, I accepted traditional rites of service without question. Now I think differently.

The inflexible worship format of "traditional" Christian churches offends the cultural sensibilities of many ethnic groups. For example, my church allows little space for spontaneity in worship. Yet this worship characteristic is familiar to Korean-Americans. For dominant-group members, participation in the Sunday morning rites can be a liberating experience; for me, as a marginal person, it is oppressive.

For example, the service is structured in such a way that I feel uncomfortable following its order. When I miss notes while singing or mispronounce a word in a responsive reading, I feel ashamed. I am afraid to make mistakes. My body is stiff and my mind becomes preoccupied with speaking each word correctly. Any mistake in Scripture reading is offensive. I must be appropriately dressed, and behave like a "gentleman" although I am a "barbarian." I am supposed to become assimilated into the dominant group by following the ritual. But this kind of assimilation is painful, like the pain of a stomach filled with stones.[5] There is no spontaneity, no freedom to express my feelings during the service. Everything has to be prepared beforehand and followed exactly in the order of the service. In this way every participant is controlled by a centralist ideology which is deeply enshrined in liturgical traditions.

Black churches seldom have such rigidity and create vivid, emotional and culturally-oriented liturgies in their communities. Likewise, Korean-Americans need to develop a more personalized worship setting for Korean churches in which spontaneity is key. Hierarchical structures which depersonalize and homogenize worship service liturgies and formats must give way to non-hierarchical politics which allow the development of new, alternative, marginal liturgies and services. It is not enough for the existing church merely to "authorize" new forms of worship. Such paternalism is offensive and unnecessary. Reform of liturgy, music, and the worship context is necessary to lift the congregation from its centralized church concepts and to allow it freedom to express its marginalization.

The church acquires status through wealth. The success of the church is often measured by the size of its membership and its budget. The more people a church has, the more power it exercises; the more money it collects, the more resources it has. This idea of success is a centralist value. Jesus never paid attention to the number of the crowds who followed him. Moreover, he denounced those who were greedy for money. Did he not tell the young rich ruler to give up what he had in order to become a disciple? Didn't Jesus say that rich people had difficulty attaining heaven? And that we cannot be faithful simultaneously to money and God? Why then does the church love money? Instead of accepting the teaching of Jesus-Christ, the church accepts the centralist ideology that values wealth as a means to salvation. The church's capitalistic structure can only alienate the poor and the weak. How can we judge the success of ministry in terms of membership and wealth? The church has become so enmeshed with centralist ideologies that it has become a business. Many churches have adopted marketing techniques and advertise to recruit members. Professional fundraisers are called in often to heighten the church's financial situation. Money, the idol of capitalism, seems to rule the church. In a society controlled by a capitalistic economy, wealth is power; and the church has become a partner in its capitalistic enterprise.

Adornment is another important aspect of centralist values. As opposed to natural beauty, artificial beauty is stressed in a centralist-value system. Church buildings are designed to reflect human creativity. Sanctuaries receive infinite attention: flowers are arranged and placed carefully; decor is crafted from expensive materials; the cross is made of precious metals. This artificial beauty which so captures the church's interest is based on the centralist value of reflecting wealth and glory. A simple wooden cross is more beautiful to me. Beauty that reflects poverty, humility, and simplicity is an expression of marginal people. As an Asian-American, a beautiful sanctuary is a simple and solitary place where worship is a spontaneous act of humble people. Beauty should reflect nature and creative order. The church, however, loves adornment and through it espouses a value for artificial beauty.

The garb clergy wear is another interesting topic. As a marginal United Methodist, I am critical of the growing liturgical movement. I notice that many ministers now appear wearing clerical collars with long robes and colorful stoles at the service. The higher the rank, the more colorful and intricately designed the robes. It seems odd to observe the bishop or the ecclesiastic leader with a splendid gown decorated with a golden cross, carrying the humble staff of shepherds, and to see ministers with long, colorful robes at a special service of worship. For a newly aware marginal person, it is a showy and symbolic demonstration of dominant ideology. Jesus did not wear a golden crown, a splendid robe, or carry a beautiful shepherd's staff. From a marginal perspective, such does not reflect the teaching and life of Jesus, but rather worldly attention to glory and dominance. When ministers and priests are more interested in their glory than in God, God is no longer glorified. Supposedly hidden behind the ideal of Jesus Christ—the margin of marginality—the church seeks the center of centrality.

Perhaps we must consider the theological seminaries that train ministers. Like the church, the seminary not only perpetuates but promotes centralist values. In seminary training, servanthood is replaced by professionalism. Seminary education, dogmatic and exclusive in its thinking, often discourages independent thinking and an open-ended approach to theology. Although it is interested in multicultural and multidisciplinary approaches, teachers in seminaries are still deeply entrenched in Eurocentric values which underestimate the values of different cultures and their religious orientations. The norm of theological education is the critical, rational, and analytical approach that has dominated for centuries. Following the secular standard of education, theological training is market-oriented, and educational priorities are often decided by demand and popularity. Such education stresses academic excellence over other qualifications, but such academic focus is based on traditional Eurocentric norms, and minority students are discriminated against when it comes to financial aid or scholarship awards. Seminary education oppresses many ethic minorities by its so-called "cult of 'perfect' language." This is a form of censorship by the white dominant group.[6] Those who will minister in their native tongues are discriminated against by "the cult of 'perfect' language" rule.

Although seminary teachers know that love and service are central to Jesus' teaching, most nevertheless seek privileges and advancements. They have a tendency to objectify love rather than to live by it, and to intellectualize justice rather than to act for it. Morality is present in the abstract but is irrelevant in practice. I know of no genuine community of love and fellowship that can be found inside a theological seminary. Even though *praxis* became a household word in theological education, it has been changed to a symbol of intellectual process.

The centralist mentality supports exclusivism, either/or, and plays a central role in critical analysis. Because of the seminary's preoccupation with a critical discipline, its education often fails to stress creative reflection and spiritual exercise. Most seminaries fail to value marginality. Poverty hardly exists in seminary life, and humility is seldom practiced, so professional achievement dominates. How, then, can seminarians learn to be new marginal people?

It is difficult for me to admit that my church is not the one of Jesus-Christ, the margin of marginality. Most churches today are the churches of the Pharisees. Jesus denounced the Pharisees, who loved to display their colorful robes before the crowd, and wanted to impress with their public prayers, and lengthy ceremonies. Haven't we become like the Pharisees? We love elaborate robes, to be understood as pious, and long prayers in the service. Are we, like they, hypocrites (Matt 23:1-36)? In the name of Jesus, do we not seek the rewards of centralism—power, glory, and wealth—rewards that marginalize the poor, women, and people of color? How can we return to being the church of Jesus, the community of marginality?

Although the church wants to be central, it is more and more being marginalized by today's secular society. The church is no longer as powerful; its voice has a diminished impact. It is the grace of God that no longer lets the church be the center of centrality. Returning to the margin, the church can become the community of new marginal people. Being Christians means to be marginal people because Jesus Christ was. One pastor who attended my workshop said, "After all, we belong where we should be. We are called to be God's marginal people, that is, God's servants. Let us be proud to be marginal people." When we realize that we are this, then we will no longer cling to centralist values. We need to discern the values of marginal people; then we can discover our true identity as new marginal people.

Today's church is caught in a vicious circle of humanistic centralism and in the webs of a dominant ideology. When the church is based on the centralist inclination to dominate and exclude others because of their race, gender, or class, it is not the church of Jesus-Christ, but the church of the centralists who crucified him.

Vision of a New Church

If we think that the authentic church should be a community of marginalized people, and that Jesus Christ is the highest of that norm, then the church should be radically reformed and restructured. When I say reform, I do not mean the same type of reformation which took place during the sixteenth and seventeenth centuries. The Protestant Reformation did not go far enough. It only went back to the orthodox tradition of the early fathers. Although the Reformation attempted to restore authority to the laity through "the priesthood of all believers," it could not overcome the hierarchical structure of social power. Ultimately, this gave sacred authority to those who already had secular authority—noblemen, rich entrepreneurs, and the like.[7] The church again settled into institutional self-interest and upheld the status quo.

Need for Radical Transformation

Thus, what we need today is radical transformation that makes the church truly a community of marginality. We must return to our Christian roots, that community restricted by no tradition, centered around the life and events of Jesus-Christ. All traditions must return to their margins of existence, because Jesus-Christ is the primordial source of traditions. Society defines the margin in terms of the center, but the church must define the center in terms of the margin; because of Jesus-Christ, the church cannot remain at the center of centrality. The center must find its existence in the margins. To rediscover the authentic church means to return to the margin where the church started.

This margin of marginality is the creative core where margins are formed and creativity takes place. Without it, the church dies, its buildings become museums, its cross becomes a decoration, its people are stiff and unmoved in pews, and liturgical services become meaningless ritual. The living church is only at the margin. When the church is not there, it becomes the rotten center of the tree. Thus, the centralist church dies like the rotten tree, but the marginal church lives like the fresh leaves that grow at the tree's edge.

The church at the center of centrality must die so that the genuine community of marginality will resurrect from its corpse. Just as resurrection is not possible without death, there is no resurrection of a new church without the death of the old church. In this respect, the centralist church can never renew itself from within: its renewal cannot be genuine because only its appearance and form change. For example, most Protestant reformations were not radical enough, because they tried to reform the church within the centralist tradition of the Roman Catholic Church. As long as a centralist tendency controls the church, the church will never transform itself. The cardinal sin—the human tendency to be at the center of centrality—must be eliminated for authentic reformation.

The church that attempts to renew itself within its orthodox tradition will never succeed. Today, we are challenged to face the task of radical reformation. This task is so radical that I compare it to what Jesus accomplished: the founding of a new community of marginality. This transformation means returning to the origin of the church. The church becomes a *kenosis* church: one that empties itself of centralist values.[8]

The community of marginality does not wholly belong to the centralist community. As with Asian-Americans in the dominant society, Jesus-Christ's church is not completely a part of the world. It is not the world per se that alienates the church but rather the centralist inclination of human beings. The lure to centrality is symbolized by evil. As Jesus said in his prayer, "I have given them your word, and the world has hated them because they do not belong to the world, just as I do not belong to the world. I am not asking you to take them out of the world, but I ask you to protect them from the evil one" (John 17:14-15). The church does not belong to the world because it opposes the evil one—the center of centrality—but it is in the world. As marginal creatures, Christians are in the world but not of it. The writer of the Letter to Diognetus observes, "They live in their own country, but only as aliens. They have a share in everything as citizens, and endure everything as foreigners. Every foreign land is their fatherland, and yet for them every fatherland is a foreign land."[9] Christian means to be an alien in one's own country. Likewise, the church as Christian community must be "in-between" the world now and the world that is to come. Both worlds, however, are one and inseparable, so it exists in-between and in-both at once.

The margin is characterized by change and transformation. The church that does not change and transform cannot be the true church: it is dead. The church is like a living organism; it is the "body of Christ." Like any living organism, the very nature of the church is transformation. We do not transform the church, but the church transforms itself if we give up our centralist tendency to dominate it. The church is like a lake that cleans itself when it is left alone. When we try to clean it, we pollute it more and disturb its natural balance. Likewise, if we let the church be the church, it will transform itself, because Jesus-Christ himself is the creative core.

A center that resists change and transformation is characterized by steadiness and security. Change and creativity create insecurity. Because we seek the center to find security, the church becomes a stable institution. Our centralist inclination prevents the church from being transformative and creative in the world. Our desire to control emerges out of our insecurity and cowardice to trust Christ in us. When we are at the margin, we give up security and rely on God. Faith is courage to trust while insecure at marginality's edge. Courage is given to marginal people. With courage they cry, "Let the church be the church!"

The Church as a Movement

If the church belonged to Jesus Christ and were a living community of marginal people, it would be a different sort of institution. Yet even as cen-

tralization is harmful in principle, it is inevitable because the church is
a human organization. Stability and security are attractive to us. What
we find comfortable and comforting we are slow to change. So plod
our institutions which often have difficulty adapting to new conditions
that arise out of unexpected global events. The church should best be
characterized as a movement of marginal people conscious of the presence of Jesus-Christ in their midst. Its current centralization should be
dismissed, in order to facilitate this movement for the transformation of
the world. We begin by returning to its New Testament origins. The
church, as a movement of marginal people, can relate to the idea of a
remnant wherein marginalized people carried out God's promise in the
world (Mic 4:6-8; 5:2-9; Isa 4:2-6; 10:20-22). The revival of this idea
seems to be reflected in the appointment of the twelve disciples, all of
whom were marginalized people. Even more marginalized were the
women who followed Jesus. As we see in the remarkable passage in
Luke, their marginality was closely connected with their service:

> Soon afterwards, he went on through cities and villages, proclaiming
> and bringing the good news of the kingdom of God. The twelve were
> with him, as well as some women who had been cured of evil spirits
> and infirmities. Mary, called Magdalene, from whom seven demons
> had gone out, and Joanna, the wife of Herod's steward Chuza, and
> Susanna, and many others, who provided for them out of their re-
> sources. (Luke: 8:1-3)

This little flock of Jesus was the *primordial tradition* of the church.
We must go back to that time to rediscover the church as a movement
of marginal people, and enact change as those first Christians did.
Jesus-Christ as Spirit who transcends temporal and spacial limitations
must become the locus of our church and the basis for our existence as
a community of marginal people. Together we must move forward and
act with him. What began as Jesus' movement becomes his again if we
live as his marginal community.

There was no formal structure in Jesus' ministry. Marginal people
spontaneously joined because of commitment to Jesus-Christ, the
margin of marginality. They were often regarded as the true children of
Abram and Sarah, the pioneers of marginality (Gal 3:6-9, 14, 16; Rom
4:11-12), and the new covenant people of Israel, who had spent
years in the wilderness (2 Cor 3:5-18; Heb 8:6-13). What kept this
group together was not dominion but the love of Jesus. His love for his

disciples and followers was the glue that bound them together. His love then becomes our love for one another.

The essence of Christianity is love: "Love one another as I have loved you" (John 15:12). Love is dynamic and embraces all, regardless of race, class, gender. It does not dominate, nor is it hierarchical or arrogant. "It bears all things, believes all things, hopes all things, endures all things" (1 Cor 13:7). Love is the principle of harmony. It alone makes a genuine community of marginality possible. Because of love, the church is always dynamic and transcends forms and structures. Because of love the church is a movement. It can never be confined in a centralist institution.

Cell Groups as Basic Units

Although the church is a movement, it cannot avoid human institutionalization. Thus its transformation does not completely eliminate the institutional element. This element, however, does not need to be centralist. By minimizing its formality and eliminating its centralist elements, the church can become movement again. We, as marginal community, need minimal structure. Any element that hinders movement toward minimal structure should be eliminated. To allow for maximum decentralization, church structure must spring from an ad-hoc foundation. Standing committees would be formed and maintained only for essential regional, national, and international coordination. Committee members would be elected from their cell groups—basic units of the church—and serve on a voluntary basis. No committee or structure would be permanent or immutable. Most decisions would be made by ad-hoc committees, which would dissolve when their assigned tasks were completed. No denominations would be needed, no doctrines necessary, no traditions permanent, and no liturgies universal. In this respect, the formal church structure would be flexible; Jesus-Christ alone is permanent and present in every cell, for he is the creative core of the new marginal people. So community diversity is harmonized in one Lord, the source for creativity and of change.

Because diverse marginal cells are brought together under one Lord, Jesus-Christ, they should be open to each other. We must allow each cell to interpret Scripture in its own way, but simultaneously interpretations are tested and reclaimed through dialogue with others. This church of radical reformation is a dynamic and living movement which should not impose any one orthodoxy or orthopraxis on others. Each cell originates from a context which provides its distinctive understanding of the Christian faith. It is not desirable to unify or universalize different understandings of the faith or different interpretations of Scripture. Any attempt to unify individual cell belief opposes the diversity of expression reflected in the original order of creation. Because a plurality of faith expressions will exist in a new marginal church, dialogue and interdependence are essential. Dialogue causes mutual growth and maturity.

A closed group is destructive to itself and cancerous to the whole community of marginal people. When this happens, a particular cell dies and causes malfunction in the whole marginal body. A living community of marginal people must relate to other communities. A dangerous but common tendency of minority communities is to become closed to gain a temporary, false emotional security to combat alienation and marginality from the dominant group. This tendency is almost as evil as seeking the center of centrality. In Korean-American churches, schisms are most common. I do not believe that schisms are always bad, but when the divided group becomes closed, it becomes cancerous. Thus, marginal cell groups need mutual interdependence to support the whole.

The transition from dominant structure to marginal structure is possible only when the power of the church is vested in cells. Today, power resides in congregation (the coalition of many cell groups) or in diocese, conference, synod, and the like. For example, in the United Methodist Church, power is vested in the annual conference which brings hundreds of churches (congregations) together, and the bishop, who presides over the conference, exercises power. This structure is based on the hierarchical ideology that marginalizes Christians. It can be eliminated if power is vested in the cell groups that make up the congregations, which again make up the annual conference. When the power of decision is vested in cells, the leadership of the church is chosen from group representatives. There is no superstructure that dominates people. The congregation is this coalition of many cell groups. Thus, regional, national, and international movements are coalitions of cell groups. Since every representative or coordinator comes from a cell group, no permanent position of power is possible. To eliminate institutionalism, there must be terms of responsibility for all representatives, and their service must be voluntary. Membership is the only permanent position. All administrative work should be done by volunteer laity.

The ministers are free from administrative responsibilities and can devote themselves to preach, advise, and counsel people in their cell, which is the congregation. These ministers are servants who assist others with humility and gratitude. As preachers, they are prophets who try to speak of justice and peace. As teachers, they are wise persons who try to guide to truth and spiritual fulfillment. As healers, they are physicians who try to heal souls and reconcile social ills. As comforters, they are friends who try to share the joy and sorrow of marginal life.

Service is not genuine unless it is performed by a servant. Likewise, a minister to marginal people must be a marginal person. Therefore, the most important qualification for becoming a minister is to be marginal and a servant. Next, a potential minister must be recommended to ministry and supported by his or her cell group. Also, a potential minister must be approved by congregational representatives—the cluster of cell groups that are then responsible for his or her theological education. Theological education must be radically transformed to meet the demands of this new ministry. Finally, a minister is called by a congregation, and should be paid according to their need. Like the cell group, one congregation will split to form another when it becomes too large for one minister. In this way, no congregation is too big, and no minister is burdened beyond his or her capacity to serve. Moreover, ministers would be expected to be in dialogue with others. In this way, the hierarchical system is eliminated, and institutionalism minimized.

Activities of the Cell Group

When we make the cell group the basic unit of the church, each group designs its own programs to its character and context. One congregation's programs could be shared with another at worship services. If a cell group is predominantly Asian-American, for example, it is essential to utilize its unique cultural and historical perspective in liturgical services, celebrated when many cells gather.

After I participated in a shamanic ritual in Korea several summers ago,[10] I began to discover my roots in shamanism and understood how natural it was for me to sing, laugh, dance, and eat as native Koreans do in this ritual. Their spontaneity could be applied to Christian ceremonies, particularly Christian Korean-American rites.

For several years, I was a minister to cell groups consisting of Korean women who were married to American servicemen, women who were triply marginalized (marginalized as Koreans in Korea, as Koreans in America, and as Korean women married to American servicemen). In my ministry, our most creative and meaningful services and activities were adapted from their ordinary lifestyle. It would have been meaningless for them to adopt traditional dominant group patterns of worship.

People like to hear stories, especially stories from the Bible, and want to tell their own as well. Preaching, teaching, and theology are often made more relevant when related in story form in which biblical stories are interwoven with those lives. An ordinary story becomes sacred when it is told among a group who believe in Christ. Most of the stories we shared were of Christian witness in our daily lives. My sermons were usually my stories or parables woven among stories of Jesus. Every story we shared was filled with the pain and alienation of marginal people. Each became a testament to our struggle for social justice.

Korean-Americans like to sing repeatedly simple gospel songs. They are not concerned so much with its meaning but with the feeling aroused by singing together. Singing gospel songs not only builds group spirit but also enhances the mood of a worship service. They want to sing without printed music sheets because these distract from the mood.

Marginal Korean-Americans like to pray. Prayers are the very foundation of their Christian life. They pray ceaselessly. They pray in various ways: in silence, through feeling, out loud. Prayers do not have to be consistent or intelligent if the Spirit is felt. The service was spontaneous because it was a part of ordinary life. People laughed, shouted, cried, or were silent during the service. They were not stiff, frozen people. It is alive and authentic. They read the Bible aloud together. They make mistakes in reading, but they are not ashamed of it. In fact, they usually laugh at the mistakes they make in the Scripture reading. Because they are marginal people, they should be themselves at worship.[11]

Marginal people in cell groups like to eat together after the service. They prepare a full meal, which is their communion. They avoid a tiny piece of bread or wine from a plastic cup. Just as Jesus ate with his own disciples, they want to eat together in the presence of Christ, the margin of marginality. As long as we recognize the presence of Christ in our midst, our meal is sacred. We give thanks for the meal, as Jesus did, and eat remembering him. A simple liturgy is sufficient. Long high-church liturgy for communion has been crafted by centralist groups. Everything is simple, natural, and ordinary. After a communion meal or love feast, marginal people discuss their social and political concerns, and plan action to improve their community. The result of planned action is reported and evaluated, and new actions are initiated. The pastor should act only as a consultant and resource person; she or he must not dominate or direct group action. The cell group is fully responsible for itself.

As they come into contact with other groups in a larger gathering in congregational life, their cell group opens itself to other groups, and each learns something from the other. In congregations, the service and activities will take a pattern similar to the cell-group services. The effectiveness of a larger congregation is dependent on how to harmonize and coordinate diverse cells. Because the cell is the church's fundamental unit, the congregation, no matter how large, cannot impose itself against the will of a cell. Each cell is distinctive and does not dissolve into the larger whole. It is individual and a part of the whole simultaneously. Thus the church, as the body of Christ, can function together under the leadership of Christ. No single group can claim its uniqueness over other groups, just as "the eye cannot say to the hand, 'I have no need of you' " (1 Cor. 12:21). In the same manner, no matter how insignificant a group is in terms of number or activity, it is as important as the next cell. In a congregational gathering, the seemingly insignificant groups are especially honored. As Paul said, " . . . Those members of the body that we think less honorable we clothe with greater honor, and our less respectable members are treated with greater respect, whereas our more respectable members do not need this" (1 Cor 12:23-24). With dialogue, cell groups learn new things, and grow and mature in Christian life.

Theological Education

Like the public-school system, where most young people are indoctrinated into centralist ideology, a definite pattern of theological thinking emerges from seminary training. A seminary is similar to a cookie cutter; they shape the same way—identically. When a seminary is modeled after the centralist ideology, one cannot expect it to produce effective ministers for marginal people. When its educational system is based on an ideology that oppresses the poor and marginal, it cannot teach, seriously, liberation theology. Many courses on liberation theology (Latin American, African-American, feminist, Asian, and third-world) are taught in the seminary, but most are taught by white professors who are influenced by the dominant theology. They are like a few blades of grass in the green yard that support the "idea" of the presence of a dandelion, although they are not and cannot become dandelions. As long as they are part of a green yard that excludes the presence of a dandelion, they still oppress the dandelion. Likewise, as long as such professors share in the privileges and resources of the dominant group, their advocacy for the liberation of marginal people has little meaning.

If the theological seminary is to educate ministers for marginal people, there must be radical change in its structure, staff, and programs. A new seminary process must emerge to meet the new marginality's needs. In this new process, commitment to theological training should focus beyond intellectual pursuit. Historical and traditional approaches to theological disciplines must be considered so that the marginal community can avoid the perpetuation of any ideology. Theological training must develop a new way to study the Bible, preach, counsel, and offer spiritual direction, as well as teach how to organize for social justice from the marginal context. Seminary should encourage students to construct their theologies, especially story theologies, from their personal context.

I also envision the seminary as a primary place to model the cell. Theological education must stress the praxis of harmonious living as servants to each other. The teacher's primary function is to advise students and to encourage individual potential that develops their talents for ministry. A traditional lecture-style of teaching should be avoided, because this one-way communication precludes challenging student potential. Rather, students should be encouraged to participate in dialogue and to keep open minds on all theological issues. Avoiding technical terminology favored by dominant-group theologians is important. A non-technical lexicon should be used to convey theological thought through stories, as Jesus used in his teaching. Students should be encouraged to prize vision and imaginative thinking, while purely abstract thought is to be discouraged. Any theological thought worth consideration must have concrete, practical implications for personal, social, or political action that eliminates dominant ideology. So holistic thinking and unity in theory and practice is vital. Rather than dualistic, analytical, and critical thinking developed by dominant groups, complementary, creative, and imaginative reflection must be emphasized in study.

My vision of new theological education supports a cell-group class of twelve to fifteen students to one instructor. On a semester basis, this cell works together studying a particular theological discipline. Since theological students are groomed as advisors and consultants to cells, they should visit as many diverse cells as possible, and report back to their seminary cell. Seminary teachers must be experienced in and deeply committed to Christian ministry. They must possess Christian character as well as moral and spiritual qualities. Most important, such teachers should be marginal and active in cell groups. Obviously, seminary students are expected also to be equipped with the virtue of Christian love, and instead of professionalism, servanthood must be stressed.

Vital to seminary admission is a candidate's demonstrated sincerity, honesty, and a desire to serve.[12] No standard test is needed, for scores from such tests have been used by centralists to control and to exclude marginal people. A seminary should accept those who are recommended by their own congregations. Competition must be avoided, and a grading system should not be used to judge student performance. The requirements should not be uniform; some students may need a longer time to complete their spiritual and practical training. Evaluations need to be a mutual process: teacher and student must agree to satisfy certain requirements in an area of study. Graduation, too, should be by mutual consent between the student and faculty members who have been involved in his or her study. Later, those who have worked as ministers can come back to the seminary for further study or to teach. Likewise, teachers must occasionally return to church work. Also, the centralist practice of tenure, which contradicts the dynamic of a changing church, needs examination. Like the cell group, a seminary must reassess constantly to meet changing context.

Financial support for students and faculty should come from voluntary cell group giving. These funds would come through congregations that support ministerial training. Seminary living standards should not surpass that of marginal people, and compensation should be based on need rather than rank. Seminaries should avoid financial support from centralist groups. They should be extensions of the marginal church, where people come to learn, serve each other, and return to the world as servants.

Finally, those interested in conventional studies within a centralist framework must enroll in a comparative study of religions or an academic study of theology that is differentiated from seminary training in ministry.

The Mission of the Church

The mission of the new marginality is the reconciliation of all by a liberation of others from social injustice and by eliminating deeply rooted dominant ideologies. Reconciliation is not possible without justice,[13] and justice is not possible without eliminating the centralist ideology of dominance. The church cannot eliminate the dominion of which it is a part. Thus, the most urgent task of the church today is to liberate itself. Such liberation, however, is inseparable from global liberation.

Radical reformation is needed. We must accept that radical reformation will occur only with a return to Jesus and his disciples to understand that the authentic church is a people's movement, especially the movement within the milieu of marginal people. Jesus' twelve disciples are the *archetype* of the cell group. In a cell group of this size, Jesus is *re-presented in Spirit*. In other words, Jesus is present in the cell group, as he was among the twelve disciples, except that in the cell group Jesus is present as the Spirit of Christ. His presence is precisely why the mission of the church must reclaim the cell as the basic church unit. Hope for the church will come through the emergence of small groups: Bible study, covenant, base community, koinonia, and others. New cell groups (communities of marginal people) emerge as the movement expands. When the cell group grows, it splits and produces a new cell group. As cells continue to multiply, the church grows. The philosophy of church growth must come from the cell-group movement. Moreover, by vesting power in the cells, which constitute the congregation, this nullifies centralist dominance, and the church becomes a community of marginal people. As long as centralist ideology dominates, there is no justice. A church without justice cannot become a community of reconciliation. Therefore, dismantling centralist ideology is essential for transformation. The mission of the church is to become Jesus-Christ's authentic church today. Let me illustrate by discussing the small-group movement in the Korean-American church.

It is often said that the phenomenal growth of Korean-American churches is due to small-group structure.[14] The small group is known as *sokhae* or *kuyokhae*, which means a regional Bible study group. The group is a basic unit that can function as church, because it is more than just a Bible study group. People gathered in such instances have a brief service—prayers, hymns, Scripture readings, a meditation, and offerings. A minister usually presides at the program.

Although I wanted lay people to preside, they appeared uncomfortable with the idea of leading anything that involved religious matters if a minister was present. This hesitancy seems to indicate that they had been deeply influenced by hierarchical ideology.

During Bible study, all kinds of personal and social issues and problems are discussed. After the study there is a splendid party with delicious food. This meal offers the members a chance to socialize and get to know others intimately. The true sense of belonging to the church comes only through the *sokhae* or *kuyokhae*. The meetings take place in members' homes, and meals are provided by the host family.

Realistically, the *sokhae* is church, for it has all the ingredients necessary to make it the body of Christ. The group's right to be the church, however, is often usurped by dominant groups within a church. By transferring the small group's power to a congregation, the congregation becomes the center, and small groups become the margins. The congregation, that coalition of cell groups, takes the power and autonomy of the small group and transfers the church locus to itself. When this happens, we are right back to God at the center of the congregation, in the sanctuary! As a consequence, the primary activities of the Korean-American church happen within a congregation setting rather than in small groups. In most Korean-American churches, the *sokhae* or the small group meets once a month, while the congregation meets every Sunday morning for worship and at other times for other activities: evening services, early morning prayers, committee meetings, and other fellowship. In my ministry to marginalized people, however, our small groups meet every Wednesday. This strengthens the small group as church.

Although the Korean-American church starts with small Bible study groups, when a congregation is established, the group loses its autonomy and becomes subsidiary and subordinate to the congregation.[15] The radical transformation I envision restores the cell group as the basic church unit and empowers its distinctive character, rather than perpetuates the so-called congregational church. When we conceive of church as a movement of cell groups, the congregation becomes a mere coalition. When the congregation becomes a mosaic of cell groups, schism within the church is not a serious problem, for schism is none other than the disharmony of cell groups.

To vest power in cell groups, people must be taught that what attracts them to the church is often the most destructive element to authentic marginal community. People are attracted by centralist ideology that promises power. Yet, they must know that centralism is the cardinal sin that destroys the authentic church. It is not the lack of professional management skills or compelling preaching that fails the church, but the attractive centralist inclination (the desire to be at the center of centrality), which fails to make the church a community of new marginal people. Paradoxically, this universal tendency to seek the center of centrality is more intensely manifested in ethnic, minority churches, especially Korean-American churches.

Most male, Korean immigrants to North America are well-educated. According to a survey in Los Angeles County, seventy percent of Korean men are college graduates and one-half of them had held professional, technical, or managerial positions in Korea.[16] However, when they arrived in the United States, they discovered they no longer had the same status. They were discriminated against because of their racial and cultural background. With their lack of English-language proficiency, often they could not find jobs, so they created their own jobs by establishing shops and stores.[17] They worked hard. Often to raise their societal status, they lived in huge houses and drove expensive cars. Nevertheless, they remained unrecognized by society at large. No matter how fine their education or how much money they earn, they are still second-class citizens. The only place where they were positively recognized was in the Korean-American community. Since more than seventy percent of Korean-Americans attend church, the church is the best place for them to get the recognition they need and deserve.[18] Although there are many reasons why Korean-Americans are churchgoers,[19] receiving recognition is an important element. In the Korean-American congregation, almost all members want to hold some kind of office. For example, there is a broad system of lay elders, deacons, and the like, in the Korean United Methodist Church, where there is no such system for laity in the United Methodist Church.[20] In one small Korean-American congregation, more than half of its members were either elders or deacons! Moreover, the schools they attended, the degrees they received, and the occupations they pursue are recognized in the church.

Women, however, are the least recognized, even though they work harder than men. One woman in the church remarked, "I already told you that most of the church work is done by women, but men tend to get all the credit. And I also think that that's just fine, because we, women, don't work for public recognition."[21] This seems to indicate that women are less inclined to seek to be at the center and more willing to accept the position of marginality.

The more Korean-Americans are marginalized, the more they seek public recognition from their ethnic congregation. A church that does not recognize this will not survive. The minister often exploits such weakness to gain financial profit. Those who are lay elders and deacons are expected to give tithes. Public recognition is given to those who tithe or make special contributions; their names always appear in church bulletins. The church thus profits by stressing the centralist values which attract marginalized people. Because they have been marginalized once, they want to be at the center in their church and give accordingly. Thus they start to climb the hierarchical prestige ladder of the congregation. Paradoxically, the church as the community of marginal people often exploits its people through the dominant ideology that marginalized and alienated them. The function of the church should not be to exploit its members' weaknesses but to help them realize that the power they seek actually marginalizes them.

The church's mission is to heighten the awareness of marginal people. Through new understanding of their marginality, people discover that it provides a distinctive identity for their group. Those who are unaware of their marginality cling to the norm of centrality and are victimized by it. When their marginality is conscientized, they discover a new perspective at the margin of their marginality. Conscientized marginal persons, therefore, think and behave differently. Because Jesus Christ is a symbol of the margin of marginality, the new perspective is a Christian perspective, and aware, marginal people are Christian in principle. Although some of them may not identify themselves as Christians, from the perspective of marginality they are anonymously Christian. To become a member of the church means to shift one's perspective from the center of centrality to the margin of marginality. At the moment of conscientization, the central perspective shifts to a marginal perspective, and people receive a conversion, or a "born-again" experience. Such causes an awakening in marginalized people, and a transforming in dominant people.[22] This transformation from the center to the margin is necessary for salvation. Salvation takes place at the margin of marginality—Jesus-Christ.

For ethnic minorities, the awareness of individual marginality is central to the mission of the church. Most ethnic, minority churches, however, are influenced deeply by the dominant ideology, and fail to see their marginality. It is a tragic reality that the church has thus lost its identity. When marginal people do not see themselves as marginal people, they are not only other-directed but also misdirected. The marginalized church, like the marginalized ethnic person, has failed to achieve individual and true identity. Let me illustrate: when I came to study in North America, I was the only person of color in the dormitory where I lived. For many years I thought and behaved as if I were a white person because everyone I saw was a white person. One day I went to California and saw an Asian policeman. I could not believe that an Asian could be a policeman! This event was my conversion experience. To know that I was different was the beginning of discovering my own identity. The ethnic minority churches, especially Korean-American churches, must rediscover or create their own identity as communities of marginalized people. They are different from the communities of dominant people. Their norm is marginality. Unless ethnic minority churches are aware of this, they cannot help church members discover themselves.

A Korean minister, who began his ministry in New York City about a year ago, explained his concern for his North American ministry. He told me that what shocked him the most when he entered the church, where he serves as minister, were these words on the wall of the church:

> Am I an American?
> No.
> Am I a Korean?
> No.
> Who am I?

When he saw it, he realized that his mission was to help young people find their identity. The Korean-American church can help Korean-Americans discover their identity only when it discovers its own and shifts its norm from a centralist to a marginal perspective. People are the church. Thus, personal discovery is the church's discovery of identity as marginal people of God. With new understanding both become truly church and truly Christian.

The Korean-American church (and all other churches) should shift its centralist norm to a marginal norm in all its activities: prayers, Bible study and commentary, worship services, hymns, liturgies, exclusive language usage, offerings, social action, Sunday school curricula, theology, consulting techniques, and puritan ethics,[23] must be reinterpreted and redesigned from the marginal perspective. This means drastic change. The Korean-American church, however, like other ethnic minority churches, is capable of a drastic change because it is still the custodian of its ethnic culture and history.[24]

Because living on the margin of marginality is the norm for ethnic minorities in America, it is certainly unacceptable for the Korean-American or other ethnic minority church to be under the supervision of dominant Caucasian-American churches. Although the marginal church must transcend denominational affiliations, currently most Korean-American churches are affiliated with major denominations. For example, the Korean-American United Methodist Church is a part of the United Methodist Church which is controlled by Caucasian-Americans. Therefore, the Korean-American United Methodist Church cannot develop its own policies, programs, and activities from its marginal and ethnic perspective, because it conflicts with the dominant perspective of the supervising church.[25] Therefore, once ethnic minority churches are conscientized, they can no longer be subject to the dominant churches. They must become independent and coexist with other churches, including Caucasian-American, African-American, Hispanic, or Native American churches. Like the cell group, the Korean-American Church must be an autonomous and open-ended community that complements other marginal communities. In this respect, when ethnic minority churches function from marginality, they become missionaries to the dominant Caucasian churches. Like the remnants of Israel, the ethnic minority churches may become the salt and light of new churches in America.

The transition by the church from a centralist norm to a marginal norm is not easy. There is strong resistance to any transition from tradition. Those in powerful and influential positions in the church will not easily give them up. Just like the young ruler who could not give up his wealth to become a follower of Jesus, those who have, want more. The awareness of marginality must begin from below and move upward, that is, to move from the margin to the center. When people accept their marginality and understand its power, they can resist the centralist church ideology, because Jesus-Christ is with them at their margin. By refusing to support any superstructure that upholds continued institutionalization, the church can become a movement and strengthen its cell-group solidarity. In this way the transition from a central norm to a marginal norm of Christianity takes place.

Finally but most importantly, the mission of the authentic church is to become the servant of the world. When the norm shifts from centrality to marginality, the church is placed at the margin of the world. To be at the margin means to be a servant of world, even of the world at the center. This idea is a paradox of the Christian faith. Jesus-Christ, who came into the world in the form of servant, leads the church to be marginal and to become servant. Because servanthood is the function of marginality, those who are marginal must be servants. However, as marginality has negative and positive, or self-negating and self-affirming, realities, servanthood has two functions: passive and creative service. The church as the community of marginality must incorporate passive and creative service when it ministers to the world. The passive aspect is negative but inevitable. We cannot be free and separate from the world. We are in the world. To deny our existence in the world is to flee reality. Thus, Paul said that Christians must respect and obey the state that represents the world (Rom 13).

However, passive service (obedience) to the world is also creative service to the world, for they are inseparable. Those who refuse to serve the world will never serve Christ, for Christ came for the world and died for the world. By serving the world, we are not serving a centralist inclination of the world but rather the world that has a centralist inclination. If we use biblical language, we do not serve evil but serve a world that contains evil. From a centralist perspective, service is passive; but from the marginal perspective, service is creative. Thus, shifting the norm from center to margin, passive service becomes creative service of the church. To refuse to serve means to decline creativity and transformation. It is the nature of love to serve, to accept, and to change. By serving the unservable, they become servable; by accepting the unacceptable, it becomes acceptable; and by changing the unchangeable, it can change. Love transforms the negative to positive, and passive to creative service. Thus the church serving the world is transforming it.

Servanthood is more than service. The servant serves, but service can be rendered by the masters as well. Mission is service. No service is authentic unless it is done by a willing servant. What is important is the willingness to serve naturally and spontaneously. On the other hand, service extended by a dominant group is necessarily and by definition partial and impersonal. It means giving what one has rather than doing what one is. That is why genuine service is not possible unless it is done by the marginal. Clearly, the church must become the servant to serve the world. Service by dominant groups is oppressive, but service by marginal people is liberative. In this way the community of marginality is always the community of the servant.

When the world is served by the church, the world is transformed into the servant, and is, therefore, marginal. Those who are at the center of centrality become the servants of the world. This is the true meaning of public service. When the church becomes the servant to the world, and the world is transformed and becomes the servant, then centrality will be overcome by marginality. When that occurs, marginality overcomes marginality.[26] Then, there is but a single norm, the margin of marginality, Jesus-Christ, who becomes the head of the body.

As I conclude this chapter, I remember the 1963 March on Washington, D.C., during the civil rights movement. This movement was the result of the coalition of many different groups of people. At that time I was a librarian at Howard University's School of Religion. I joined the thousands and thousands of people who came to Washington, D.C., to show their belief in and solidarity with the unity and harmony of all people. Black and white, yellow and brown held hands together as brothers and sisters, and marched to the Lincoln Memorial, where we heard Martin Luther King, Jr.'s, famous speech. His voice of inspiration, eloquently recalling the American dream, still rings in my ears.[27] We then sang "We Shall Overcome" together. I want to see the church, like the civil rights movement, become a movement of countless cell groups, "marching" to overcome marginality by marginality. This will be not just "a" movement but a permanent movement, a movement that never ends.

7. CREATIVE TRANSFORMATION

Overcoming Marginality through Marginality

> Every valley shall be lifted up,
> and every mountain and hill be made low,
> the uneven ground shall become level,
> and the rough places a plain.
> *(Isa 40:4)*

The church as the dynamic community of new marginal people will be the servant of the world. This does not mean, however, that the new marginal people will serve the community of centralists who dominate the world. Rather, the church serves the world, though it is dominated by centralists. The community of new marginal people should be the agency that saves the world from centralist domination. Accomplishing that, marginal people liberate themselves but also liberate centralists from their obsession to be at the center. What does it mean to overcome marginality through marginality? How is it possible? What guidelines are used to conquer marginality? I will attempt to answer these questions and to provide a vision of the new world symbolized in Jesus' teaching of God's reign on earth.

Marginality as Transforming the World

We have a tendency to think that marginalized people are saved or rescued by centralist people, because centralist people dominate our society. Since central-group people have marginalized the poor, the weak, and the different, we naturally think that they have the power, the wealth, and the ability to rescue the same. Likewise, central-group people expect marginal people to ask for mercy and compassion because their salvation depends on the centralist will. By marginalizing others, central-group people cause marginal group dependence. However, the more we depend on centralists, the more we lose our autonomy and conform to centralist values, norms, and idealogy. As long as we accept centralist ideology as normative, it will be impossible for the marginalized to be free. From the centralist perspective, liberating marginal people makes them centralists who, in turn, can marginalize others. As long as centralist ideology dominates the world, there will be conflict and dichotomy between marginal people and central-group people.

When centralist ideology is normative, everyone wants to be at the center. The center's power, wealth, and glory pulls people like a magnet. The margin as a symbol of the weak, poor, and despised repels people. Because everyone struggles to achieve the center of centrality, competition is inevitable and the only means to achieve survival. Moreover, competition creates conflict, and conflict creates struggle for victory. Even when one attains the center, struggle is constant to maintain it. Life can become a struggle toward a center that does not really exist. The center sought is not authentic but a mind-set produced by centralist ideology.[1] This centralist inclination to seek the center is, as I said, the carnal sin that enslaves us, oppresses us, and marginalizes us in our society. Such a value structure has been made normative. History is filled with vicious cycles of violence and conflict, that is, centralist competition.

Marginal people who subscribe to the centralist perspective cannot gain it until and unless they, too, occupy the center. Even if marginal people become conscious of their predicament and assert their freedom from dominant people, they will never be free as long as they share the same norm as the dominant group. Those who do gain center then dominate others and become oppressor. For example, the Exodus story does not end with the liberation of the Hebrews. It continues with the conquest of Canaan and the oppression of its native people. The liberated through the Exodus become the oppressors: the Israelites, liberated from the oppression in Egypt, became the oppressors of Palestinians. Likewise, Irish people who were oppressed by the British people in their homeland came to North America and became oppressors of other ethnic minorities. Historically, once-oppressed proletarians became oppressors of the bourgeoisie under Communist rule. As long as centrality's center is considered normative, no liberation for either group is possible. If one group dominates, the other is necessarily oppressed.

Genuine liberation comes only when the norm shifts from the center to the margin. Once there, liberation of marginal people is possible. However, instead of moving up from the bottom, one moves down from the top. Instead of moving from the margin to the center,[2] one moves from the center to the margin. Or, one descends into the valley rather than climbing up the mountain. The margin is the locus which the spirit of God fills with mighty power. Isaiah wrote, "Every valley shall be lifted up, and every mountain and hill be made low; the uneven ground shall become level, and the rough places a plain" (40:4). When heights descend to the valley, the valley is filled and lifted, the mountain is lowered. Everything becomes even. Just so, dominant ideology is abolished, and everyone becomes a servant. From the marginal perspective, every person is marginal to each other, and each becomes a servant to another, for new marginality is depicted in the symbol of the suffering servant, the margin of marginality. When everyone becomes marginal, there is no centrality that can marginalize anyone. Thus, marginality is overcome through marginality.

Shifting the perspective from centrality to marginality does not create a new center at the margin. Marginality will never become centrality because it is inclusive. Centrality is based on hierarchical value, while marginality is based on egalitarian principle. Centrality is interested in dominance, while marginality is interested in service. Centrality vies for control, while marginality seeks cooperation. Because of such polarity, the margin cannot be the center. Thus I have avoided calling the margin the "new center." The margin does not have a center. When one margin meets another, there is the margin of marginality, the creative core, which is Jesus-Christ's presence. No real liberation for marginal people exists unless and until central people join them at the margin. In other words, central people must be freed of their inclination to dominate and control, and instead become servants to all people. Then all people will be served as brothers and sisters equally. Everyone will be marginal, and marginality will overcome marginality. This approach can liberate all people and provide the possibility of peace globally.

The Creative Potentiality of Marginality

How does the marginal approach transform the world? Marginal people seem powerless to do anything that affects positively socio-political structures. From a marginal perspective, however, its people exist to do more than serve and support the dominant group; they have the potential to change and transform the world. The marginalized realize their potential when they are conscious of themselves as part of a creative core—the very creativity of God manifest in Jesus-Christ. Such consciousness affirms them as new marginal people and connects them to the power of divine creativity.

As new marginal people, they see themselves as the subject of salvation history. They understand servanthood as intrinsic to themselves and as the means to eliminate dominant ideology. Marginal service is dedicated to breaking distorted ideology and creating a new world.

Marginal creative potential comes from the experience of being in-between two or more dominant ideologies. Being outsiders, marginal people are acute and able critics of dominant ideology. Immigrant, marginal people also live in-between worlds and affirm both the dominant culture of their residence and the ancestral culture of their roots. They can creatively combine the knowledge and insight of the insider with the critical attitude of the outsider.[3] The creative synthesis of these conflicting cultural values can provide the potential for new visions and creative energies. Life in-between is characterized by a neither/nor or total detachment, while life in-both is characterized by a both/and or total attachment. The creative movement of human life comes when both total detachment and total attachment are simultaneously experienced. It is the moment when total negation (total detachment) and total affirmation (total attachment) are brought together. When negation and affirmation or negative and positive are united, they produce creative energies that transform the world. Because the very locus of marginality is creative, God became the margin of marginality in Jesus-Christ in order to transform the world.

Historian Arnold Toynbee recognizes the creative potentiality of marginal people. He believes that marginal people are not only self-assertive and spiritually strong but also endowed with the potentiality of new visions and creative energies because they have had to deal with uncertain conditions and conflicting cultural values.[4] Victor Turner, a well-known anthropologist, helps us understand this creative potentiality of marginality by using the term *liminality*, derived from the Latin language, *limen,* a threshold, chasm, or margin. In rites of passage, persons pass from one stage to another (for example, from infancy to childhood), and the liminality or "in-between-ness" which separates one stage from another is poised with extraordinary strength or a supernatural power.[5] As liminal agents, marginal people are like the remnant of the Israelites. They can be the creative minority in God's plan for salvation. As Halford E. Luccock once said, "God's instrument has been a creative minority. No limits can be set to the achievement of a small group of lives, possessed of the spirit of God, imbued with the idea of the Kingdom, dedicated to the person of Christ."[6] Marginal people, as a creative minority, can become catalysts to transform the world and to shift the axis from centrality to marginality.

Since creative potential of marginal people ultimately rests in Jesus-Christ, the church as genuine community of new marginality (the *communitas* of liminality) must serve as a creative agency for transforming the world. To become an agent of transformation, the first task is to become the "anti-structural" communitas of liminality.[7] Today's church is structurally "bureaucratic, patriarchal, and hierarchical in the extreme."[8] The communitas of liminality as an anti-structural movement can become an agency for deconstructing central ideology. The importance of this movement stems less from its size and more from the intensity of its commitment to Jesus-Christ as the creative core of marginality. The genuine commitment of these creative minority groups (or cell groups) to the sacramental community of love or *koinonia* (sharing) is the key to success for transformation of the world.

The community of new marginality, the communitas of liminality, is always in a dialectical relationship with the world. It is in the world but not of it. It is the agent of global transformation but never identifies with the world. So the communitas of liminality continuously cracks the recurring symbols of centralist ideology to liberate the world. This agent never stops. The transformative process will continue until every one is free.

The source of this transformative, marginal power is love, because God is love.[9] The beloved community of new marginality (or *koinonia*) transforms itself and the world out of love. Love is the dynamic catalyst that transforms the power of centrality. The love of new marginality is inclusive, while the power of centrality is exclusive; the former serves, while the latter dominates; the former cooperates, while the latter controls; the former derives from spirit, while the latter drives from matter. The power that controls, dominates, and excludes others is based on a centralist ideology. When power is transformed, centrality becomes marginality, as marginality becomes new marginality.

Overcoming Marginality Through Love

We understand how love works through the teaching and life of Jesus-Christ. As he commanded us: "Love one another as I have loved you" (John 15:12, 17), so our love is modeled after his love. We can overcome centrality by following his way of love.

First of all, Jesus' love was expressed in his service to others. He was born in the form of servant (Phil 2:7) and as servant, he suffered and died on the cross. His love descends and spreads to reach people where they are. It is contrary to the centralist order of ascent.[10] Love reverses the centralist value of power. As Jesus said: "The first becomes last, the last becomes the first; the greatest becomes the least and the least becomes the greatest." Jesus-Christ came to serve: service is his love. The centralists who use racism, sexism, or classism as their means of power to dominate people of color, women, and the poor want to be served rather than to serve. The more they are served by marginal people, the more they want power, to continue to dominate. Love resists service to centralists who use that service to benefit themselves. It serves only people who need service. Jesus did not serve Pharisees, Sadducees, and other centralists who were wealthy and powerful. Love that serves marginal people resists service to the powerful. By resisting, marginal people serve one another and activate solidarity. If the power that dominates is racism, the communitas of liminality must refuse to serve it. If it is sexism, it must resist through love. Resisting dominant ideology by love is a creative response, while resistance by power is a reaction that creates waves of contrapuntal reaction. It provides room for centralists to repent and redirect themselves to serve the needy. Thus, the community of new marginality has to analyze centrality's power structure and target its resistance. Such movement should continue until centrality's dominance is gone. When it is, each becomes a servant to the other. Government officials become true public servants; business leaders become servants of the poor; and scholars become the servants of students. When all become servants to others, everyone acts as a marginal person, but no one is marginalized; so, marginality has been overcome by marginality.

The love that Jesus-Christ exemplified contrasts with the power of centralists. Love cooperates for the benefit of the whole. New marginality's love is communitarian and, therefore, relational and pluralistic. It acts and thinks inclusively in terms of the community as a whole. Centrality's power is hierarchical and individualistic; centralists think and act exclusively, in terms of individual interests. As such, they promote competition, individualism, singularity, and sameness. Just as an exclusive category of either/or must function within the inclusive category of both/and, the power of individualism must be confined within the love of wholeness. The love that includes the exclusive and changes the individualistic to wholeness belongs to Jesus-Christ. Altering the value system from individualism to communitarianism and accepting the love manifested in Jesus-Christ, marginal people can liberate themselves from dependency upon the power of centrality.

The commitment of marginal people to the communitas of love (*koinonia*) is the power to overcome marginalization. No individual marginal person can alone fully overcome individual marginality. It is overcome in solidarity with marginality; Jesus-Christ is present in their midst and acts as love to transform marginal people and central-group people. Any force that causes a break in the group's solidarity is the enemy. In our capitalist society, the power that destroys solidarity is greed for money, the most seductive symbol of dominance.[11] Ethnic minorities in this country, especially Asian-Americans, are lured by money and leave marginal solidarity. As they succumb to this lure, they are ensnared by the centralist system and become dependent on it. The more money they desire, the more selfish they become; the more selfish they become, the more individualistic their lifestyle. The more individualistic they become, the more marginalized they are by the dominant group. Greed causes pain and alienation rather than easing our marginality. As said in the Bible, "For the love of money is a root of all kinds of evil, and in their eagerness to be rich some have wandered away from the faith and pierced themselves with many pains" (1 Tim 6:10). It is not money itself but greed for money that destroys the solidarity of the family, of the communitas of liminality, and of *oikomenia* or the household of God. Money is the driving force of capitalism. It can destroy communal life and deprive everyone of cultural depth.[12]

Unless consumer capitalism is overcome, marginal people will never be liberated from central-group people. To overcome consumer capitalism, we must alter its value system. New marginal people value simplicity, naturalness, and spirituality. Clearly, the two groups' values are at odds. My cultural roots tell me that true beauty is in simplicity and naturalness. I still remember seeing a simple flower in a pot when I visited a Zen monastery. Pointing to the flower, a monk said, "Beauty is in simplicity and naturalness. What is true is also simple and natural." The monk's life seems to exemplify each quality. I also remember a Korean Methodist bishop, H. K. Yew, who came from Korea to preach at my church in Toledo, Ohio. I went to the airport to pick him up. When I met him as he got off the airplane, he was carrying a small briefcase. After greeting him, I said, "Let us go to claim your luggage." He said, "Oh, no. This is all I brought with me." Then he asked me to carry his briefcase. I asked him how he could survive two weeks in America without luggage. He told me how easy it was for him to travel: "Much bag creates more problems." He has to carry it to airports, wait for it to be picked up, and then carry it everywhere he goes. "I become a slave to it," he said. For him, it was better and easier to travel simply. He wore wash-and-wear clothing. When he stopped at a hotel, he washed his garments before going to bed and donned them the next day. "I can wear the same things for two weeks without trouble. All I need is to spend a few minutes washing them every evening. That is much easier for me than carrying a big bag around everywhere I go." Certainly, he exemplified the simple life that all Christians should value.

If we value simple and natural things and devote more time to what is spiritual, our lives will be easier and healthier, and will promote a cleaner environment. The community of marginal people must demonstrate that a simple and natural life based on the spirit of love is superior to compulsive consumerism based on greed. We don't have to own more than we need. For example, we need a few pairs of shoes or a couple suits of clothes. We can use them until they wear out. We don't have to follow fashion. We can drink cold water rather than soft drinks and eat less often in restaurants. We can use public transportation, walk, or bike short distances, and at the same time socialize with others or exercise for good health. By sharing space with others, we nurture the spirit of communitas. We must learn to share expensive items, to use public libraries and other public facilities more often to minimize living expenses. Most of all, we must learn to enjoy natural beauty and simple living. These things must happen as part of the solidarity movement among marginal people. By changing values and committing ourselves to the spirit of love, we marginal people can liberate ourselves and defeat the centralist ideology of dominance. When this happens, marginality is overcome through marginality, and central-group people enter the community of new marginal people.

Love is inclusive. Like water it soaks in everywhere. Love is irresistible. It penetrates human hearts and opens them. Marginality and centrality can be brought together through love, for love reunites. The love expressed in the margin of marginality is responsive, spontaneous, and kind. It does not compromise justice, for love without justice in action is romance. Love waits patiently, pliantly until centrality responds with openness. Through love, dialogue takes place, for love is dialogue.[13] Dialogue based on love demands total, mutual participation. Because love works through empathy, marginality participates in centrality and centrality participates in marginality. In this mutual participation, the potentiality of transformation is possible through the conscientization of marginality. For example, when centralized white persons empathetically participate in the cultural and ethnic activities and lives of Asian-Americans, they experience marginality and discover their identity distinct from the marginalized Asians in America. If they participate through love, they become aware of injustice they have created and are motivated to liberate themselves from centralist domination. Thus, love acts to transform domination.[14] On the other hand, when Asian-Americans participate in activities of the dominant group, they reinforce their marginality. They become convinced of their responsibility to transform the present order of injustice to the new order of a just world where all people, regardless of their racial origins, sexual orientations, or class distinctions, live together in harmony and peace. The creative potentiality of marginality is realized through conscientization and dialogue. We must use whatever means are available through education or politics to work in solidarity as a creative minority toward a just world empowered by love.

Finally, love or agape is like water that flows downward. It touches the lowest first and then reaches out to the highest until everything is inundated. As the high places are lowered and the low places are lifted up, everything becomes even. Again, as Isaiah said, "Every valley shall be lifted up, and every mountain and hill be made low; the uneven ground shall become level, and the rough places a plain. Then the glory of the Lord shall be revealed, and all people shall see it together, for the mouth of the Lord has spoken" (40:4-5). This vision is certainly new; it is possible through love. In it, no conflict exists between centrality and marginality, between the rich and the poor, between white and colored, nor between female and male. All are equal members of the family of God and share the same privilege and power as brothers and sisters. So everyone is marginal and a servant to the other. God alone is the creative core of marginality. Creativity continues because of God, but it operates within the complementary framework of a harmonious whole. Thus the true vision of reconciliation is what the communitas of liminality hopes to achieve. We must bring this vision to life, as Jesus-Christ asked us to pray: " . . . Your kingdom come. Your will be done, on earth as it is in heaven" (Matt 6:6-10).

Overcoming Suffering with Suffering

Until this vision is realized, one of the continuing struggles intrinsic to marginal people is suffering. The Old Testament seems to indicate that suffering is a result of the fall (Gen 3). If we reinterpret the fall as original sin, suffering seems to be the consequence of our sins. The perception of suffering as a consequence of sin seems to be central to Scripture, transmitted by dominant groups in biblical history. According to this interpretation, suffering can be terminated when we eliminate our sins. Because the root of suffering is sin, the problem of suffering is the problem of sin, which appears to indicate that the intensity of suffering should be proportionate to the intensity of sin. Or the more we sin, the more we suffer; the less we sin, the less we suffer. This kind of reasoning, however, is flawed. We know that suffering falls on all kinds of people. Associated as it is with sin, suffering is often regarded as evil. Nevertheless, we know that good people often suffer more than bad people. So this interpretation of suffering does not always work. Protest against this interpretation is clearly expressed in the Book of Job.[15]

We can assume that suffering is an existential reality, and that it falls to anyone who is not perfect. When there is imperfection, there is suffering, for suffering is due to imperfect relationship. From the marginal perspective, the creation story in Genesis does not deal with perfection or completion of creation. Rather, it is the *beginning of creation*,[16] for creation continues even today. The continuing creative process itself contains suffering. As long as creation continues toward perfection, suffering is a part of that creative process. If we are created to be creative, we must be created to be marginal because marginality is creative. The creative process itself, therefore, contains suffering as does marginality. Suffering as a part of the creative process—unlike suffering due to socio-political or economic alienation—is creative and inherent in the creation. In this respect, suffering does not begin with the fall but with creation. For example, the suffering of childbearing for women and of toil for men should not be regarded as a result of sin (Gen 3:16-19). They are procreative and creative work which have their origins in creation. Some suffering is unavoidable if we are involved in creating. I believe creative suffering can be a positive power for transforming the world. An attempt to avoid suffering, then, by sheltering in the center, is not only contrary to but also destructive of creativity.

Although suffering is inevitable, people naturally seek to avoid it. The progress of our civilization can be attributed primarily to the human attempt to avoid suffering. For example, medicine and technology exist to please the senses and eliminate suffering. One of the prime objectives of medicine is to alleviate patient pain and suffering. Automobiles and airplanes are made to ease the suffering of legs. Any advance that promotes our convenience can be regarded as alleviating inconvenience, pain, and suffering. But nothing can completely eliminate suffering. For example, aspirin use does not always remove pain. Any attempt to completely remove suffering from life is a centralist attempt to eliminate one episode of suffering for another. Such is a perspective of either/or thinking. If suffering and life are inseparable, the exclusion of suffering is the exclusion of life. Suffering cannot be overcome by the centralist mind-set.

On the other hand, marginal people consider suffering inevitable. To be marginal means to be suffering servants. To be marginalized means to have to endure some kind of suffering, whether socio-political or psychological. If we judge marginality by the dominant norm, it means to be outside the norm, different, abnormal. Being outside of so-called normal relationship means to suffer, as suffering stems from distortion of normal relationship. Buddhists help us understand suffering as the act of distorted relationship. Suffering is known as *dukkha*, which literally means "disjoined" or disjoined relationship. When arms or legs are disjoined, every movement is suffering. Marginal people are culturally, racially, and socially disjoined to the dominant group. They are people in-between two worlds. To be in-between means to be disjoined, and to be disjoined means suffering. Because they are forced to be in-between, they are innocent sufferers. Those who are marginalized because of their ethnicity or race or gender suffer innocently, for they are born to be different and are naturally different. Suffering due to difference is other than creative suffering inherent in creation. Marginal people endure both kinds: from centralist ideology of dominance

and from the creative process. Thus marginal people are acutely aware
of suffering in life. There is no way to be free from some suffering as
long as they live. To be free from suffering is to be non-existent.

Marginal people live life in-between and in-both and know suffering
in each sphere. It is their both/and understanding that deals with life's
suffering. Suffering can be overcome sometimes by living through it.
How? There is an Oriental saying that heat is overcome by heat, and
cold is overcome by cold. In Korea some people drink a hot tea in the
summer to overcome the summer heat. I was once asked to put my
frostbitten hands in ice water, as part of the curative process. These
illustrations seem to convey that an extreme situation may begin to find
relief by one's remaining in the extreme position for a short time. Perhaps this has something to say to us about how to deal with suffering.
How so?

I use the word "overcome" because suffering cannot be solved. To
overcome means to confront it and struggle with it. This struggle to
confront suffering is a lifelong process. We become more adept at confronting and struggling with suffering as we experience it, and gain a
confidence to overcome it again and again. Our struggle with suffering
certainly trains our will and character to deal with life and gives new
meaning to existence.

Jesus-Christ was the pioneer of suffering. Called the suffering servant, he confronted and struggled with suffering regularly and overcame it even on the cross. Marginal people are called to share and
participate in his suffering, in the very depth of his suffering. Jesus said
that he must undergo great suffering at the hands of the elders and
chief priests and scribes (Matt 16:21). He did not avoid suffering. He
knew that avoidance was not the way of God but the way of humanity,
especially centralist people. Therefore, he said to Peter, "Get behind
me, Satan! You are a stumbling block to me; for you are setting your
mind not on divine things but on human things" (Matt 16:23). The
power that overcame suffering was not the crown but the cross, not
glory but tragedy, not wealth but humility, and not hate but love.[17]

As marginal people, we are called to join in the suffering of Jesus-
Christ. We join him when we follow him. Our cross is rugged, the centralist's cross is adorned; our cross is heavy, their cross is light; our
cross demands much, their cross demands little. Our cross is a symbol
of divine suffering, their cross repudiates distress. Our cross symbolizes
sacred power, their cross represents weakness. Our suffering can be
overcome through the cross.

Many years ago, when my children were interested in riding the roller coaster, I went along with them. I was afraid to ride it because it moved so fast that my body was pulled in the direction opposite my resistance. Then I decided not to resist. I relaxed into the movement and pushed myself, mentally, to move faster than the roller coaster did. This done, I overcame my fear and enjoyed the ride. Like riding the roller coaster, we must avoid resistance to suffering. Then we overcome our suffering. We overcome suffering in the creative core of our suffering.

Our suffering is eased when shared with others, because it often produces true friendship, which supports a spirit of endurance. Jesus was our true friend, for he suffered for us and gave his life for us (John 15:13). In the shared human support of suffering, true friendship is formed. As is sometimes true with those who suffer together in wars or concentration camps, deep closeness that endures can result. Likewise, suffering in a marginal community should strengthen true friendship. Conversely, those who avoid suffering will seldom have true friends, which is why, among the dominant group, genuine friendship is rare. True friendship often comes only through suffering together, because suffering touches the depth of our hearts. In suffering people learn to trust each other. Suffering is easier when shared. As Jesus said, "Come to me, all you that are weary and are carrying heavy burdens, and I will give you rest. Take my yoke upon you, and learn from me; for I am gentle and humble in heart, and you will find rest for your souls. For my yoke is easy, and my burden is light" (Matt 11:28). In our friendship and sharing with Jesus-Christ, our suffering is easier and overcome.

Finally, suffering is overcome through suffering because suffering is a part of love. Those who avoid suffering do not know how to love. The more we love, the more we expect to suffer. Because God is love (1 John 4:17), God also suffers. To use Kierkegaard's words, "Those whom God loves he makes to suffer."[18] In suffering we experience love, for love and suffering are inseparable. If God loved us so much as to give us Jesus (John 3:16), the Creator *must* have suffered for us. In God's suffering, we find meaning in ours. Suffering without love has no meaning and no redemptive value at all. When we find the meaning and redeeming value in suffering, we can endure the suffering and overcome it.

To return to my earlier analogy, love is like water that reaches down to the lowly people first and lifts them up to make them level with kings. Love moves downward, because it is part of suffering. Those who suffer are people at lower social levels, the marginalized. God loves marginal people, authentic sufferers who belong to God's loving care. Although God's love is universal, it manifests itself differently. Because God's love is suffering, those who avoid suffering avoid that love. God's love is intensely manifest in the marginal sufferer, because love is part of suffering. Like a parent who loves and defends a young child mistreated by an elder child, God sides with the weak and loves the innocent sufferer more intensely than the one who causes suffering. Conversely, like a parent who punishes the elder child who hurts a younger sibling, God's love is expressed as righteous anger toward those who cause the suffering of others, although the same love is manifested as compassion toward those who suffer innocently. Jesus' suffering love, therefore, also manifested itself as anger at the oppressor of the innocent victim. Anger against unjust suffering contains an element of healing and eases suffering because this anger is part of suffering love. When there is a long, vicious accretion of unjust suffering, it can generate an intense rage which can burst out like a violent volcano, as in the case of the Los Angeles riots after the acquittal of officers charged with brutalizing Rodney King. But, when coupled with suffering love, this accumulated anger explodes with volcanic power in non-violent resistance, which completely smothers and paralyzes the centralist system. Also, anger is expressed in other constructive ways: in satiric humor, in laughter. Humor releases pent-up frustration against unjust suffering. Laughter often transcends distress and pain.[19] By laughing loudly and often, marginal people escape moments of suffering and reconcile the irony of injustice.

Overcoming suffering means coping with it, finding meaning and support through community fellowship, and believing divine presence is with us. In Jesus-Christ, the unjust suffering of marginal people is united with his suffering love and becomes creative suffering. Such returns the world to the original order of creation, where justice and peace prevail over injustice and undeserved suffering.

Transforming the Personal Experience of Marginality

Certain emotions or feelings are associated closely with marginal people in situations of innocent or undeserved suffering. They include: rejection, humiliation, alienation, loneliness, nothingness, wholeness, and a vision of new life. All are found in my parable of the dandelion in chapter 1. While these emotions are not unique to marginality, they are particularly typical of the marginal experience. The following personal episodes will illustrate the feelings aroused in a human being because of marginalization, and will draw on the life of Jesus-Christ, as an exemplary model for overcoming the experience of marginality.

Rejection is the first warning signal that awakens the conscience of marginal people. Rejection comes through various forms of exclusivism which set apart those who are different. The dandelion was rejected because its shape and color were different from that of the grass. Like the dandelion, I was deeply hurt when I was rejected by white people because of my racial and cultural difference. However, unexpected rejections are often blows that not only disorient but startle consciousness of one's marginality; this was certainly the case for me.

More than fifteen years ago, I visited Winston-Salem in North Carolina to see a white woman, Beatrice Bruteau, who wanted to discuss my manuscript. When I got to the city with my wife and two children, it was about four o'clock in the afternoon. Although it was early, I wanted to secure a room before having supper. I stopped at a Holiday Inn. A clerk looked me up and down and said, "Sorry, all rooms are occupied. Try some other place." I went to a few other motels, but all responded the same. I was rejected by one after another. I finally decided to take my family to a restaurant for dinner, for it was almost six o'clock. We waited for almost an hour, yet no one came to serve us. My children were furious, my wife was impatient, and I was angry. I was so angry that I almost slammed the door as we left. I decided to call Beatrice Bruteau before leaving town. She asked me to wait at the phone booth for a few minutes. She called me back soon and said, "I reserved a room for you and your family at the Holiday Inn." It was the same hotel that had rejected me. Beatrice was successful where I was not, because she was white and belonged to the centralist group. Now, whenever I hear "Winston-Salem" in cigarette advertisements, I am reminded of that incident and my marginality.

Marginalization occurs in the church. In June, 1961, when I finished my theological education, I was supposed to be ordained an elder at the Ohio Conference of the Methodist Church held at Lakeside, Ohio. I was to be admitted to full conference membership. Before the admission, there was a final review of candidates by the Board of Ministerial Qualifications. When I met with board members in a small cottage in the Lakeside campground, I answered all the questions they asked me.

When the questioning session ended, the chairman of the board asked me to wait for a few minutes, then he could let me know of their decision. I knew that I had met all their requirements, so I did not expect anything but good news. When they returned to the conference table, the chairman told me, "We definitely think that you are qualified and meet all the requirements for ordination and full membership in our conference. You have attended the Methodist seminary and done quite well. You were ordained a deacon a year ago and served the Methodist church as an associate minister for two years. You also answered all the questions we asked you. As far as we are concerned, you have met all qualifications for full membership in our conference. However, you must know that once you have been admitted to our conference, our bishop is responsible for appointing you to a local church, and there is no congregation in our conference that wants you to be their pastor. You know what we mean."

"Why?" I was a bit emotional.

"You should know that you are different," the chairman said with arrogance.

"Yes, I know. I am yellow."

I was so angry that I became almost irrational. At the end of our argument, I said, "I do not wish to be a part of a conference that discriminates against me because of my racial origin. You are worse than Pharisees." I slammed the door as I left. A few days later, however, the bishop intervened and accepted me into the conference. To this day, I believe he did so merely because he felt he had to in the face of my obvious qualifications.

Why was it so painful for me to be rejected by the central group of the church? It hurt because until then, I had thought I was a part of that group. The more I wanted to be a part of the central group, the more I was denied and rejected. There was a great gap between what central-group people thought of me, and what I thought of them. The gap was so wide and deep that even the so-called ministers of the gospel could not cross it, nor could I bridge the gap, because it is crossable only by those who create it. Until they accept me, I must accept their rejection.

Jesus, rejected by his own people, became the stone that the builders rejected and the cornerstone (Luke 20:17). He was rejected by the people of his hometown (Mark 6:1-6), by Pharisees and other central-group people, and was betrayed and rejected by his own disciples and by the world (John 1:11). Even the crowd who had followed him ultimately rejected him by accepting Barabbas (Luke 23:18). Because Jesus anticipated their rejection, he accepted it rather than denying it. He overcame rejection by accepting it for what it was.

The second emotion felt by marginal people is humiliation. The dandelion in the parable was not only rejected but deeply humiliated. The dandelion was pulled out many times and thrown onto the roadside. Seeing what happened to the dandelion, the grass laughed. Like the dandelion, I was rejected and humiliated. When I slammed the door and left the cottage after my rejection by the Board of Ministerial Qualifications, I was so upset that I hardly knew what was happening to me. Once angry emotions subsided, others arose. I became depressed, and depression was followed by humiliation and dehumanization. I began to question my worth and the meaning of life in this country. Becoming acutely self-conscious and suspicious of central-group people, I sensed that the arrogant ministers of the board were talking behind my back. Humiliation is certainly a dehumanizing process. I lost my ability to trust those with whom I had to work. I was unprepared to accept humiliation as inevitable.

Although the bishop received me into the conference, he did not want to appoint me to a church. I was an unappointable minister. One day, the district superintendent in Cleveland asked me whether I would be willing to accept a position as a janitor in a huge university church. I was humiliated. My instinctive response was "No!" "I was ordained to be a minister of the gospel, not to be a church janitor," I told myself. Now, I regret my decision not to accept that job. I would have learned to be a humble servant had I taken the janitorial job. I could then have changed humiliation into humility.

Jesus, the pioneer of our marginality, was humiliated in every possible way. He endured and accepted humiliation from the Sanhedrin, from the Roman soldiers, from crowds on his way to Calvary, and on the cross—each with humility. He was not ashamed of humiliation because he had a different value system. He taught us to be humble: " . . . All who humble themselves will be exalted" (Matt 23:12). Humiliation is used by centralist people to dehumanize marginal people, but humiliation is overcome when it is accepted with humility. When the disgrace of humiliation is accepted as the grace of humility, the norm shifts from centrality to marginality.

The third feeling explicit to the marginal experience is alienation. Like the dandelion in the green grass, my complete sense of alienation followed a humiliating experience. This time I alienated myself from the central group which had alienated me. I began to keep a distance myself from the white ministers of our denomination. I felt that I would forever be a stranger in this country. Some years ago, I used to attend the monthly meetings of United Methodist ministers. Whenever I went there, the first thing they asked me was: "When are you going back?" One day I told them angrily, "I am not going back. I am going to stay here for good." My ministerial colleagues were so upset that they even stopped greeting me. Although I have taught white students in colleges and universities in this country for twenty-five years, I am still regarded as a stranger. Whenever I complain about injustice to minorities in this country, white people say, "Why don't you go back home?" I am a stranger here because of my face, my skin color, my cultural background. It does not matter how long I have lived in this country; I will be forever a stranger, an alien, because I am different. However, my alienation is no longer painful because I celebrate my difference as God's gift and as a part of God's original design of creation.

Jesus was alienated from centralist people. Jesus was a stranger to his home (John 1:11-12). He suffered outside the gate to save people (Heb 13:12). As a friend of outcasts, the sick, the poor, and sinners, Jesus was completely alienated from the dominant group of his time. However, Jesus seemingly accepted alienation as inevitable and took it as a means to affirm his distinctive mission in the world. He overcame alienation by accepting it as an essential aspect of his mission. We, Christians, must also accept alienation as an inevitable part of becoming true disciples of Jesus-Christ.

Another emotion is loneliness which results from total alienation. Being the only yellow flower in the whole green yard, the dandelion symbolized the loneliest of creatures. The dandelion was alienated not only from its roots but also from the green grass. In the same manner, my experience of loneliness was the result of double alienation: centrality in this country and from people in my ancestral country. When I was alienated by the central group in this country, I wanted to return to my homeland to find security there. When I returned to Korea, I discovered that I had become an alien in my homeland because of my Americanization. Although I once moved back to Korea with a permanent teaching job in Seoul, I had to return to North America. I have discovered that I belong neither to my homeland nor to North America. I am twice marginalized. I am truly in-between two worlds, and to be in-between means to be lonely. Loneliness, therefore, is an essential characteristic of marginal experience, the experience of in-between.

Loneliness is overcome by confronting it, not by avoiding it. The more we want to avoid loneliness, the more we need to be a part of that which rejects us. I have felt that I was climbing up an icy hill. The more I climb the hill, the more I slip downward. Thus there was constant insecurity because I wanted to be a part of those who rejected me. It is, therefore, best to overcome loneliness through loneliness. We must transform loneliness to an attitude of meditation, the total detachment from all people. In meditation, we become creative and can reach to the depth of our being. Jesus was also lonely. He was not only rejected by the central group, by his people, but also by God. When Jesus was desperate for help, the Creator was absent. "My Father, if it is possible, let this cup pass from me" (Matt 26:39). However, God did not respond. Jesus felt utterly alone. He was truly in-between. Yet, he accepted loneliness and overcame and transformed it through prayer. It is, therefore, meditations or prayers which touch the depth of our being and give us the courage to stand alone. When loneliness is met with loneliness, loneliness exhausts itself in meditation and connects us to the ultimate ground of our being. Thus, meditation in loneliness yokes us to the divine. When loneliness is yoked to the divine, loneliness is overcome.

A fifth feeling is nothingness. Nothingness is an extreme form of the marginal experience. The experiences of rejection, humiliation, alienation or loneliness do not deny the existential reality of marginality. Yet, the experience of nothingness denies it. The dandelion in the parable did all it could to contribute something to brighten up the whole yard, but it could do nothing right. Rather, it was more destructive than constructive. The best way for it to contribute to the green yard was to extinguish itself, to become nothing, or to be pulled out. Like the dandelion, I, as a marginal person, am asked to become nothing, or to not exist in the mind of central-group people. The negation of my existence is the worst form of exclusivism that I endure in my marginality. Whenever I have been invited to social gatherings of central people, I try to make all kinds of excuses to avoid it, for nothingness becomes most intensively felt in social gatherings, where I become an invisible person. Central people often think, talk, and behave as if I do not exist. I become like a ghost, who sees them but is unseen by them.

I remember one Christmas party where more than a hundred people attended. All the guests, except me, were white. I felt utterly alone for more than two hours. I was like a ghost at that party. Even when being introduced, most people did not expect me to speak. Although I lis-

tened to them, they seemed unconcerned about whether I listened or
not. To be a marginal person means to be a ghost—invisible.

Jesus-Christ, as the pioneer of marginality, no doubt experienced
nothingness in his life. His death on the cross is the supreme example
of his nothingness. His existence was truly and totally denied at his
death. Symbolically, Christians must die with him in baptism, for death
or existential negation is essential for becoming Christian disciples.
Jesus did not deny death but accepted its inevitability. Nothingness
must be overcome by nothingness. Central-group people regarded
Jesus' death as the negation of his existence, but Jesus-Christ regarded
it as the fulfillment of his mission in the world. As marginal people, we
must also give nothingness a positive meaning. Although seeming to be
worth nothing, the empty canvas can be indispensable for creating. In
a like manner, we must transform the centralistic negation of nothingness to the marginal affirmation of nothingness. Nothingness then becomes the potentiality of fullness.

The sixth sensibility is allness, which is the opposite of nothingness
and is possible because of it. Thus, allness is the fullest expression of
nothingness and is the affirmation of marginality. The worthless dandelion in the parable becomes a beautiful and bright flower—like the
golden sun—when it is seen from this new perspective. The one who
wanted to eliminate the dandelion became its admirer. Likewise, nothingness from a centralist perspective can become allness from a
marginal perspective. From a marginal perspective, a neither/nor is expressed in a both/and, and total detachment becomes total attachment.
In the experience of allness, I, as a marginal person, can affirm my
place in the world. Although I am a marginal person, I am no longer an
alien, a stranger, or the other. Just as the dandelion had faith in affirming the soil as its own, I can root deeper and more strongly into the
land of North America even as I am dismissed and pulled out, because
I received this land from God, who is its real owner. When I affirm this
land as my own, I can then affirm my right to be a true citizen of this
country. The sensibility of allness allows me to be a citizen of the
world. I am not only an American but also an Asian. I am always a both/
and person, which helps me overcome my marginality.

In allness, I affirm my entirety. What I am, God made me to be. My
cultural heritage, my physical makeup, my skin color, my language and
values are all what they should be for me to be who I am. I am a full
human being because I have the characteristics I was created to have.
In this respect, I become complete by being who I am rather than who

others think I should be. In this respect, my "all" is a re-affirmation of my original creation. I must, therefore, celebrate what I am rather than what I am not. Moreover, to affirm myself is to affirm the dignity of all human beings and to affirm the differences of other people. In allness I affirm not only people of color but also white people, both male and female. Being completely human is understood only from a both/and viewpoint, which is my transformation from nothing to all.

If Jesus-Christ's death ultimately symbolized his nothingness, Jesus-Christ's resurrection represents his allness. Death and resurrection are united on the cross, as nothingness and allness are inseparable in marginality. The negation of negations is manifested in the affirmation of affirmations. If Jesus' emptiness signifies the nadir (the servant of all servants), his fullness symbolizes the zenith (the lord of all lords). In Jesus-Christ's allness, all people are reconciled at the margin of marginality, where central and marginal people meet and transform. In him an enemy becomes a friend and conflict becomes complementary. To be in Jesus-Christ or in his body means to be united with him and to become the marginal people of God.

The final characteristic of marginal experience is to realize the vision of new life which was inaugurated in the resurrection of Jesus-Christ. In the parable the dandelion could not have continued to tolerate the suffering unless it had a vision of new life. The vision was to live wherever it chose and in harmony with all other plants. My vision is the American dream of liberty, equality, justice, pursuit of happiness, and peace that all people desire. When I was naturalized in Boston more than twenty-five years ago, the judge reminded me that the vision I had was the vision of all Americans. What makes me different from the forefathers and foremothers (white Europeans) who founded and built this country was that I happened to come later to this country of immigrants. Despite disappointment and occasional despair, I never forget that the vision I have is realizable. It is a collective vision, a communal vision, that is lived and grounded in the shared struggle of all humanity. It is like a lamp that guides people in darkness and gives them hope to struggle together. It gives us meaning in our suffering, strength in our weakness, courage in our disappointment, and faith in our doubt. Unless we keep this vision alive, marginality cannot be overcome; reconciliatory redemption will never take place; and the world will not be transformed into the reign of God.

Holding the vision of new life alone is not enough. We must work toward its realization here and now. We cannot be sojourners or pilgrims who seek our final homeland somewhere outside the world.[20] Work toward the vision of new life empowers and joins us; it makes us creative. Jesus asked us to pray that the reign of God will come on earth as it is in heaven. This vision of a new world is not of a utopian life without struggle but a new life of creativity with struggle. It is not a life that receives service but one wherein we serve one another. It is not a life of being loved, but one of our loving one another. The new life is not to unify but to harmonize differences.

The beauty of the new life is not found in a green yard or a rose garden but in the garden where all plants grow together. A park I often visit symbolizes this new life. In the park different plants of all shapes and colors grow together: dandelions, lilies, wild roses, daisies, trees, and bushes. They seem to live harmoniously, having their own places in the park. Like the park, the new world values difference and allows room for all kinds of people to live together in harmony and peace. This vision must be kept alive if we are to overcome our marginality.

No matter how much I have committed myself to marginality or to the Christian faith, my personal experience of marginality can not be fully overcome without my solidarity with the community of marginality. My personal struggle to overcome my marginality complements the communal struggle. I am always the I of plurality or the I of community. I am communal: I am relative to and dependent on the whole. We do this together. Likewise marginal people's work must be part of central-group effort, for they are inseparable from the whole. When centralist people understand that the center they seek is not real, they will be liberated from centrality and seek the creative center. When this transformation happens, centrality changes to marginality, and marginality changes to new marginality, and all people become marginal. Marginality is overcome through marginality, and all are marginal to God manifest in Jesus-Christ. When all of us are marginal, love becomes the norm of our lives, and service becomes the highest aspiration of our creativity. We then become servants to one another in love.

CONCLUSION

In the past I, like most theologians, interpreted the Christian faith from the center, but in this book I interpret it from the margin. To illustrate, I have used the image of a pond in the park near my town. In the small pond are waves coming from the center and reaching out to the margin or the periphery of the pond, but I have learned to see that the same waves return to the center after they have reached the margin. As a marginal person, it is natural for me to observe and to think of everything from the margin. In the past I was deprived by central-group people not only of my marginal perspective but also of my Christian faith, which is deeply grounded in the marginality of Jesus-Christ. Just as Jesus-Christ was "a marginal Jew,"[1] I am a marginal Asian-American. In marginality Jesus-Christ and I meet: my marginality participates in his marginality. A proper approach to theology for me is marginal and autobiographical.

A theological approach to a marginal autobiography is different from a centralist autobiography. An autobiographical approach from the perspective of centrality is exclusive, stressing the uniqueness of the individual and his or her personal perspective. It creates not only parochialism but also discontinuity with others. It also has a tendency to elevate one's experience above others by placing it at the center. Thus, a centralist autobiographical approach to theology is disastrous. A theological approach, however, through a marginal autobiography is inclusive and open-ended. It does not stress the uniqueness of an individual's personal experience over others' experiences. It creates an engagement with others in community. From a marginal perspective, I am always the I of others, the I of plurality, or the I of community, for

171

marginality is defined by two or multiple worlds (a neither/nor and a both/and). A marginal autobiography always includes a marginal socio-biography or communobiography.

Throughout the book I demonstrate that the theological method of a marginal theology rooted in autobiography is truly a praxis-oriented approach. If theology is a reflection on praxis, theology must be autobiographical. No one can reflect, with credibility, on the poor unless he or she is poor; likewise, no one can reflect on the oppressed unless he or she is oppressed; and no one can reflect on the marginalized unless she or he is marginalized. Marginal theology can only be written and lived by a marginal person, just as a centralist theology can only be written and lived by a central-group person if either is to be genuine. No central-group person can write an authentic theology of marginality.

Likewise, liberation theology must be done by the oppressed. When liberation theology is done by the dominant group of scholars who preside over the structure of oppression, it becomes an abstract intellectual exercise of their academic discipline without praxis. Oppressors who claim their solidarity with the oppressed can write a theology *for* or *with* the oppressed, but they cannot write or live a theology *of* the oppressed as oppressors. Just as misogynists cannot do a theology *of* women, oppressors cannot do a theology *of* liberation. If Jesus-Christ was a marginal person, Christian theology must be assessed, written, and lived by marginal people. Thus, an authentic theology must be marginally autobiographical.

Unlike the centralist approach, which is interested in a finished product, the marginal approach stresses an unfinished work, as exemplified in this book. Nothing can be finished or completed from the marginal perspective, because marginality is a process of movement, creativity, and change. No matter how much I want this book to be comprehensive, it will remain incomplete. So, I have discussed essential topics that lay a foundation for marginal theology; I have attempted to add a stone to the cornerstone—Jesus-Christ—in building a new and authentic structure of theology. Others will add other stones to it toward the fuller expression of this theology.

A marginal approach to theology can be also compared to an ever-expanding mosaic, where my work represents one piece of its pattern. New pieces will be added toward the perfection of this mosaic vision. No matter how many stones or small, inlaid pieces are added and connected, the process will never end. Marginal theology is never finished;

it continues as long as Jesus-Christ exists as the margin of marginality among marginal people.[2]

In this book I have also attempted to describe the unity of incarnation and creation in marginality. Both incarnation and creation are divine marginalizations: incarnation is the subjective or inner marginalization of the divine, while creation is the objective or outer marginalization of the divine. Human beings as God's creatures are marginal. Any attempt to avoid human marginalization results in reversion to centralist inclinations, which distort the original order of creation and salvation. The more we seek the center, the more we are alienated from the divine presence; the more we seek dominion, the more we are afraid of others; the more we gain material wealth, the more we become spiritually bankrupt. The history of salvation does not belong to the glory of King David in Jerusalem but to the humiliation of the suffering servant in Galilee. The essence of a marginal God is suffering love, symbolized by the cross. We are bearers of the cross: centralist people bear a beautiful cross, while marginal people bear a rugged one. The centralist Christ wears a crown of gold, while the marginal Christ wears a crown of thorns.

For marginal people, suffering is more meaningful than pleasure, and love is more fundamental than power. Marginal people have learned to find meaning in suffering and power in love, while centralist people want to eliminate suffering from pleasure and find love in power. Because both pleasure and suffering as well as power and love are inseparable, marginal people are also inseparable from centralist people. The ultimate victory of suffering love transforms central-group people to marginal and marginal people to new marginal people, so all become marginal people of God. When all are marginal, all become servants to one another in Jesus-Christ, who is the servant of all servants (Matt 20:28; Phil 2:5-11). By becoming servants to one another, tears of sorrow change to tears of joy, an in-between is transformed into an in-both, and suffering is overcome in the fellowship of suffering. When all become servants to one another, the dualistic, exclusive, and dominant ideology of centrality is overcome. Joy is found in service, freedom becomes an inalienable right of human beings, differences are as valuable as similarities, and beauty is discovered in the harmony of mosaic. This service-oriented vision of marginality, in contrast to the utopian vision of centrality, is deeply rooted in the life and mission of a marginal Jew, Jesus of Nazareth, who is known to marginal people as the margin of marginality.

NOTES

Introduction

1. The demographic shift in New York City illustrates the drastic changes taking place in our time. The population shift in New York City in the last decade (from 1980 to 1990) illustrates how other large cities in this country are changing. For example, in the Bronx, New York City, there was a 32.2 percent decrease in the white population, while there was a 5.6 percent increase in the black population, a 32.4 percent increase among Hispanics, an 87.8 percent increase among Asians, and a 45.4 percent increase in other ethnic groups. Bergen County, N.J., which is regarded as one of the most prestigious places to live in that state, showed a dramatic change in demography within ten years. There was a 10.6 percent decrease in the white population, in comparison to an increase of 18 percent in the black, 73 percent in the Hispanic, 165.6 percent in the Asian, and 23 percent in other ethnics such as Native Americans, Eskimos, and Aleut. See *New York Times*, April 17, 1991. The Asian population grew more rapidly than any other ethnic group. In 1970 there were only 1.5 million Asians in America. By 1980 the population more than doubled and reached 3.5 million people. In 1985 it reached 5.1 million, and by 2000 it is estimated that the Asian population in this country will reach 9.9 million. See Wesley Woo, "A Socio-Historical Starting Point for a Pacific and Asian American Theology" (unpublished manuscript, delivered at Pacific and Asian American Theological Conference at Berkeley, California, January 23–25, 1987), 9.

2. Mearle Griffith, *A Church for the Twenty-First Century: A Planning Resource for the Future* (Dayton, Ohio: Office of Research, the General Council on Ministries, 1989), 3.

3. See *Living: Press and Sun-Bulletin Sunday*, Binghamton, N.Y., October 22, 1989.

4. The method and content of theology are inseparable. As Gutiérrez said, "The great hermeneutical principle of faith . . . is Jesus Christ." See Gustavo

Gutiérrez, *The Power of the Poor in History* (Maryknoll, N.Y.: Orbis Books, 1983), 61. See also chapter 3 of this book.

5. Some early theologians regarded theology as an objective discipline, pursued independently and without personal bias. They called theology one of the objective sciences, following the popular idea of scientific study of religions. Karl Barth, for example, begins his theology in *Church Dogmatics* with this notion. However, even so-called objective science is no longer objective in a strict sense. In modern science, pure objectivity is no longer viable, since the discovery of the indeterminacy principle by Werner Heisenberg. According to this principle, personal observation is one of the factors that determines the location and speed of sub-atomic particles.

6. See Paul F. Knitter, *No Other Name? A Critical Survey of Christian Attitudes towards the World Religions* (Maryknoll, N. Y.: Orbis Books, 1985), xiii.

7. The dissertation was published under the title *God Suffers for Us: A Systematic Inquiry into the Concept of Divine Passibility*, by Martinus Nijhoff in 1974.

8. Their interest in the personality type of marginality reflects their bias against Asians in America. The characteristics of the marginal people they describe include ambivalence, restlessness, irritability, moodiness, lack of self-confidence, and so on. They saw negative characteristics of the marginal person from the perspective of the dominant group. For detail, see " 'In-between': the classical definition" in the second chapter of this book.

9. For example, Goldberg raised the question in regard to the classification of the American Jew as a marginal man. See M. M. Goldberg, "A Qualification of the Marginal Man Theory," *American Sociological Review*, 6: 52–58.

10. See chapter 4. This idea is also implicit in John P. Meier, *A Marginal Jew: Rethinking the Historical Jesus* (New York: Doubleday, 1991).

Chapter 1   I Am: The Autobiographical Context
of Theology

1. *Oori* (or *Uri*) is more than "our" in English. It is used as a corral for livestock. As Byung Mu Ahn says, "We don't say 'my home,' 'my wife.' Rather, we say 'our home,' 'our wife.' 'I' and 'you' are not important in our thinking. *'Oori'* (we) is more important." See Byung Mu Ahn, *Minjung Shinhak Yiyaki* (The Story of Minjung Theology) (Seoul: The Korean Theological Study Institute, 1988), 70.

2. See my *Sermons to the Twelve* (Nashville: Abingdon Press, 1988), 15–20.

3. Quoted in Russell H. Conwell, *Why and How* (Boston: Lee and Shepard Co., 1971). See also Linda Perrin, *Coming to America: Immigrants from the Far East* (New York: Delacorte Press, 1980), 7, 8.

4. See Tricia Knoll, *Becoming Americans* (Portland, Ore.: Coast to Coast Books, 1982), 14, 15.

5. See Gunther Barth, *Bitter Strength: A History of the Chinese in the United States, 1850–1870* (Cambridge, Mass., 1964). See also his "Chinese So-

journers in the West: The Coming," *Southern California Quarterly*, 46 (1964), 55-67.

6. See Perrin, *Coming to America*, 21ff.

7. See Stanford Lyman, *The Asian in North America* (Santa Barbara, Calif.: ABC-Clio, Inc., 1977), 11-24.

8. It is difficult to know the exact statistics, but it appears that at least half of the Chinese men who came to America were married. See Mary Coolidge, *Chinese Immigration* (New York, 1909), 17-20.

9. The census reported 33,149 male Chinese in 1860; 58,633 in 1870; 100,686 in 1880; 102,620 in 1890; 85,341 in 1900. Between 1860 and 1900 the ratio of Chinese males per female was alarmingly high: 1,858:1 in 1860; 1,284:1 in 1870; 2,106:1 in 1880; 2,678:1 in 1890; and 1,887:1 in 1900. U.S. Department of Commerce, Bureau of the Census, *Sixteenth Census of the United States*, "Characteristics of the Non-White Population by Race," 7; see also Stanford Lyman, *The Asian in North America*, 68.

10. Lyman, *The Asian in North America*, 70.

11. See Thomas Sowell, *Ethnic America: A History* (New York: Basic Books, Inc., 1981), 139.

12. Knoll, *Becoming Americans*, 21.

13. See Albert S. Evans, "From the Orient Direct," *Atlantic Monthly* (Nov., 1969). Quoted in Perrin, *Coming to America*, 13.

14. Ronald Takaki, *Strangers from a Different Shore: A History of Asian Americans* (Boston: Little, Brown and Company, 1989), 101.

15. Stanford Lyman, *Chinese Americans* (New York: Random House, 1974), 71.

16. See "Twelve Hundred More" in *The Blue and Grey Songster* (San Francisco: S. S. Green, 1877). Quoted in Perrin, *Coming to America*, 32-34.

17. Perrin, *Coming to America*, 36-37.

18. At that time Perry brought with him a number of gifts to the Emperor— modern guns, machinery, steam locomotives, and the like. The Emperor of Japan was impressed with American civilization and sent a small number of students to America between 1860 and 1870.

19. William Petersen, *Japanese Americans* (New York: Random House, 1971), 15.

20. Unpublished interview with Noriko Oma (Princeton: Visual Education Corp.).

21. All Asians were not eligible for citizenship, even though the people who were born in Africa or of African descent could become citizens. The eligibility for citizenship of African born or African descent was passed in the year 1870.

22. See *Sacramento Bee*, November 28, 1921; quoted in Perrin, *Coming to America*, 79.

23. The imbalance of the sex ratio was not as great as with the Chinese, but it was a problem for the Japanese immigrants in America. There were seven times more males than females in 1890 and twenty-four times more males than

females in 1900. However, in 1910 there were only seven Japanese men to every Japanese woman, and by 1920 the ratio was two-to-one.

24. Roger Daniels, *Concentration Camps, USA* (New York: Holt, Rinehart and Winston, 1972), 46n.

25. Jeanne W. and James D. Houston, *Farewell to Manzanar* (Boston: Houghton Mifflin, 1973), 27–29.

26. Carols Bulosan as quoted in "Introduction" by E. San Juan, Jr., *America Journal*, 6 (May 1979), 26.

27. Sixteenth Census, *Characteristics of the Nonwhite Population by Race*, 105. Quoted in John Modell, "Class or Ethnic Solidarity: The Japanese American Company Union," in *The Asian American: The Historical Experience,* ed. by Norris Hundley, Jr. (Santa Barbara: Clio Books, 1976), 68.

28. They were An Ch'ang-ho, Kim Kyu-sik, Pak Yong-man, and Yi Sung-man, the first president of the Republic of Korea.

29. The first shipload carried 101 in December, 1902; fifteen additional shiploads in 1903 brought 1,133; thirty-three ships brought 3,434; and the number of immigrants in 1905, the final year of direct immigration to Hawaii, was 2,659.

30. In 1906 the Gentlemen's Agreement was made to prevent embarrassment for the United States and Japanese governments. California was forced to back down on the segregation of Japanese and other Asians in the San Francisco Public School system, while Japan agreed to limit emigration to those who had relatives in America.

31. The imbalance in the gender ratio for Koreans in Hawaii was high: Out of 7,226 Korean immigrants, 6,048 were male adults, 637 women, and 541 children.

32. Warren Y. Kim, *Koreans in America* (Seoul, Korea: Po Chin Chai Printing, 1971), 82.

33. During the nine years following the Japanese annexation of Korea in 1910, only 541 Korean students came to this country to study. By 1945, some 3,000 Koreans on the mainland and 6,500 in Hawaii were reported.

34. The Korean Methodist Church of Hawaii was established in November 1903, the Korean Episcopal Church in January 1905, and Korean Christian Church of Hawaii in 1918. The Korean Methodist Church of San Francisco had its first service in October 1905, and the Korean Presbyterian Church was established in Los Angeles in 1906.

35. Won Moo Hurh and Kwang Chung Kim, "Religious Participation of Korean Immigrants in the United States," *Journal for the Scientific Study of Religion*, 29, 1 (1990), 19–20.

36. See Won Moo Hurh, Hei Chu Kim, and Kwang Chung Kim, *Assimilation Patterns of Immigrants in the US: A Case Study of Korean Immigrants in the Chicago Area* (Washington, D.C., University Press of America, 1978).

37. For example, Drew University has about eighty Korean students who are presently working toward professional degrees or advanced academic degrees in theology. Princeton Theological Seminary has more than 100 Korean stu-

dents. Boston University has about fifty students who study in theology. It is rare to find any U.S. theological seminary that does not have Korean students studying for ministry.

38. From 1961 to 1964, about 10,000 Koreans came to this country. From 1965 to 1970, 24,000 arrived, including large numbers of professionals. From 1970 to 1975, there were about 122,000 Koreans seeking jobs in this country. In 1980, the census indicated a Korean population of 354,000, five times the 1970 population. Korean population in 2000 will reach about 1.3 million. See Robert Gardner, Bryand Robey, and Peter S. Smith, *Asian Americans: Growth, Change and Diversity* (Washington, D.C.: Population Reference Bureau, 1985).

39. Interview with May Ching in *They Chose America*, Vol. 1 (Princeton: Visual Education Corp., 1975).

40. *Report of the National Advisory Commission on Civil Disorder* (New York: Bantam Books, 1968), 1.

Chapter 2   In-between and In-both: Defining Marginality

1. This is not so for all ethnic groups. For example, most Caucasians from Europe may have different ethnic orientations but have the same racial origin. Their racial orientation, in this case, does not play a significant role in their ethnicity, for they belong to the dominant group in North-American life.

2. Sexism and racism are inseparable. bell hooks said: "The ideology of sisterhood as expressed by contemporary feminist activists indicated no acknowledgement that racist discrimination, exploitation, and oppression of multiethnic women by white women had made it impossible for the two groups to feel they shared common interests or political concerns." See bell hooks, *Feminist Theory: From Margin to Center* (Boston: South End Press, 1984), 49.

3. See Joe R. Feagin, *Racial and Ethnic Relations* (New York: Prentice-Hall, 1978), 9.

4. See Manning Marable, "The Rhetoric of Racial Harmony: Finding Substance in Culture and Ethnicity," *Sojourners* (August–September, 1990), 16.

5. See Feagin, *Racial and Ethnic Relations*, 6.

6. In some other countries, biological traits do not play an important part in social categories. For example, in South Africa, Japanese people were considered by the regime as "white," whereas Chinese were classified as being "colored." In Brazil, the people of color could be white, mulatto, or black, depending upon their income, vocation, and education level. See ibid.

7. See Won Moo Hurh, "Comparative Study of Korean Immigrants in the U.S.: A Typological Study," in B. S. Kim, and others, eds., *Koreans in America* (Association of Korean Christian Scholars in North America, 1977), 95. See also "Called to Be Pilgrims" in *Korean American Ministry*, ed. Sang H. Lee (Princeton: Consulting Committee on Korean American Ministry, Presbyterian Church, 1987), 93.

8. The primary source for this theory is found in Robert Ezra Park, *Race and Culture* (Glencore: The Free Press, 1950).

9. See Israel Zangwill, *The Melting Pot: A Drama in Four Acts*, revised edition (New York: Macmillan Company, 1939). The original edition of this book was published in 1909.

10. Ibid., 184–85.

11. Robert E. Park, "Our Racial Frontier on the Pacific," *Survey Graphic*, 56, 3 (May 1, 1926), 196.

12. Park failed to take institutional racism seriously. Moreover, he neglected the idea of race *per se*. He did not acknowledge the uniqueness of ethnicity. In other words, his idea was to apply the European immigrant analogy to all without reservation. See the critiques of Park's dominant ethnicity-based theory in Michael Omi and Howard Winant, *Racial Formation in the United States: From the 1960s to the 1980s* (New York and London: Routledge and Kegan Paul, 1986), 9–24.

13. Michael Omi and Howard Winant, *Racial Formation in the United States*, 20, 104–105.

14. See especially Rose Hum Lee, *The Chinese in the United States of America* (Hong Kong: Hong Kong University Press, 1960). For further discussion, see Stanford M. Lyman, "Overseas Chinese in America and Indonesia," *Pacific Affairs* (Winter, 1961–62), 380–89.

15. Many leading journals focus their attention on race relations and politics in this country. See the cover story of *The Atlantic Monthly* (May, 1991) or the cover story of *Newsweek* (May, 1991). Manning Marable, professor of political science and sociology at the University of Colorado, said that the central characteristic of race relations in the 1990s is "interaction without understanding" or "the rhetoric of racial harmony without the substance of empowerment for the oppressed." See his "The Rhetoric of Racial Harmony," *Sojourners* (August–September, 1990), 14–18.

16. See Michael Omi and Howard Winant, *Racial Formation in the United States*, 21–24.

17. Roy I. Sano, *From Every Nation without Number: Racial and Ethnic Diversity in United Methodism* (Nashville: Abingdon Press, 1982), 26–38.

18. Brewton Berry, *Race and Ethnic Relations* (Boston: Houghton-Mifflin Co., 1965), 135. See also Stanford M. Lyman, "The Spectrum of Color," *Social Research*, 31 (Autumn, 1964), 364–73.

19. Stanford M. Lyman, *The Asian in North America* (Santa Barbara, Calif.: ABC-Clio, Inc., 1977), 26.

20. See J. Hector St. John de Crevecoeur's *Letters from an American Farmer* (New York: E. P. Dutton and Co., 1957), 39.

21. See his "I Know Who I Am," in *Trends*, March/April 1973, 10.

22. Oxford and New York: Oxford University Press, 1979.

23. It is important to know that assimilation is different from cultural assimilation or acculturation. The term "assimilation" later came to be termed "structural assimilation" to distinguish it from acculturation.

24. One of the most embarrassing sights that I saw in America was the public display of love between a boy and girl on a college campus.

25. Mary Paik Lee, "A Korean/Californian Girlhood," edited by Sucheng Chan, *California History,* 77:1 (March 1988), 45–46.

26. Ronald Takaki, *Strangers from a Different Shore: A History of Asian Americans* (Boston: Little, Brown and Company, 1989), 271.

27. See Linda Perrin, *Coming to America: Immigrants from the Far East* (New York: Delacorte Press, 1980), 25.

28. "Twelve Hundred More," *The Blue and Grey Songster* (San Francisco: S.S. Green, 1877). See also Takaki, *Iron Cages,* 103.

29. According to Kwang Chung Kim and Won Moo Hurh, "First, if Asian-Americans are successful, they no longer need public policies designed to benefit deprived minorities—the benefit denying function. Second, Asian-American success validates the widely held assumption that the United States is a land of opportunity—the system preserving function. Third, in this land of opportunity, if a minority group fails to achieve a high socioeconomic status, then the minority is responsible for its own failure—the minority blaming function." Quoted in "A Socio-Historical Starting Point for a Pacific and Asian American Theology" by Wesley Woo (unpublished manuscript, edited from transcript of the presentation at Pacific and Asian American Theological Conference at Berkeley, Calif., January 23–25, 1987), 11.

30. See Michael Omi and Howard Winnant, *Racial Formation in the United States,* 64–69.

31. See Joshua A. Fishman, *Language Loyalty in the United States* (Hague: Mouton, 1966), 29–31.

32. See Donna Dong, "The Asian-American Bi-Cultural Experience" (unpublished manuscript based on her panel presentation on April 20, 1974). See *The Theologies of Asian Americans and Pacific Peoples: A Reader,* compiled by Roy Sano (Berkeley: Asian Center for Theology and Strategies, 1976), 12.

33. L. C. Tsung, *The Marginal Man* (New York: The Pageant Press, 1963), 158–59.

34. Stanford M. Lyman, *The Asian in North America* (Santa Barbara, Calif.: ABC-Clio Inc., 1977), 12.

35. Robert Park, "Introduction," to Everett V. Stonequist's *The Marginal Man: A Study in Personality and Cultural Conflict* (New York: Russell and Russell, 1961), xvii.

36. Ibid., 8.

37. According to a study of social interaction between white and yellow people, the more closely an Asian identifies with white friends, the more intense become the Asian's feelings of marginality and alienation. See Won Moo Hurh, "Comparative Study of Korean Immigrants in the United States: A Typology" (San Francisco: R. and E. Research Associates, 1977), 91.

38. See *Hankuk Ilbo* (Korean Newspaper), February 28, 1979.

39. See the discussion of this by Kazuo Kawai, "Three Roads, and None Easy," *Survey,* May 1, 1926, pp. 164ff. See also Stonequist, *The Marginal Man: A Study,* 105.

40. Joanne Miyamoto, "What Are You?" *Roots: An Asian American Reader*, a project of the UCLA Asian American Studies Center, published by University of California in Los Angeles, 1971. Quoted in *The Theologies of Asian Americans and Pacific Peoples*, l.

41. See Ada María Isasi-Díaz, "A Hispanic Garden in a Foreign Land," in *Inheriting Our Mothers' Gardens: Feminist Theology in Third World Perspective*, Letty M. Russell, et al., eds. (Philadelphia: Westminster Press, 1988), 92.

42. See Stonequist, *The Marginal Man: A Study*, 139. See also Alan Kerchkoff and Thomas McCormick, "Marginal Status and Marginal Personality," in *Social Forces*, 34, (October, 1977), 48–55. Quoted in Sang H. Lee's "Call to Be Pilgrims" in *The Korean Immigrant in America*, ed. by Byong-suh Kim and Sang Hyun Lee (Montclair, N.J.: AKCS, 1980), 39. A similar idea is also found in Werner Heisenberg's Uncertainty Principle. According to this principle, "the more accurately you try to measure the position of the particle, the less accurately you can measure its speed, and vice versa." See Stephen Hawking, *A Brief History of Time* (New York: Bantam, 1988), 55.

43. Yusuke Hidaka describes "identificational differences," relating to three identificational categories among American-born Asians. He believes that the traditionalists who follow the norms, beliefs, values, symbols, and identity of their immigrant ancestors are different from marginal persons who belong to a different category. Although traditionalists may not consciously be aware of their marginality, I believe that they certainly have a collective sense of marginality. See his unpublished manuscript, "Developing Ministries with Americans of Asian Ancestries" (originally presented to Korean Ministries Administrative Council, October, 1984), 2.

44. Donna Dong, "The Asian-American Bi-Cultural Experience," 12.

45. Stonequist, *The Marginal Man: A Study*, 217.

46. Quoted in Manning Marable, "The Rhetoric of Racial Harmony," 16. A similar observation is made on the natives of Brazil who lived among Europeans and developed two personality patterns. See Max Schmidt, *Primitive Races of Mankind: A Study in Ethnology* (Boston, 1926), 189–90.

47. See Charles H. Cooley, *Human Nature and the Social Order* (New York, 1922), 184. Quoted in Stonequist, *The Marginal Man: A Study*, 145.

48. Stonequist, *The Marginal Man: A Study*, 149.

49. Ibid., 155.

50. The Chinese laundryman depicted by L. C. Tsung in his *The Marginal Man* is a perfect image of the marginal person as understood in the classical definition. It is, however, important to know that he is more than a man in-between two worlds, for he is also in-both worlds at the same time. His physical presence in North America and his cerebral presence in China place him in-both worlds. He is excessively in-between, but is recessively in-both.

51. Again, when I say Asian-Americans, I do not mean every Asian-American who came to this country. As I said previously, I am confining myself to Chinese, Korean, and Japanese ancestries, because to include every person coming from Asia as an Asian-American is meaningless. For example, people from India

are also categorized as Asian-Americans, according to the mentality of the dominant people. People from India have almost totally different racial roots and cultural backgrounds. Their skin color is different, and their physical features are different from Chinese, Korean, or Japanese. When I write Asian-Americans, I mean Chinese-Americans, Korean-Americans, and Japanese-Americans, because I closely identify with them. Since this book is autobiographical, I support my experience with data from those who share a similar racial and cultural background. In short, when I say Asian-Americans, I mean Northeast Asian-Americans, not South Asians or Southeast Asians.

52. Francis Naohiko Oka, *Poems* (San Francisco: City Lights, 1970), 31.

53. Genny Lim, "Children Are Color-blind," *The Forbidden Stitch: An Asian American Women's Anthology*, ed. by Shirely Geok-lin Lim, Mayumi Tsutakawa, Margarita Donnelly (Corvallis, Ore.: Calyx Books, 1989), 196.

54. See the first chapter of this book. Refer also to the author's *Sermons to the Twelve* (Nashville: Abingdon Press, 1988), 15–20.

55. Robert Fulghum, *All I Really Need to Know I Learned in Kindergarten* (New York: Villard Books, 1988), 67–69.

56. I don't think Robert Fulghum was aware of the profound implications to the contemporary meaning of marginality when he told the story of dandelions.

57. Diana Chang, "Saying Yes," quoted in *Asian-American Heritage: An Anthology of Prose and Poetry*, ed. by David Hsin-Fu Wand (New York: Washington Square Press, 1974), 130.

58. See *Negro History Bulletin*, 31, 5 (May, 1968), 17.

59. I have used a genuinely pluralistic society, in order to distinguish it from a majority pluralism. Paul Nagano helps me see that the pluralism which Anglo-Americans advocate is different from a genuine pluralism that ethnic minorities envision. The Anglo-Americans have their own strategy of pluralism, which he calls a majority pluralism. Through the majority pluralism the white Anglo-Americans continue to dominate racial, ethnic minorities by control of values and color preference. See Paul Nagano, "Identity and Pluralism from an Asian American Perspective" (unpublished manuscript, 1989), 38.

Chapter 3   In-Beyond: New Marginality and Theology

1. We have been taught that the two opposing views cannot coexist in a sensible definition. As I will explain further, this kind of mind-set is deeply embedded in the exclusive thinking of centralist people. This kind of thinking was further supported by the Aristotelian logic of the excluded middle and was used by the dominant group as an intellectual tool to maintain strict categorical distinctions of all things for an efficient control and domination of marginal people.

2. See Bill Bradly, "Economic Relations in the Pacific Rim," *The Commonwealth* (March 29, 1989), 141 and 142. See also Paul Nagano, "Identity and Plu-

ralism from an Asian American Perspective" (unpublished manuscript, 1989), 71.

3. The Asian-American population has drastically increased. The population was only 3,466,421 in 1980, occupying 1.5 percent of total U.S. population; in 1985 it increased to 5,147,900, about 2.1 percent of U.S. population, and it is expected to reach 9,850,364 in 2000, about 4 percent of the total population of America. The 1980 census was taken by *Bureau of the Census* 1980 Census of the Population, PC80-S1-12. The Asian-American population in 2000 was projected by Leon F. Bouvier and Anthony Agresto in their "Projection of Asian American Population, 1980–2030" in their *Asian and Pacific Immigration to the United States*. Quoted in Paul Nagano, "Identity and Pluralism from an Asian American Perspective," 6–7.

4. According to Roy Sano, Roger Daniels, and Harry H. L. Kitano, this two-category system is based on race. The system is divided between white and colored people in America. See Roy Sano, *From Every Nation without Number: Racial and Ethnic Diversity in United Methodism* (Nashville: Abingdon, 1982), 30–32; Roger Daniels and Harry H. L. Kitano, *American Racism: Exploration of the Nature of Prejudice* (Englewood Cliffs, N.J.: Prentice-Hall, 1970), 5–28.

5. For a paradigm shift in racial formations, see Michael Omi and Howard Winant, *Racial Formation in the United States: From the 1960s to the 1980s* (London and New York: Routledge and Kegan Paul, Inc., 1986), 89–108.

6. See Abraham H. Maslow, *Toward a Psychology of Being* (New York: Van Nostrand, 1968), 40.

7. The common assumption is that second-generation Asian-Americans reject their ethnic roots and strive for full assimilation in the dominant American culture. That is why they are in the state of being in-between. However, third-generation Asian-Americans, secure in citizenship, seek their roots in ethnicity. This is often called "the law of third-generation return." This assumption was made in early days, but is no longer true. According to my own experience of raising two second-generation Asian-Americans, they experience both worlds simultaneously. Even the third-generation Japanese-American with whom I shared my marginal experience told me that he also experiences the alienation and rejection that the first- or second-generation Asian-American experiences. Perhaps the intensity of negative experience might be different from person to person or from generation to generation, but it is not possible to live the positive experience of marginality without the negative, as a marginal person.

8. Charles V. Willie, *Oreo: On Race and Marginal Men and Women* (Wakefield, Mass.: Parameter Press, 1975), 32.

9. Ibid.

10. Asian-Americans usually fall into three distinctive categories: the traditionalist who adheres to the norms, beliefs, and values of Asia, the marginal person who does not belong to either Asia or America, and the new Asian-American, who finds a new identity by creating new norms, beliefs, values, and

symbols through the synthesis of Asian and American culture. See Yusuke Hidaka, "Developing Ministries with Americans of Asian Ancestries" (unpublished manuscript, revised, 1984), 2, 3; "Second Generation Issues Related to the Korean-American Churches," in General Assembly Minutes of Presbyterian Church in the U.S. (Atlanta, Ga.), 317. This linear progress from one stage to another is logical, but unrealistic. The discovery of one's identity and positive self-esteem cannot remove him or her from marginal status, from being in both cultures, from being an "and."

11. Ronald Takaki, *Strangers from a Different Shore: A History of Asian Americans* (Boston: Little, Brown and Co., 1989), 6.

12. I have intentionally used the hyphen when I describe Asian-Americans. This is to indicate that Asian-Americans are "both" Asians and Americans.

13. See "An Interview with Harry Kitano," in *Roots: An Asian American Reader* (Los Angeles: University of California Press, 1971), 88.

14. Caucasian-Americans are not marginal people, because they belong to the dominant group. However, if they take their hyphenated ethnicity or "and" seriously, they cannot identify themselves as Americans. Conceptually, Caucasian-Americans are marginal people, but practically, they are not.

15. David Ng, "Sojourners Bearing Gifts: Pacific Asian American Christian Education," in Charles R. Foster, ed., *Ethnicity in the Education of the Church* (New York: Scarrit Press, 1987), 14.

16. Some women speak of the value of their in-between or nothingness experience. In such they seem to find a new orientation and a new sense of self. See Carol P. Christ, *Diving Deep and Surfacing: Women Writers on Spiritual Quest* (Boston: Beacon Press, 1980), 9-14. See also Sang Hyun Lee, "Called to Be Pilgrims: Toward an Asian-American Theology from the Korean Immigrant Perspective" in *Korean American Ministry: A Resource Book*, ed. by Sang Hyun Lee (Princeton: Consulting Committee on Korean-American Ministry of the Presbyterian Church, 1987), 99.

17. Mark C. Taylor, *De-Constructing Theology* (Atlanta: Scholars Press, 1982), 29.

18. Perhaps the so-called postmodern philosophy, following the development of quantum mechanics, may lead to the direction of non-dualistic interpretations. Quantum theory seems to reject the absolutist and categorical approach of an either/or logic: "Planck's quantum theory and Einstein's theory of relativity led to the Aristotelian 'either/or' being questioned. The result of the first was that the axiom, *natura non facit saltus* (nature makes no leaps) became untenable. As a consequence of the quantum theory, we know today that nature is very capable of making such leaps. This was the first intrusion into the Aristotelian 'either/or.' . . . We know today that matter is not merely a spatial element but also a temporal one. It is corpuscular as well. In 'this as well as that' lies the impetus that led to questioning the Aristotelian 'either/or.' " See Jean Gebser in P. J. Saher, *Eastern Wisdom and Western Thought: A Comparative Study in the Modern Philosophy of Religion* (New York: Barnes and Noble, 1970), 10.

19. Asians have always been interested in a holistic way of thinking. A typical example of this is found in Mencius' thinking. "Thinking in Mencius' context involves not only the heart and the mind but also the body. It signifies a holistic and integrated way of learning." See Tu Wei-ming, "The Value of the Human in Classical Confucian Thought," in *Humanitas* (15 May 1979), 168.

20. See Maxine Hong Kingston, *China Men* (New York, 1980), 100ff. Quoted in Ronald Takaki, *Strangers from a Different Shore*, 8.

21. No-thinking or no-mind is deeply rooted in classical Taoism. It has a profound impact on Ch'an or Zen meditation. Zen Buddhism is often regarded as the religion of nothingness, symbolized by nirvana. An extensive study on the idea of nothingness has been made by the Kyoto School, especially by Nishitani, who claims nothingness as a unique contribution of Buddhist philosophy. See Keiji Nishitani, *Religion and Nothingness* (Berkeley: University of California Press, 1982). See also Donald W. Mitchell, *Spirituality and Emptiness: The Dynamics of Spiritual Life in Buddhism and Christianity* (New York: Paulist Press, 1991), 31-52.

22. Under General DeWitt's command, all persons of Japanese ancestry were ordered for evacuation: "Pursuant to the provisions of Civilian Exclusion Order No. 27, this Headquarters, dated April 30, 1942, all persons of Japanese ancestry, both alien and non-alien, will be evacuated from the above area by 12 o'clock noon, P. W. T., Thursday, May 7, 1942." See Ronald Takaki, *Strangers from a Different Shore*, 392.

23. See Ronald Takaki, *Strangers from a Different Shore*, 402.

24. Ibid. See also John Tateishi, *And Justice for All: An Oral History of the Japanese American Detention Camps* (New York, 1984), 161.

25. Central people use an "either/or" logic as an intellectual tool to analyze and validate truth; they cannot deal with the holistic and open-ended approach to reality. Thus, they often characterize the "both/and" and "neither/nor" way of thinking as a mystical approach. Mystics, who transcend the either/or way of thinking, share similar characteristics of thinking with marginal people. However, they are not culturally, socially, or racially marginalized. They usually belong to a privileged group whose primary interest is to gain the mental or spiritual experience of marginality.

26. This is a transcript from an informal conversation I had with her at her office in the Pacific School of Religion in Berkeley, California, on February 17, 1992.

27. Gustavo Gutiérrez, *The Power of the Poor in History* (Maryknoll, N.Y.: Orbis Books, 1983), 61.

28. According to the centralist way of thinking, the transcendence and immanence of God are expressible only in terms of mystery or paradox. According to the either/or way of thinking, God is either transcendent or immanent; God cannot be both transcendent and immanent at the same time.

29. In a patriarchal society, the dominant partner in a marriage is often incapable of real love by virtue of his or her dominant status. Many second-generation Asian-Americans have experienced the lack of their father's love,

because the father is a dominant figure in the traditional Asian family. On the other hand, they have experienced mother's love, for she is a marginal figure who is capable of love.

30. Quoted in R. Feild, *Last Barrier* (New York and San Francisco: Harper and Row, 1976), 97.

31. Open-ended thinking is also an important part of scientific discipline. In his *The Structure of Scientific Revolutions,* published in 1970, Thomas Kuhn shows how scientists obtain their most effective achievements through the application of a paradigm or pattern of images. Using images and symbols such as "fields," "waves," and "atoms," they interpret the behavior of the natural world. The paradigm is "open-ended" in that it is a developing phenomenon dependent upon continuing research and repeated application. . . . The time then comes when the original paradigm is replaced by a new one." See A. Shorter, *African Christian Theology* (Champman, 1975), 135–36.

32. Although terminologically similar to Charles Willie's notion of a new marginal person, this idea is quite different. See text at n. 8 above.

Chapter 4   Jesus-Christ: The Margin of Marginality

1. "Jesus as the Christ" is commonly used to understand the relationship between Jesus and the Christ. This term has a tendency to stress the Christ over Jesus. He is not only Jesus as the Christ but also the Christ as Jesus. To stress the "Christly" function of Jesus over the "Jesusly" function of the Christ can be attributed to the centralist tendency to elevate power and majesty over weakness and lowliness. As the new marginal person, Jesus-Christ is the hyphenated one, who reconciles both the powerful and the weak or the central and the marginal.

2. When I refer to the historical background of Jesus' birth, I do not mean the critical study of the historical Jesus or formal or textual criticism performed by scholars of centrality. I am neither a biblical scholar nor a historian. My interest is to present a marginal perspective based on my re-reading of the Scripture. Thus, I have taken the Scripture, particularly the Gospels, seriously as a sole source of knowing Jesus and his life.

3. The illegitimacy of Jesus as a viable thesis has been suggested by recent scholars. However, according to John Meier, the charge of illegitimacy is not new. In *Contra Celsum*, Origen reported that Celsus had heard that Jesus' mother, Mary, was driven out by the carpenter husband because she had committed adultery with a Roman soldier. Meier believes that such a story was already circulating among certain Hellenistic Jews around the second century. See John P. Meier, *A Marginal Jew: Rethinking the Historical Jesus* (New York: Doubleday, 1987), 222–29.

4. Matthew dated the time of Jesus' birth during the time of Herod the Great, who reigned from 40 to 4 B.C. Luke, on the other hand, dated it with the taking of the census organized by Quirinius after Archelaus's deposition in A.D. 7. It is certainly difficult to provide historical accuracy of Jesus' birth date or place. Various attempts to reconstruct the historicity of Jesus have failed. That is

why I do not take the story of Jesus' nativity as a fact but as a meaningful statement, for I have faith in him. Bethlehem as the place of Jesus' birth is also problematic. From the centralistic perspective, Jesus' birth in Bethlehem is
important because of a symbolic connection with Davidic messiahship. Thus,
"Jesus' birth at Bethlehem is to be taken not as a historical fact but as a *theolo-
goumenon*, i.e., as a theological affirmation (e.g., Jesus is the true Son of David,
the prophesied royal Messiah) put into the form of an apparently historical narrative." See John Meier, *A Marginal Jew*, 216.

5. See Ernest F. Scott and Robert R. Wicks, "The Epistle to the Philippians,"
in *The Interpreter's Bible*, vol. 11 (Nashville: Abingdon Press, 1955), 47–52.

6. Among Buddhist scholars, the Kyoto School of Thought is more active in
dialogue with Christian scholars in this area. Their primary interest is in the
absoluteness of divine nature rather than in the idea of incarnation. Many
books and articles have been written on this topic. Some of them are: *Buddhist
Emptiness and Christian Trinity*, ed. by Roger Corless and Paul F. Knitter
(New York: Paulist Press, 1990); Keiji Nishitani, *Religion and Nothingness*
(Berkeley: University of California Press, 1982); Kitaro Nishida, *Intelligibility
and the Philosophy of Nothingness* (Honolulu: East-West Center Press, 1958);
Kitaro Nishida, *Last Writings: Nothingness and the Religious Worldview* (Ho-
nolulu: University of Hawaii Press, 1987); John B. Cobb, Jr., and Christopher
Ives, eds., *The Emptying God: A Buddhist-Jewish-Christian Conversation*
(Maryknoll, N.Y.: Orbis Books, 1990); Masao Abe, *Zen and Western Thought*
(Honolulu: University of Hawaii Press, 1985); Hans Waldenfels, *Absolute Noth-
ingness: Foundations for a Buddhist-Christian Dialogue* (New York: Paulist
Press, 1980); Paul O. Ingram and Frederick J. Streng, eds., *Buddhist-Christian
Dialogue: Mutual Renewal and Transformation* (Honolulu: University of
Hawaii Press, 1986); Frederick Franck, ed., *The Buddha Eye: An Anthology of
Kyoto School* (New York: Crossroad, 1982); Seiichi Yagi and Leonard Swidler, *A
Bridge to Buddhist-Christian Dialogue* (New York: Paulist Press, 1990);
Donald Mitchell, *Spirituality and Emptiness: The Dynamics of Spiritual Life
in Buddhism and Christianity* (New York: Paulist Press, 1991).

7. My argument is that the real comparison between the Buddhist concept
of sunyata and the Christian concept of kenosis is easily misunderstood unless
we have to clarify the distinctive emphasis in each tradition. As far as I know, in
Buddhism, especially in Mahayana tradition in East Asia, emptiness is the essence of the Buddha nature. In other words, emptiness can be regarded as the
original nature of Buddha. However, from my reading of Philippians 2, emptiness is not the original nature of God. It is the consequent nature of God. That
means the Son of God was *not originally self-emptying* but emptied himself,
so that his emptiness was fulfilled through exaltation. His self-emptying process was *temporary*, according to my reading of Philippians 2. Masao Abe, for
example, reads it quite differently. According to him, the very original nature of
the Son of God "is essentially and fundamentally self-emptying or self-negating
. . . The Son of God becomes flesh simply because the Son of God is originally
self-emptying." See Masao Abe's "Kenotic God and Dynamic Sunyata," in *The*

Emptying God: A Buddhist-Jewish-Christian Conversation (Maryknoll, N.Y.: Orbis Books, 1990), 10-11. It is a fascinating idea to think of emptiness as the essential and original nature of the Son of God, because it is exactly fitting to the Buddhist notion of emptiness as the original nature of Buddha. This facilitates the Buddhist-Christian dialogue and ecumenical horizons of different religions. I am completely for dialogue, and encourage this kind of intellectual pursuit. However, what troubles me is to relate this idea—emptiness as the original nature of the Son of God—to other passages such as the prologue of John and Christmas stories in the Gospels. For example, it is difficult to think of the Word or Logos in John as emptiness if we take seriously the context of its origin. It is possible to interpret the Word or Logos as emptiness from a Buddhist or an Eastern perspective, but, if we do, we do injustice to the original intent of it. If the Word or Logos has its origin in Hellenistic thinking, we try to understand it from the perspective of Hellenistic philosophy. The same issue can be applied to stories of Jesus' birth in the Gospels. Is emptiness, as the original nature of the ultimate reality (Son of God), a normative interpretation of Christianity as it is in Buddhism? Is it possible to interpret Philippians 2 in isolation from all other relevant passages that deal with the same topic in the Scriptures? Can we dismiss the historical and cultural context when we compare an idea or ideas of different religious traditions? I suggest that one of the basic tenets of centralism is to provide a single norm for everything. In other words, Christian centralists want to universalize their perspective, while Buddhist centralists want to do the same. I agree that the dynamic nature of sunyata gives a new insight for Christian understanding of Jesus-Christ, although I have reservations.

8. Quoted from NRSV.

9. See Jung Young Lee, *Sermons to the Twelve* (Nashville: Abingdon Press, 1988), 32-33.

10. Quoted from NRSV.

11. Again, it is not my intention to provide historical evidence of this passage. It might be added by the editor to justify Jesus-Christ as the Messiah who fulfilled the promise in the Old Testament. What I hope to do in this book is to re-read and re-understand the Gospels of Jesus-Christ as witnessed and written in the New Testament.

12. In Mark 6:3, Jesus was known as a carpenter: "Is not this the carpenter, the son of Mary and brother of James and Joses and Judas and Simon, and are not his sisters here with us?" We often get the image of a poor Jesus because he was a carpenter. However, this image should be revised. According to Meier, there were three classes in the socio-economic structure of Galilee at the time of Jesus: a small group of the very wealthy, a middle-class composed of craftsmen and farmers, and slaves. "On this rough scale, Jesus the woodworker in Nazareth would have ranked somewhere at the lower end of this vague middle, perhaps equivalent to a blue collar worker in lower-middle class America. . . . His was not the grinding, degrading poverty of the day laborer or the rural slaves."

Meier, *A Marginal Jew*, 282. However, what made him different from others was that he renounced his economic security and became poor.

13. Traditionally, repentance is closely related to the remission of sin, and baptism has been used since the time of the early church for the remission of original sin. However, it was probable that the baptism of Jesus was meant to signify the need of repentance by the whole nation. See Sherman E. Johnson, "The Gospel according to St. Matthew," in *The Interpreter's Bible*, vol. 7 (Nashville: Abingdon Press, 1951), 268.

14. In all synoptic Gospels it is said, "You are my Son, the Beloved; with you I am well pleased" (Mark 1:11; Luke 3:22; Matt 3:17). It is difficult to justify adoptionist theory from this passage. It is very clear to me that God reaffirms or confirms Jesus' sonship at baptism.

15. The devil is often known as the prince or the ruler of this world (John 12:31). It was probable that evil was then figured in the ruler of the Roman Empire or other powerful nations. See S. MacLean Gilmour, "The Gospel according to St. Luke," *The Interpreter's Bible*, vol. 8 (Nashville: Abingdon Press, 1952), 85. In this respect, the devil is regarded as the center of centrality.

16. Desmond Stewart thinks that the temptation deals with power. "The three temptations were linked by power; the power to solve man's economic problems; the power to impress by prodigies or magic; above all, the power to rule men." See his *The Foreigner: A Search for the First-Century Jesus* (London: Hamish Hamilton, 1981), 65. The power to impress by prodigies or magic is to show off, that is, to glorify oneself in front of other people.

17. George A. Buttrick thinks that the pinnacle is a tower (used by Roman guards?) on which a man could be seen by crowds in Jerusalem. Jesus could imagine the crowds watching: "Surely he is not going to jump! Look, he has jumped! He is safe! Is this the Messiah?" See his "The Gospel according to St. Matthew," *The Interpreter's Bible*, vol. 7 (Nashville: Abingdon Press, 1951), 271–72. If this kind of imagination became true, he would be certainly glorified by the crowds. Jesus was not impressed by this kind of temptation.

18. The following passages seem to imply that the crowds were more interested in miracles and prodigies from Jesus than in his teachings: "An evil and adulterous generation asks for a sign, but no sign will be given to it except the sign of the prophet Jonah" (Matt 12:39). "Why does this generation ask for a sign?" (Mark 8:12). "Unless you see signs and wonders you will not believe" (John 4:48).

19. See Rabindranath Tagore, *Gitanjali: A Collection of Indian Songs with an introduction by W. B. Yeats* (New York: Macmillan Co., 1971), 30.

20. Dietrich Bonhoeffer said, "He does not enter in the royal clothes of a 'form of God.' . . . He goes incognito as a beggar among beggars, as an outcast among the outcast, despairing among the despairing, dying among the dying. He also goes as sinner among the sinners, yet in that he is *peccator pessimus*, as sinless among the sinners. And here the central problem of christology lies." See his *Christ the Center* (New York: Harper and Row, 1966), 111.

21. In early Korea, the emissary of the king, Ameng-usa, was sent out as a beggar to investigate the conduct of officials in various provinces. In Hindu tradition, the beggar Sanyasin was regarded as an enlightened one, the sage, who was respected as a divine being. In Asian tradition the beggar was, therefore, given a special status.

22. My aunt used to manage a huge hotel in Korea. She wanted to help a young beggar whose life was wasted on the street. She invited this young beggar in, and gave him the room and a job in the hotel, but he ran away saying "I want freedom as a beggar more than a job that binds me."

23. Matthew adds "in spirit" after "poor" and "righteousness" to "hunger now." Scholars question whether Matthew and Luke had different sources or whether Matthew added these words to the Q source. See Sherman E. Johnson, "The Gospel according to St. Matthew," 280.

24. For Asian-Americans, this principle of reciprocity and reversal is deeply rooted in Asian tradition. Especially, classical Taoism is based on this principle. Because of inevitable reversal, Taoism stresses the weak, lowly, humble, and marginalized. The best symbol of the Tao or the way is described as: water flowing lower and penetrating into the depth of existence.

25. I am afraid that this is also happening in America. When the so-called marginal group of Asian-Americans succeeds in business and other areas of life, penetrating into the very structure of centrality, we see alarm expressed in anti-Asian racism. The rise of anti-Asian racism is directly connected with the idea of "model minority," which allows the penetration of Asians into the life of centrality. One newspaper article said, "Japan-bashing politicians and stereotypes that paint Asian-Americans as a 'model minority' have fueled widespread and growing discrimination and racial violence in the United States, the U.S. Commission on Civil Rights reported Friday after a two-year investigation." See "Anti-Asian Bias Called Rising Threat" in *San Jose Mercury News*, Saturday, February 29, 1992, 1D.

26. Rituals become complex as the church moves toward the center. The closer to the center, the more complex the ritual. For example, established churches striving to be at the center, such as the Roman Catholic church, Episcopal Church, or Methodist Church, make their rituals very complex, while non-established churches or churches at the margin seem to keep it simple.

27. Ron Tanaka, "I hate my wife for her flat yellow face," in *Gidra*, September, 1969. Reprinted in *Roots: An Asian American Reader*, ed. by Amy Tachiki, et al. (Los Angeles: UCLA Asian American Studies Center, 1971), 46–47.

28. Mary Paik Lee, "A Korean/Californian Girlhood," ed. by Sucheng Chang, *California History* 77:1 (March 1988), 45–48.

29. Although he was not physically dead at the moment he cried to God, his death and cry coincided. He reached non-being, where there is complete detachment—death. Thus, Mark wrote, "Then Jesus gave a loud cry and breathed his last" (Mark 15:37).

30. This new center may help us understand the idea of the Trinity in terms of relationship rather than substance. I said it in terms of divine empathy

(God's in-feeling) as a force centering itself to create the inner-community of the Trinity. See Jung Young Lee, *God Suffers for Us: A Systematic Inquiry into a Concept of Divine Possibility* (The Hague: Martinus Nijhoff, 1974), 72–74.

31. Here, I would like to remind the reader that the idea of empty or nothing is not the original nature of God but the consequent nature of God. God emptied himself to become a servant. Thus emptiness is the original nature of the servant (margin of marginality) rather than of God. However, because God became the servant, emptiness can be applicable to God and the servant. What is needed is to maintain unity with a clear distinction between the original nature of God as fullness and the consequent nature of God as emptiness. See my argument in notes 6 and 7 in this chapter.

Chapter 5   True Discipleship: The New Marginal People of God

1. Creation is closely related to order, just as order is related to peace. For example, Walter Brueggemann believes that God solves the problem of chaos by imposing order. See Walter Brueggemann, *Living toward a Vision: Biblical Reflections on Shalom* (New York: United Church Press, 1984), 86.

2. The spoken word of Yahweh is never an empty sound but an operative reality. The word "*dabar*" possesses creative dynamism. See Edmond Jacob, *Theology of the Old Testament*, tr. by Arthur W. Heathcote and Philip J. Allcock (New York: Harper and Brothers Publishers, 1958), 127–28.

3. See Jacob, *Theology of the Old Testament*, 129.

4. It is important to know that the traditional doctrine of *creatio ex nihilo* has very little to do with the story of creation in Genesis. The idea of *creatio ex nihilo* is found explicitly affirmed for the first time in 2 Maccabees (7:28); "Consider the heaven and the earth . . . and know that God has not made them from existing things." See Edmond Jacob, *Theology of the Old Testament* (New York: Harper and Brothers Publishers, 1958), 143, note 1.

5. The image of God as relationship is maintained only in one's relationship with God. According to Jacob, "the *imago Dei* means for man a relationship with, and dependence upon, the one for whom he is only the representative." See Edmund Jacob, *Theology of the Old Testament*, 171. Karl Barth, in particular, defined the concept of the image of God in terms of *analogia relationis*, which takes place in humanity in two different individuals, the man and woman. See Karl Barth, *Church Dogmatics, III/1*, tr. by G. W. Bromiley and T. F. Torrance (Edinburgh: T. and T. Clark, 1936–1961), 196. See also Jung Young Lee, "Karl Barth's Use of Analogy in His Church Dogmatics," *Scottish Journal of Theology*, 22, no. 2 (June 1969), 129–51; Jung Young Lee, *God Suffers for Us: A Systematic Inquiry into a Concept of Divine Possibility* (The Hague: Martinus Nijhoff, 1974), 99.

6. See Maria Lugones, "Playfulness, 'World'-Travelling, and Loving Perception," in *Hypatia*, 2, no. 2 (Summer, 1987), 14.

7. This passage belongs to the Priestly source. Man is created in the image and after the likeness of Elohim. If the P or priestly writer were responsible for

editing the Hebrew Bible, bringing different documents together, Elohim and Yahweh must represent the same God of the Hebrew people. However, in Gen 1:26-27 the idea of God is closely connected with the plurality of Godself. See Jacob, *Theology of the Old Testament*, 166-73.

8. The Korean word *uri* or *Oori* means more than *we*. It is close to *I* in plurality. See chapter 1 of this book.

9. Today we begin to see the importance of difference and plurality in the dynamic and changing world. According to quantum physicists, the difference between the positive and negative charges is as between matter and anti-matter. This not only presupposes plurality but also becomes the basis for plurality. In other words, difference and plurality are the very essences of understanding the world of change and transformation. See Werner Heisenberg, *Physics and Beyond: Encounter and Conversations* (New York: Harper and Row, 1971), 163; Werner Heisenberg, *Philosophic Problems of Nuclear Science* (New York: Pantheon Books, 1952), 15. See also Jung Young Lee, *The I Ching and Modern Man: Essays on Metaphysical Implications of Change* (Secaucus, N.J.: University Books, Inc., 1975), 60-82.

10. In view of the ecological crisis in our time, the word "dominion" is often replaced by "stewardship." See Douglas John Hall, *Imaging God: Dominion as Stewardship* (Grand Rapids, Mich.: Wm. B. Eerdmans for the Commission on Stewardship, NCCCUSA, 1986). What bothers me the most is not the word "dominion" but the way it is used in selfish interest to control and manipulate other creatures. Unless we change our attitude, the change of word or symbol has little effect on our ecological problem today.

11. In the center of marginality, we become parts of marginality in a creative process. We are not separated from the marginal creature. This means human beings are part of nature and are above it because of their central position. In the center of centrality, we no longer identify with nature but act as if we are independent from it. In this kind of position we want to dominate nature as if it has only an instrumental value. For example, if one considers that plants and animals merely exist for the benefit of human beings. For a detailed explanation of the center of centrality, see chapter 2 and chapter 3.

12. One of the most common expressions of this type is "What is good for us must be good for you." This kind of attitude is expressed in American foreign policy. People can interpret it as an expression of benevolence and sharing their goodness with other people. This kind of benevolence is based on false naivete. Of course, our theological education and church mission have often been based on this attitude. What the postmodern world and plurality have done is to help us see the importance of diversity. In this respect, postmodernity seems to move closer to the original design of creation.

13. For example, an extreme form of racism was manifested in Nazi Germany during the Second World War and in the Serbian war against Moslems in Yugoslavia. Frequent displays of the swastika in American cities are symbolic expressions of white supremacy over ethnic minorities, especially Jewish people. As we will discuss later, marginalization is a part of Jewish history.

14. The singularity and plurality of God is a mystery to us, even though the both/and thinking of marginality is helpful to demystify our perception of divine nature. When the story of creation is understood from the perspective of the Word (the Son of God), the concept of the trinitarian God is implicit in creation. In the trinitarian idea of God, God is not only one but also three at the same time. The trinitarian formula "one-in-three" is also "three-in-one," and is best described as the plurality of Godself.

15. See Cain Hope Felder, ed., *Stony the Road We Trod: African American Biblical Interpretation* (Minneapolis: Fortress Press, 1991), 32.

16. Ur was Abram's ancestral city located at the southern end of the Euphrates River in Mesopotamia. Archaeological studies witness the brilliant civilization in that city. When the glory of the Sumerian Dynasty (c. 2800–2360 B.C.) ended, the third dynasty of Ur (c. 2060–1950 B.C.) began. Amorites invaded the Mesopotamian plain and established the first Babylonian Dynasty, whose last and greatest king was Hammurabi (c. 1728–1686 B.C.). It is probable, according to Bernhard W. Anderson, that Abram's migration into the land of Canaan was connected with the Amoritic invasion into Mesopotamia. See Bernhard W. Anderson, *Understanding the Old Testament*, 2d ed. (Englewood Cliffs, N.J.: Prentice-Hall, Inc., 1966), 22–23.

17. Walter Breuggemann, *The Land: Place as Gift, Promise, and Challenge in Biblical Faith* (Philadelphia: Fortress Press, 1977), 14.

18. Some feminist theologians and third-world theologians claim that the Bible as the official history of Israelites supports rulers' ideologies to dominate the poor and marginal people. See Phyllis Trible, *Texts of Terror: Literary-Feminist Readings of Biblical Narratives* (Philadelphia: Fortress Press, 1984), 93–116; Nam Dong Suh, "A Counter-theological Approach in the Story-telling," from *In Search of Minjung Theology* (Seoul: Hangilsa, 1983), 299.

19. See Sang Hyun Lee, "Called to Be Pilgrims: Toward a Theology within the Korean Immigrant Context," *The Korean Immigrant in America*, ed. by Byong-suh Kim and Sang Hyun Lee (Montclair, N.J.: AKCS, 1980), 48ff.

20. Sang Hyun Lee, "Called to Be Pilgrims," 49.

21. Jerusalem, the seat of the Davidic kingdom, was regarded as the center of the ruling class, the seat of highest authority, and the locale of the wealthy. The people of Galilee, on the other hand, were marginal people, oppressed by the ruling elites of Jerusalem. See Joachim Jeremias, *Jerusalem in the Time of Jesus* (Philadelphia: Fortress Press, 1981), 74–76, 95–97.

22. David's death gave rise to the hope that a Messiah ("Anointed One") would come, who would be of David's lineage, who would reunite the tribes of Israel, and who would restore Jerusalem to a position of prestige among the nations (see Isa 9, 11). See also Bernhard W. Anderson, *Understanding the Old Testament*, 149.

23. Not all prophets were critical of the establishment or the status quo of the centralist idealogy of the Hebrews. There were prophets who supported the royal court. In Kings, "the 400 prophets are the central figures, whose enquiry of God can be guaranteed to produce an answer correspond-

ing with the king's own wishes" (1 Kings 22:6). On the other hand, Mica-
iah was a marginal figure, to whom the king said, "I hate him, for he never
prophesies anything favorable about me, but only disaster" (22:8). See R. A.
Coggins, *Introducing the Old Testament* (Oxford: Oxford University Press,
1990), 73.

24. Tracing Jesus from Davidic genealogy creates a problem, because it was
traced from Joseph, who was not his biological father. Moreover, the emphasis
on his birth at Bethlehem, the city of David, is problematic. See John Meier, *A
Marginal Jew: Rethinking the Historical Jesus* (New York: Doubleday, 1991),
214-19.

25. John Meier's judicious historical scholarship shows that Jesus was a marginal Jew. See ibid.

26. James Cone said, "Because the church is a community called into being
by the "Crucified God," it must be a crucified church, living under the cross."
See his 'The Servant Church,' in *The Pastor as Servant*, ed. by Earl E. Shelp and
Ronald H. Sunderland (New York: The Pilgrim Press, 1986), 76.

Chapter 6   Authentic Church: The Community of
New Marginality

1. In this chapter, I will use the term "institutional" to indicate the static,
unchanging, and centralized state of the contemporary church. To this, I contrast the dynamic and decentralized state of a church of marginality.

2. See Jung Young Lee, "Lead Us Not into Temptation," *The Lord's Prayer
Series*, Discipleship Resources of the United Methodist Church, Nashville,
Tenn., 1985.

3. Justo L. González, *Out of Every Tribe and Nation: Christian Theology
at the Ethnic Roundtable* (Nashville: Abingdon Press, 1992), 107-108.

4. I taught at a state university for seventeen years before I came to teach in
a United Methodist theological seminary. Based on my experience, seminary
teachers are more authoritarian and interested in the status quo than state university professors. I also found that seminary teachers are more dogmatic and
arrogant than state university teachers. I believe my experience is not an isolated case.

5. Elizabeth Tay said, "Assimilation was an attempt to fill my soul with
stones. My soul was filled, but with stones." See Elizabeth Tay, "Sharing Our
Stories" in *Asian and Asian American Women in Theology and Ministry:
1992 Annual Conference*, March 6-8, 1992 (M. Alverno Conference Center,
Redwood City, Calif.), 17.

6. Many first-generation non-Caucasian immigrants suffer from "the cult of
'perfect' language," which is "a form of censorship based on racism, sexism,
classism and colonialism in the U.S." See Jung Ha Kim, "Labor of Compassion:
A Case Study of Churched Korean-American Women" (unpublished manuscript), 3.

7. Justo L. González, *Out of Every Tribe and Nation*, 108.

8. Paul Vidales calls it "Kenosis church." He said, "We need a church that is poor. We need a church that does not claim to hold the key to political, social, cultural, economic, or even ethical problems. We need a church of Kenosis, a church emptied of self, a church reduced to and embracing 'nothingness.'" See his "How Should We Speak of Church Today?" in *Faces of Jesus: Latin American Christologies*, ed. by José Míguez Bonino (Maryknoll, N.Y.: Orbis Books, 1984), 152.

9. See *Letter to Diognetus* 5:1–6:1, Eugene R. Fairweather's translation. Quoted in Edward Pl. Blair, *The Illustrated Bible Handbook* (Nashville: Abingdon Press, 1975), 500.

10. Shamanism or *Mutang* is the native religion of the Korean people. The indigenous ethos of the Korean people is found in shamanistic rituals. After more than twenty years of life in America, I returned to Korea to study shamanism in order to rediscover my roots. See my *Korean Shamanistic Rituals* (New York, Paris, and Berlin: Mouton Publishers, 1981).

11. Let me illustrate the spontaneous act of marginality based on experience in this country. I still remember the first Christmas Eve program I attended. As I was sitting in the pew and hearing the beautiful Christmas carols, I suddenly recalled a Christmas Eve service in Korea. I had a strong urge to sing "Silent Night." During the program, I raised my hand. The minister, who knew me, came and said, "Put down your hand. What do you want?" I said to him, "I want to sing." The minister sternly said, "No. You can't." I again insisted, in my strong accent, "I want to sing." The program was suddenly disrupted and everyone's eyes were directed toward me. A few people said, "Let him sing." The minister had no choice. He let me go up to the stage. The pianist said, "I cannot play without rehearsal." I said, "I don't need a rehearsal and I don't need a piano." I sang it in Korean as it came out. After it was over many giggled and laughed behind me. The minister was embarrassed at my marginal act. The program continued, but it was never the same. When the program was over, many people said that my singing was the best part of the program, and suggested that we should be more spontaneous in the program. Of course, it never happened again. For marginal people, however, structured programs do not work. They kill the spontaneity and dry up the unifying spirit.

12. The greater a desire to study, the greater the intensity of learning that takes place in study. This desire to learn is the beginning of wisdom. In the conventional education under the centralist system, qualification for admission to school is primarily academic achievements and leadership skills. However, in seminary training for leading a community of marginal people, one's sincere desire for study should be the most important qualification for admission. Buddhism in Asia followed this practice for many centuries. One of the best known traditions of proving sincerity for learning is found in the story of Hui-ko, the first disciple of Bodhidharma, who came to China to teach Buddhism. In order to show his sincerity, Hui-ko cut off his arm and gave it to the master. Impressed with Hui-ko's sincerely, Bodhidharma admitted him to discipleship. See Heinrich Dumoulin, *A History of Zen Buddhism* (New York: Random

House, 1963), 72–76. In training Christian ministers, we need to test their sincerity for learning before admitting them to the seminary.

13. In traditional Western theology, which has been dominated by centralist people, reconciliation was conceived on a personal basis without considering social justice. However, reconciliation without justice is a fiction. As Yan Jin, a Chinese-American woman, who was a victim of the "Cultural Revolution" in the 1960s and witnessed the Tiananmen Massacre, said, "I cried and cried. That was the very first time I cried for the dead, for hundreds, probably thousands of innocent Chinese who were brutally killed by a few powerful men. My dream for reconciliation was greatly challenged by the cruel reality. I realized that I had been dreaming of a reconciliation without justice. I was awakened by the cry of the dead." Yan Jin, "Sharing Our Stories," in *Asian and Asian American Women in Theology and Ministry, 1992 Annual Conference, March 6–8, 1992,* p. 5.

14. Korean immigrant churches in the United States grow faster than the Korean-American population. They grew from about seventy-five churches in 1970 to about two thousand churches today—about twenty-seven times their initial size. See "Koreans Here Embrace Christianity" in *Philadelphia Inquirer,* May 30, 1988, sec. B.

15. What makes the Korean-American congregation different from the Caucasian-American congregation is that the Caucasian-American church begins from the top. All plans, including surveys of potential membership in a particular region for the establishment of a local congregation, are directed by the annual or district cabinet meetings, who then appoint a pastor to cultivate a congregation. On the other hand, the Korean-American congregation begins with a Bible study group, usually consisting of three or four families. In this respect, the Korean-American congregation is less centralized than its white counterpart.

16. Randolph Nugent, "Model Minorities or Model Disciples?" in *Report on 1987 National Convocation of Asian American United Methodists,* January 16–19, 1987, Inglewood, Calif., 82.

17. In 1978, for example, more than forty percent of all Korean heads of household in Los Angeles County were self-employed. Ibid., 81.

18. According to a sociological study of Korean immigrants in the Chicago area, about seventy percent of Korean-Americans are affiliated with the church. See Won Moo Hurh and Kwang Chung Kim, "Religious Participation of Korean Immigrants in the United States" in *Journal for the Scientific Study of Religion,* 29, no. 1 (1990), 26.

19. Reasons for the rapid expansion of Korean-American churches are many: (1) the historical tie of Korean immigration with the church; nearly half of the 101 immigrants on the first ship were from the Yongdon church in Inchon, Korea; (2) the Korean church serves as a social center; (3) it serves an educational function; Korean languages are taught for second-generation and third-generation families, and English is taught to the first generation of Koreans; (4) it keeps Korean nationalism alive; (5) it gives psychological support. See Hurh

and Kim, "Religious Participation of Korean Immigrants in the United States," 20–23.

20. This system of lay officers was no doubt inherited from the Presbyterian Church, which is the largest Protestant denomination in Korea. Many Korean United Methodist churches keep a separate file for officers who are not recognized by the Methodist Church, which seems to indicate that the unified system based on centralistic ideology does not work for all people. Especially, those of cultural diversity and with special ethnic needs that can be met only with church inclusivity.

21. Jung Ha Kim, "Labor of Compassion," 4.

22. The most famous transformation is Paul's conversion experience on the road to Damascus. This dramatic transformation from a dominant-group person to a marginal person shows the shift of perspective from the center of centrality to the margin of marginality. After it, Saul became Paul, centrality became marginality, and the master became the servant. See Acts 9:1–22.

23. The Korean church is regarded as one of the most conservative evangelical churches in the world. Recently, the Methodist Church in Korea excommunicated two professors: one who advocated inter-faith dialogue between Christianity and Buddhism, and another who supported postmodernism. However, it is often said that the Korean church in the United States is more conservative than the Korean church in Korea. Most Korean Protestant churches still retain the same puritan ethics, theology, and liturgies brought to them by American missionaries at the end of the nineteenth century. See Jung Young Lee, "The American Missionary Movement in Korea, 1882–1945: Its Contributions and American Diplomacy," in *Missiology: An International Review*, 11, no. 4 (October, 1983), 287–402; see also Donald N. Clark, *Christianity in Modern Korea* (Lanham, Md.: University Press of America, 1986).

24. The Korean-American church is perhaps the only place where Korean-Americans communally celebrate most of their national holidays, work toward the unification of the divided Koreas, teach Korean languages to their children, and perform other cultural events. See various church newspapers such as *Hanminjung* (One People), published by Korean Community Council in America; *Saemmul* (Spring Water), published by New York Korean Churches; *The Socio-Theological Thought* (New York: Korean Socio-Theological Study Center); or *Encounter* by Charleston Korean United Methodist Church. See also Justo González, *Out of Every Tribe and Nation*, 103.

25. Many attempts have been made by the Korean-American United Methodist Church to have a separate independent language conference, in order to develop its programs and policies. However, the centralist-structured United Methodist Church has denied their proposal. The Korean-American United Methodist Church appealed again in 1993. Although it has been given an autonomous conference, such cannot be truly autonomous unless it permits its members to give up the centralist ideology that is part of that church.

26. I will explain this more fully in the next chapter, which deals with overcoming marginality through marginality.

27. See my "Transcending Vision," in *Salt*, 13, no. 1 (anuary 1993), 19.

Chapter 7 Creative Transformation: Overcoming Marginality through Marginality

1. Karl Mannheim holds that the original idea of ideology comes from Bacon's idea of *idola*. He said, "Bacon's theory of the *idola* may be regarded to a certain extent as a forerunner of the modern conception of ideology." See Karl Mannheim, *Idealogy and Utopia: An Introduction to the Sociology of Knowledge* (New York: A Harvest/JBJ Books, 1985), 61. The idols denote perceptions, which denote the sources of error derived either from human nature or from a particular individual or individuals which constitute society. See Hans Barth, *Truth and Ideology*, tr. Frederick Lilge (Berkeley: University of California Press, 1976), 23-24. Karl Marx identified ideology with the distorted ideas used by the ruling class as weapons against the exploited masses and as a manifestation of false consciousness' refusal to see reality as it is. Since ideology originated in the ruling class, it influences the intellectual production and distribution of ideas. Marginal people are excluded from creating an ideology of knowledge and culture. There is no representation of marginal groups in the political and economic philosophy in the past. Even the views of marginal people are hardly traceable in the Bible. See Dorothy E. Smith, *The Everyday World as Problematic: A Feminist Sociology* (Boston: Northeastern University Press, 1987), 17-18. See also Karl Marx, *The German Ideology: In the Marx-Engels Reader*, ed. by Robert C. Tucher (New York: W. E. Norton and Co., 1972), 136-37.

2. The approach of most liberation theologies, including feminist theology, is based on the centralist norm. One of the most attractive titles which seems to represent a feminist approach to liberation is bell hooks' *Feminist Theology: From the Margin to the Center* (Boston: South End Press, 1984).

3. See Everett Stonequist, *The Marginal Man: A Study in Personality and Culture Conflict* (New York: Charles Scribner's Sons, 1937), 154-55.

4. See Stonequist, *The Marginal Man: A Study*, 219-20. See also Sang H. Lee, "Called to Be Pilgrims," *The Korean Immigrant in America* (Montclair, N.J.: AKCS, 1980), 48.

5. See *The Ritual Process* (Hawthorne, N.Y.: Aldine Publishing Co., 1969). See also Tom F. Driver, "Justice and the Servant Task of Pastoral Ministry," in *The Pastor as Servant*, ed. by Earl E. Shelp and Ronald H. Sunderland (New York: The Pilgrim Press, 1986), 48-49.

6. Halford E. Luccock, "The Gospel according to St. Mark," *Interpreter's Bible*, vol. 7 (Nashville: Abingdon Press), 707.

7. The communitas of liminality is an alternative structure, which Victor Turner speaks of as anti-structural. See Tom F. Driver, "Justice and the Servant Task of Pastoral Ministry," 53-54.

8. Tom F. Driver, "Justice and the Servant Task of Pastoral Ministry," 58.

9. If God is love, love should transcend all forms of power. To classify love as a form of power is misleading. From a perspective of ontological analysis, the power of being is inclusive of love. In this respect, "Love is the moving

power of life" or "Love is the drive [moving power] toward the unity of the separated." See Paul Tillich, *Love, Power, and Justice: Ontological Analysis and Ethical Applications* (Oxford: Oxford University Press, 1954). From a Christian perspective, love can transform power because God is love.

10. In the classical treatment of Christian love, Nygren attempts to define agape love as a descending movement, the movement from God to humanity, in contrast to eros love as the ascending movement of love. However, he failed to see that agape love not only moves from God to human beings but also moves downward in human relationships as well. See Anders Nygren, *Agape and Eros*, tr. by Philip S. Watson (Philadelphia: Westminster Press, 1953).

11. The hierarchical structure of our social order is very much based on money, although race and gender are closely related to it. In some other societies the hierarchical order is based on lineage, on religion, on education, and the like. See Tom F. Driver, "Justice and the Servant Task of Pastoral Ministry," 50.

12. According to Robert N. Bellah, modern consumer capitalism creates in North America a monoculture, which is not Caucasian but modern consumer capitalist. All cultural diversity and multi-ethnicity seem to be subsumed in what he calls, in *Habits of the Heart,* utilitarian and expressive individualism. He tries to fight it by teaching Old and New Testament sociology and the sociology of early Confucianism in his sociology of religion course. He expressed this concern in his letter on July 9, 1992. See also Bellah, et al., *Habits of the Heart: Individualism and Commitment in American Life* (Berkeley and Los Angeles: University of California Press, 1985).

13. Paulo Freire said, "Love is at the same time the foundation of dialogue and dialogue itself." See Paulo Freire, *Pedagogy of the Oppressed* (New York: Seabury, 1970), 77.

14. See bell hooks, *Feminist Theory*, 161.

15. A popular treatise on the problem of evil and suffering is the book *When Bad Things Happen to Good People* by Harold S. Kushner (New York: Schocken Books, 1981), which takes up the Book of Job. Kushner's solution is to limit the power of God, which is the centralist approach.

16. "It is also possible to look at the stories of 'creation' in the early chapters of Genesis, not as 'the story of creation,' but as 'the story of *the beginning of creation*.' Indeed, it is in such terms that early Christian writers such as Irenaeus and others consistently refer to the Genesis narratives." See Justo L. González, *Out of Every Tribe and Nation: Christian Theology at the Ethnic Roundtable* (Nashville: Abingdon Press, 1992), 70.

17. It seems distinctive of Christianity to stress the significance of suffering and death on the cross. Arnold Toynbee once said, "This Christian glorification of suffering in the cause of love can be very shocking to non-Christians. I once heard the following story told of an English family living in China who engaged a Chinese nurse for their small children. As soon as this Chinese woman came into their house, they saw that she was much disturbed by something, and, as the hours and days passed, she showed signs of being more and more upset.

Naturally, they were anxious to discover the reason, but she was very shy of telling them. At last, with great embarrassment, she said: 'Well, there is something that I just cannot understand. You are obviously good people; you obviously love your children and care for them; yet, in every room in this house and even on the staircase as well, I see repeated reproductions of a picture of a criminal being put in death by some horrible form of torture which we have never heard of in China; and I cannot understand how you—responsible people and loving persons as you obviously are—I cannot understand how you can expose your children to these pictures, at every turn, at this early impressionable stage of their lives.' " See Arnold Toynbee, *Christianity among the Religions of the World* (New York: Scribner, 1956), 26-27.

18. See Søren Kierkegaard, *Attack upon Christendom* (Boston: Beacon Press, 1957), 157.

19. In Asia, laughter is very important for releasing frustration and anger. The idea of cosmic laughter in Zen and the use of satiric laughter in mask dances are common. See Conrad Myers, *Zen and the Cosmic Spirit* (Philadelphia: Westminster Press, 1973); Commission on Theological Concerns of the Christian Conference of Asia, *Mingjung Theology: People as the Subjects of History* (Maryknoll, N.Y.: Orbis Books), 1983; *An Emerging Theology in World Perspective: Commentary on Korean Minjung Theology*, ed. by Jung Young Lee (Mystic, Conn.: Twenty-Third Publications, 1988).

20. The pilgrimage motif of the perfect city of God is expressed in the centralist vision of new life. This motif reappears in other writings of marginal people. See Sang H. Lee, "Call to Be Pilgrims," Korean American Ministry (Princeton: Consulting Committee on Korean American Ministry, Presbyterian Church, 1987), 93.

Conclusion

1. See John P. Meier, *A Marginal Jew: Rethinking the Historical Jesus* (New York: Doubleday, 1991).

2. Systematic theology, as a task of central groups, is different from marginal theology. According to Peggy Billings, "Systematic theology is a result of systems thought, tending toward hierarchy and reliance on rationality. Reflecting the action of God from the margin is a process, provisional and extemporaneous, for it knows its life to be conditional, continuing only by accident and the grace of God." See Peggy Billings, "A Reflection from the Margin," *Social Questions Bulletin*, 83, no. 3 (May-June 1993), 4.

INDEX